Regnum, Religio et Ratio

Essays Presented to
Robert M. Kingdon

Habent sua fata libelli

Volume VIII
of
Sixteenth Century Essays & Studies
Edited by Jerome Friedman

General Editor: Charles G. Nauert, Jr.

The book has been made possible through a gift from
Gela Sessler in memory of her husband, the Rev. Dr. Jacob J. Sessler;
contributions from the Ph.D. students of Robert M. Kingdon;
and the generous support of Northeast Missouri State University

ISBN 0-940474-08-5

Composed by Paula Presley, NMSU, Kirksville, Missouri
Designed by RUS
Printed by Edwards Brothers, Ann Arbor, Michigan
Text is set in Bembo II

The paper used in this publication meets the minimum requirements of the American National standard for Permanence of Paper for Printed Library Materials Z39.48, 1984.

Contents

Introduction

It is hardly necessary to introduce Robert M. Kingdon to readers of this volume. His publications (a complete list is included on pages 171-79) place him at the forefront of Reformed tradition scholarship. He is known to every early modernist as editor of *The Sixteenth Century Journal*, a periodical which has risen to international prominence in large part because of his efforts. Kingdon has also served on the board of editors of other journals, including the *Archive for Reformation History*, *French Historical Studies*, and the *Journal of The History of Ideas*.

While some know Kingdon best through his own publications or journal activity, others know him as an officer of several professional organizations. He has served as a council member, Secretary, Vice-President, and President of the American Society for Reformation Research; as President of the American Society of Church History; as a board member of the The Meeter Center for Calvin Studies; as Vice-President of the Society for French Historical Studies; and as council member and Executive Board member of the Renaissance Society of America. Less well known is Kingdon's service to foreign professional associations which include the Société de l'histoire du protestantisme française and the Société d'histoire et d'archéologie de Genève. Kingdon has been awarded grants by such prestigious organizations as the Guggenheim Foundation, the American Council of Learned Societies, the Folger Shakespeare Library, and the American Philosophical Society. As befitting his status as one of the most respected American scholars of the Protestant Reformation, on May 26, 1986 Kingdon was awarded an honorary doctorate from the University of Geneva in celebration of the 450th anniversary of that city's acceptance of Protestantism.

Kingdon is also a prominent teacher and respected colleague. He is a professor in the University of Wisconsin's prestigious Department of History and director of that university's Institute for Research in the Humanities which is housed in that university's wonderful Old Observatory. Before arriving in Madison, Kingdon taught at the University of Massachusetts and the University of Iowa and has been a visiting scholar at a host of institutions both here and abroad including Amherst, Stanford, and the University of Adelaide in Australia. And before sharing his knowledge with others, Kingdon earned a Bachelor's degree from Oberlin College (*summa cum laude*) in 1949, where he was also inducted into Phi Beta Kappa. He received a Master's degree in 1950 and a doctorate in 1955 from Columbia University, where he wrote his dissertation for Garret Mattingly. All of this is well known.

Anyone who has had contact with Kingdon in any of his many capacities will tell you that he is a professional, the historian's historian. Only a few of us realize that Bob Kingdon will celebrate his sixtieth birthday this year; but then, few know him as do those who have contributed to this volume. We received our doctorates from Robert Kingdon and it is to honor him on his sixtieth birthday that we have come together to share with him the fruits of our labors, or more precisely, the fruits of his labors, one step removed. As editor of this project, it falls to me to introduce this birthday gift but since Kingdon's most productive years are still before him, it is still too early to assess his full influence on current Reformation scholarship. Rather, in these next few pages I would like to share with the general community of scholars what we, his students, feel about this singular man, what it was to study with him, and why he continues to mean so much to us.

There is no more profound influence in the life of a graduate student in history than a graduate advisor. This curious "Parent-Confessor" affiliation is a complex blend of professional, familial, personal, and heroic elements where the advisor often serves as a paternal figure, as a confessor and confidant of secrets, and as a partner in the finished product. This complicated relationship can last anywhere from one to six or seven years and involves almost daily contact. Such was the relationship between Kingdon and his students. The association which we had with our advisor was intensely close yet not obviously personal and was complicated by the fact that we were dependent upon Kingdon for fellowships and for simple affirmation of our scholastic value at a time of life when dependency is often resisted and resented. Even more, Kingdon is a very private man and not easy to know and then, never quickly. While each of us knew him as a lecturer and as a critic and as the author of The Timetable of Papers, that schedule by which chapters of one's thesis and dissertation were to be completed, he also served as our goal and as our window into a world we hoped to share. Among ourselves, we spoke about him constantly, trading any bit of gossip anyone heard, mock-arguing with his professional opponents, taking pleasure in his accomplishments. He was the magical agency that would turn students into historians and the pattern upon which we would attempt, much later, to work with our own students.

When asked to submit incidents from their graduate school experience of studying with Kingdon, almost everyone indicated that the central facet of every student's relationship with Kingdon, indeed, the core of his graduate program, is that dreaded, if beneficial, crucible known as the "continuing seminar." Meeting once a week, all graduate students from the greenest master's student to those veterans completing their doctoral dissertations were enrolled in this common class. In the first part of the semester Kingdon would concentrate on a general theme cutting through the period as a whole or on different technical skills such as paleography, that particularly nasty trick the dead play upon the living. Lynn Martin remembers the easy atmosphere of this first phase when seminar meetings were held in Kingdon's apartment and how "the informality of the setting prompted the students to take turns bringing cookies and cakes to the seminars, while Kingdon supplied the drinks, usually tea, served in his grandfather's Korean tea set." Kingdon would also utilize the experiences of his advanced students when choosing seminar topics. Those students returning from research abroad would contribute their own expertise from their research and travels to the seminar and Merry Wiesner remembers "his structuring his seminars around the specific interests of his graduate students, especially if we were fresh back from the archives and ready to tell the world. The year I came back the seminar was on women, the year Tom Safley came back, on the family, etc." This part of the course was fairly traditional because we were essentially students taking notes but all this changed in the second half of the semester when students presented new chapters from their theses and dissertations before the seminar. Each week another student would photocopy and distribute his masterpiece a week in advance of his presentation according to a timetable created at the beginning of the semester. Things were different now and several people commented how "the character of the seminars changed dramatically during the second semester and the seminar now met in . . . a much more formal setting."

The atmosphere of these formal seminar meetings was often very tense because every student understood that this was the prime occasion to impress both Kingdon as well as one's peers. Neither task was very easy. Bob Linder remembers his own experiences as Kingdon's student at Iowa. "As I recall, all of his seminars were quite religious experiences—he scared the hell out of us! He seemed to know so much and we seemed to know so little." Kingdon was rarely the worst problem, however, if only because he knew better than to expect too much from new students. Far more critical was each week's discussion leader, also chosen in advance, who carefully checked citations, translations, and general understanding of the material and led that week's assault. Given the diversity of interests and levels of skill and experience among Kingdon's students, a student of intellectual history might challenge a student of military history or a student of economic history might face a critic more interested in literature. The potential for conflict was enormous and was further compounded by student rivalry. One student wrote the following about a particular seminar meeting that many of us remember: "In the seminars Kingdon was quite often able to sit back and watch his students criticize each other's papers and reports, and on occasion he had to intervene when the criticism threatened to get out of hand. On one occasion he did not intervene, and the students responded by doing a thorough hatchet job on a report that was at the same time exasperatingly arrogant and embarrassingly awful. In a word, the offending student was crucified by his peers."

Most seminar sessions passed easily enough and without too much bloodshed, but Kingdon's point was that scholars must get used to the hostile criticism of peer review. And yet, the seminar also taught us to depend upon one another and help each other. Maryanne Horowitz wrote that "generally, student comments on seminar papers brought improvements in the re-writes and we began to rely on each other for editing tips." Perhaps one reason so many Kingdon students present papers at professional meetings is because we all did so at least once a semester for several years. The seminar was, in reality, a conference session consisting of people working in vastly different areas. Convince them and you were home free. Fail, and you had next semester to do better. It was Kingdon's insistence that there was always a better way to do things that motivated most of us to work harder than we ever had. Bob Schnucker wrote that in Iowa he did "a paper on *die Meidung* as practiced by the Anabaptists. For that, I read every single issue of the *Mennonite Quarterly Review* and even delved into sixteenth-century Dutch documents even though I could not read a word of Dutch." The reason was simply an awareness "of the need for thoroughness, precision, and attention to detail." Bob Linder sums it all up: "I think that is the essence of what he taught me in his seminars—to be careful and thorough in my own work. In some ways it has been a curse for I suspect that I could get much more done if I did not have these Kingdon habits so deeply ingrained in me." Almost everyone did improve over time but each September saw new master's students, still too green to know about the continuing seminar, and the silent absence of some recently departed older students who should have known better.

If the seminar would forge the critical, analytical, and writing skills so important in our profession, Kingdon's most enduring importance for most students was the close relationship they enjoyed while writing their dissertations. By this time both student and teacher understood what to expect of each other and it was possible to communicate about the significance of the material in question without all the complications involving student egos characterizing class work, tests, and comprehensive examinations. One would have assumed that this foremost scholar of the Reformed tradition would have many students working in the area of Swiss and French Protestantism. Yet, curiously, despite his own interest and prominence in the Reformed tradition, Kingdon encouraged his students to find their own areas of interest. Joseph Freedman wrote, "I am not sure how many scholars would allow students to work in a field far removed from their area of specialization" and expressing what so many of us have thought, Merry Wiesner noted, "We are not all psychic clones, as the students of certain members of our profession seem to be." Perhaps for this reason, years after leaving Kingdon's care, each student continues to believe that he or she enjoyed a very special relationship with Kingdon because of their individualized scholarly relationships during the progress towards the dissertation. Rudolph Heinze remembers that he wished to work on Tudor royal proclamations, "but, since Kingdon was not a specialist in the early Tudor period and did not claim to know anything about royal proclamations, I was reluctant even to suggest that topic. However, once I learned to know Kingdon, I realized that I had no reason to fear suggesting a topic that interested me no matter how far removed it was from his research interests. He not only readily accepted my topic but encouraged it." My own experience was similar. I was interested in radicals and radicalism and expressed little interest in the more usual intellectual currents of the day. When Kingdon suggested that I might look into Tridentine statutes regarding Anabaptism, I remember thinking it was half a good topic and thought I was very witty when I asked why I need bother with Trent. Kingdon thought this less humorous than I did but, then, he thought my dissertation more humorous than I did. In any event, Kingdon permitted—indeed, demanded—that his students identify their own areas of interest in what we all hoped would be a lifetime's commitment to scholarship.

And yet, this does not do real justice to Kingdon. However well developed the seminars and however helpful a dissertation advisor Kingdon might prove to be, Kingdon's influence on his students extends past his resourcefulness as a teacher and past the lessons learned in seminar meetings. Perhaps because he is so grand an example of the serious scholar, he provides his students with a personal representation of the broad range of professional virtues and values he was trying to instill in each of us. Kingdon was willing, for instance, to use himself as a model and put himself up for criticism much as he was demanding of his students. Joseph Freedman reports that "in the Spring Semester of 1971 Kingdon brought a draft of an article which he had written to his seminar. It was entitled 'Toward a Structural Study of the Reformation.' He asked us to do a public critique of it. I submit that very few professors of his stature would be willing to do such a thing."

In other ways, too, Kingdon was never too proud to share his personal experiences with his students. Lynn Martin reports, "As a student I heard Kingdom describe his initial experiences working at the archives in Geneva . . . [and] as a result of his experience and advice, I went to Rome well-prepared to do research in the Jesuit Archives." Indeed, one of Kingdon's more valiant efforts had been to teach his students paleography and the vagaries of sixteenth-century language usage. Martin was terribly discouraged when he discovered that he still was experiencing great difficulties and Kingdon wrote to him that "your discouragement at this stage is perfectly natural. It reminds me of my own reactions after my first month in the Geneva archives and of Garret Mattingly's reactions (as reported to me recently by his wife) after his first month in the Annency Archive."

Kingdon is also a living demonstration of the social virtues of scholarly fellowship. A good research historian must possess skills and languages, of course, but must also maintain active contact with other members of the early modern confraternity. Wherever we travelled and did our research, Kingdon encouraged us to meet scholars in other universities and in other countries and he was always willing to help us make initial introductions. I doubt there is a single student who has not benefited from Kingdon's contacts with the scholarly world. Heinze writes how "he made sure that I was in contact with the best scholars in the field. Consequently, I was sent to G. R. Elton and J. F. Larkin who provided me with the critical assistance that not only made possible a competent dissertation but eventually provided the guidance and help I needed for my future scholarly contributions." This same thing happened over and over again. At one point Kingdon insisted that I visit Roland Bainton, then in retirement at Yale University. At the time I thought Kingdon was sending me to Bainton to be read the riot act. In fact, he was putting me in touch with the one authority who better than anyone else could help me develop my ideas. Indeed, it was Roland Bainton's reading of my Servetus manuscript several years later that settled its publication. Other students had the same experience with Richard Popkin, J. H. Salmon, John Tedeschi, and so many other important scholars. The same lesson was made several years later when Alain Dufour of Droz Press in Geneva visited the United States and attended a spring meeting at the Newberry Library in Chicago. Despite language differences, and Mr. Dufour's shyness, Kingdon lined us up and introduced each of us and our work to Mr. Dufour. In fact, several of us went on to publish with Droz. This was to be expected of Kingdon; a complete teacher does more than instruct.

"The world knows him as a scholar," one student wrote, "but we know him as a gentle man." Despite the competitive rigor of his seminars and the strenuous demands of a heavy writing schedule, Kingdon was also willing to facilitate an easy social atmosphere between students and himself. It is only now that I am roughly the same age Kingdon was when I was his student, and have my own needs for privacy, that I can appreciate how much of himself he was willing to share on a social level. "Some of the charming things I remember," writes Merry Wiesner, "are his pride in his house (he bought his first house while I was in Madison), his willingness to throw it open to any and all parties (as long as we remembered the paper plates), his killer mulled wine, and his ability to make people feel welcome." Lynn Martin recalls Kingdon's students when he first came to Wisconsin from Iowa in the 1960s. "As a group Kingdon's students were at the same time extremely close with each other and extremely competitive with each other. They partied together, had lunch together, and went to games and on outings together. To celebrate the end of the academic year we had a picnic and baseball game (Martin struck out while Friedman starred), followed by a party at Kingdon's apartment." [Editor's note: Kingdon pitched.] It is easy to dismiss such non-academic activity as just so much frivolity but Maryanne Horowitz expressed what we all have come to understand when she wrote, "I realized only years later that Kingdon was setting us on the path to become colleagues rather than just fellow students." In later years these close ties were renewed and strengthened when on the Thursday night before the annual meeting of the Sixteenth Century Studies Conference we would gather in Bob Kolb's apartment above the Center for Reformation Research. We were no longer in Madison, but the seminar continued.

The large number of his students maintaining active ties with Kingdon over the years must indicate the measure of unceasing respect and affection his students have for him. Rather than receiving our degrees and each of us going our own way, we remain in touch with the man whom we continue to see as our teacher and as a well of inspiration and collegial help. For his part, rather than pushing us out of the nest and wishing us well, Kingdon has been more than willing to work with his students. He has co-authored articles and books with some, planned conferences with others, and edited journals with yet others. He is a tireless writer of letters of recommendation and despite a heavy schedule, Kingdon has been willing to continue reading his former students' manuscripts. He would indicate he was busy, how long it would take to get to it and when it would be done. And it was. After indicating how little he knew of the subject, he always found sources that were untapped and secondary sources worth rereading. But then, this should hardly surprise anyone; before he was editor of the journal, he was an editor for his students. Or, is it the other way around? Where once he advised only his students, as editor of *The Sixteenth Century Journal* he now serves as advisor to the profession as a whole.

This birthday present volume is as an act of respect, continuing admiration and esteem to a teacher who has formed so many professional careers and to an individual whose entire professional life stands as a model for us to emulate no less today than when enrolled in his seminar. Hopefully, this volume which is dedicated to so complete a scholar will have something for everyone. Those respecting the man are presented with his picture. Those respecting institutions of learning and scholarly method are presented with pictures of the Institute's observatory and its telescope. Students of the Reformed tradition are presented with a complete list of Kingdon's publications, and Kingdon himself is presented with a series of mini-reviews of his work to remind him how well his works have been received by his peers and not merely by his students. His students are presented with an opportunity to demonstrate their respect and appreciation to this most singular man, and subscribers to the journal get an additional (free!) issue. It is hoped this diverse collection of essays will also satisfy the scholarly interests of a varied sixteenth-century constituency and reflect the broad currents of scholarship Kingdon has loosed. It stands to reason that there could be no single theme or direction to this volume dedicated to so important a teacher. Nothing more than the diversity of Kingdon's students can express how mighty trees send their branches in many directions.

In addition to those contributing articles, this volume would simply not have appeared without the help, advice, and judgment of Professor Robert V. Schnucker, another individual needing no introduction to readers of *The Sixteenth Century Journal*. Other individuals, met the financial burden of this publication. Despite his position as editor of this journal, Kingdon himself gets no technical thanks at all because for the last two years these many contributors and benefactors worked in secrecy and without his knowledge. Indeed, so that this birthday gift would remain a surprise to the general editor of *The Sixteenth Century Journal*, only two people knew all the details of this project with even contributors and benefactors knowing only that publication would take place, but not how, when, or where. After two years' effort and secrecy, all that remains for this introduction is to ask, "now, isn't it a dainty dish to set before the King?"

Happy Birthday!!!

Jerome Friedman
Cleveland Heights, Ohio

The Final Demise
of the Medieval Knight in France

Frederic J. Baumgartner
Virginia Polytechnic Institute & State University

Hans Delbrück maintained that the appearance of a true French cavalry—the use of tactical bodies composed of horsemen—dated to the era of the French Wars of Religion. This article places the transformation a little earlier, in the reign of Henry II, 1547-59. That king, despite his love of medieval pageantry, romances, and tournaments, was forced by his wars with Charles V and Philip II to find new military tactics. In several battles in the middle years of his reign the French forces, especially the heavily armored *gens d'armes* (knights), whom Henry regarded as the heart of his army, took heavy casualties from the German pistolers, the *reîtres*, serving in Charles's army. After the disastrous French defeat at Saint-Quentin in 1557, Henry decided to recruit a great number of German *reîtres* and develop his own corps of pistolers. A year later the French army included eight thousand *reîtres*.

Henry's death in July, 1559, while jousting, dealt a further blow to the style of knightly fighting. It created a sharp reaction against the mystique of jousting, which had supported the traditional values and skills of the lancer. Without the reinforcement provided by the tournament, the nobles let the old style of fighting die out. Thus during the religious wars French mounted troops more and more adopted the pistol, so that by the accession of Henry IV in 1589 the pistoler had effectively replaced the knight.

IN HIS MAGISTERIAL *HISTORY OF THE ART OF WAR*, Hans Delbrück spoke of the transformation of knights into cavalrymen in the sixteenth century.[1] He defined the change as the shift from individual mounted warriors to tactical bodies composed of horsemen, while acknowledging that with mounted troops the existence of cohesive tactical units is less easy to perceive than for infantry. Delbrück concluded that the first to achieve the transformation were the pistol-carrying light horsemen of Germany, whom the French called the *reîtres*. Hired by the thousands during the French religious wars, he argued, the *reîtres* spurred the French on to develop their own true cavalry by 1600. While there is nothing manifestly wrong about Delbrück's scenario, the key period for the transition in France from the traditional knight to the cavalryman was somewhat earlier, during the reign of Henry II, 1547-59.

It is ironic to present Henry's reign as the era of the final demise of the medieval knight, for in several respects he was in his attitudes the most medieval of the French kings since the end of the Hundred Years War. Henry loved

---

[1]Hans Delbrück, *History of the Art of War*, trans. Walter Renfroe, 4 vols. (Westport, Conn.: Greenwood Press, 1975-85), 4: 117-45.

to joust, and virtually no court festival took place without a tournament. Once, in the midst of war, he was forced to celebrate a marriage of an important courtier without a tournament because most of the usual participants were with the army. He was reported as "much saddened" by it.[2] Henry was also greatly enamored of the romance *Amadis of Gaul*, sometimes called the last medieval romance. Its hero does little besides jousting with friend and foe alike. The existing specimens of Henry's personal armor are regarded as among the finest ever made.[3]

Far more than was true of the other French kings of the century, Henry had an affinity for the persons and lifestyle of the great nobles who dominated his court and government. He regarded the heavily armored knights, the *gens d'armes* whose principal weapon was the long lance, as the real defenders of the realm. In 1554 after a review of his gens d'armes he expressed his "incredible pleasure and contentment that he was defended by so great and courageous a nobility."[4] For Henry the heart of the royal army remained the gens d'armes, the armored lancers who like the medieval knights still depended upon the weight of their charge in a long thin line—*en haie*—to break the enemy's lines. Encased in plate armor, astride a great war horse, the men-of-arms thought themselves lords of all they surveyed, although by 1547 there was considerable reason to question that attitude. But that vague sense of vulnerability had little effect on their arrogant and often foolhardy disdain for the other arms of the military at that time. In attitude at least the French gens d'armes of 1547 had changed little from their ancestors whose arrogance had brought about the disastrous defeats of the Hundred Years War. Despite heavy casualties in recent battles inflicted on them by commoners, the French men-of-arms remained convinced that they were the lords of the battlefield. Blaise de Monluc, after a successful career as a captain of infantry and a worthy siege master as well, declared that the gens d'armes were the principal defenders of the realm[5] He was far from alone in that opinion. Certainly Henry II believed it.

The men-at-arms were organized into companies of lances. Except for three or four companies commanded by the highest ranked officers, which had 100 lances, the companies consisted of 50 lances or a total of 125 men—50 knights and 75 archers (that is, a ratio of 2 to 3). Since the so-called archers were cavalrymen who wore light armor and used the short lance, they were

---

[2]*Calendar of State Papers Relating to English Affairs Existing in the Archives of Venice and Northern Italy*, ed. Rawdon Brown, (Liechtenstein: Nendeln, 1970, reprint), 5:497.

[3]S. Grancsay, "The Armor of Henri II of France from the Louvre Museum" *Bulletin of the Metropolitan Museum of Art* 2 (1952): 68-80.

[4]François de Rabutin, *Commentaires des Guerres en la Gaule-Belgique*, 2 vols., (Paris: Honoré Champion, 1932), 1: 303.

[5]Blaise de Monluc, *Commentaires*, ed. Paul Courteault, (Paris: Bibliothèque de la Pléiade, 1964), 297.

usually petty nobles because their expenses were not very high. Service in the companies of lances was a function both of wealth and blood; therefore, the number of gens d'armes could not be increased very rapidly. Upon Henry's declaration of war in 1552 against Charles V, there were 51 lance companies totalling 5,975 men, knights and archers. After eighteen months of war, with little serious fighting, the number had reached only 6,900 men. The gens d'armes in the lance companies were part of a standing army and were paid 1,200 livres a year.[6] In addition the king could summon the *ban* and the *arrière-ban*—the feudal levy—if in dire straits he needed more manpower. The rest of the nobility was then obliged to serve, providing the king with several thousand poorly trained and ill-disciplined cavalrymen. By 1547 the French king also had in his service several thousand native mounted harquebusmen (*harquebusiers à cheval*) who provided some measure of firepower for the lance companies.

In fact the infantry had become the master of the battlefield by 1547, as reluctant as the king and the nobles were to admit it. The French army had to depend heavily on foreign mercenaries for both pikemen and musketeers. Ever since the notorious peasants' revolt of 1357, the French nobles had been reluctant to arm their peasants for service as infantry. This prejudice remained strong into the sixteenth century, and the French peasantry had not developed a tradition of service in the infantry except for Gascony, where the English had used Gascon infantrymen in the Hundred Years War. Thus the monarchy in Henry's time found it difficult to recruit good French infantry except among the Gascons. French military captains like Blaise de Monluc, himself a Gascon, did not have a high regard for French infantry, and they preferred to see the monarch recruit mercenaries from abroad. France had a treaty with the Swiss Confederation that permitted the recruitment of up to thirty thousand Swiss pikemen, but Swiss infantrymen were more expensive than those of other nations, and they had a very small proportion of musketmen.[7] Henry tended more and more toward hiring the German landsknechts, who had the additional virtue of serving longer without pay than did the Swiss.

Although Henry was very much attached to the knightly style of fighting, he was first of all motivated by his hatred of Charles V. As the Venetian ambassador wrote in 1553,

---

[6]Bibliothèque Nationale, Fonds français 3127, fol. 3; Ferdinand Lot, *Recherches sur les effectifs des armées françaises, 1494-1562* (Paris: SEVPEN, 1962), 247-48.

[7]A Swiss infantryman cost the king 11.5 *livres* a month; a German, 9 *livres*, and a French footsoldier, 8.5. These rates are calculated from the cost of infantry companies found in BN, Fonds français 3090, fol. 12, which included the pay of the captains, usually 100 *livres* a month, and other officers, so the pay of the ordinary footsoldier was less than the above sums.

The King wishes the Emperor every evil that it is possible to desire for one's mortal enemy. This virulence is so deep that death alone or the total ruin of his enemy can cure it.[8]

Henry burned with hatred for the emperor—largely a consequence of the four years that he spent as a prisoner in Spain as a hostage for his father. Henry always felt that he had been badly mistreated there and blamed Charles. There was also the legacy of a century of wars and feuding between their ancestors to fuel the rivalry.

Motivated by his hatred Henry was willing to make any changes in his military that enhanced his power. For instance he was deeply interested in the artillery, at one point personally touching off several pieces during a siege. His advisers were furious with him for ignoring the clear danger that both enemy fire and the possibility of a cannon bursting presented.[9] On the advice of Jean d'Estrées, his grand master of artillery, the king moved to create order out of the enormous confusion in the types of cannon by establishing the six calibers of French guns that remained standard well into the next century.[10]

In regard to his mounted forces, it appears that the first important incident occurred in October, 1552, at the battle of Saint-Vincent in Lorraine. One of the Guise brothers, François d'Aumale, had been ordered to reconnoiter the army that Charles V was bringing to invest the city of Metz, occupied by Henry earlier the same year. D'Aumale, with a force of seven hundred gens d'armes and a similar number of light cavalry, encountered a slightly larger force of *reîtres*, led by Duke Albrecht of Brandenburg. The *reîtres*, from the German *ritter*, were the successors of the "black horsemen," so-called because of their dark shiny armor. They had been a light cavalry force that had used the short lance but had adopted the pistol by 1552. The wheel-lock pistol of the era was clumsy, inaccurate, and unreliable, but a horseman carrying three or four of them in his hands and boots had some effect at very close range. Using the pistol required less training than did the lance, and a pistoler's horse did not have to be as strong as a lancer's.[11]

Attacking in their standard formation that often was seventeen ranks deep, the *reîtres* decimated the French horsemen at Saint-Vincent and captured d'Aumale. François de Rabutin, a French participant, stated that the gens

[8]N. Tommaseo, *Relations des ambassadeurs Vénitiens sur les affaires de France au XVIe siècle*, 2 vols., (Paris, 1838), 1:385.

[9]Brantôme, *Oeuvres Complètes*, ed. Lalanne, 10 vols., (Paris, 1867), 1:164.

[10]Carlo Cipolla, *Guns, Sails and Empires* (London: Minerva Press,1965), 29n. On Estrées, see *Discours des villes, chasteaux et forteresses batues, assaillies et prises par la force de l'artillerie durant les règnes des roys Henri second et Charles IX* (Paris, 1568), in BN, Collection Clairambault, 1080. As an example of the enormous range of guns available, see the list of artillery pieces surrendered by the English at Boulogne in 1550. Thomas Rymer, *Foedera publica inter Reges Anglicae*(London, 1749), 6/2: 217.

[11]Delbrück, *Art of War*, 4:120-22.

d'armes could not stand up to the numerous blows from the pistols. Henry II was astounded to hear that a force of pistolers not much larger than his own gens d'armes had so easily defeated them. He ordered Constable Anne de Montmorency arrange for every French company of gens d'armes to include an accompanying unit of *reîtres*. In 1554, however, a muster of the army noted only two hundred *reîtres*.[13]

The extent to which Henry actively recruited *reîtres* between 1552 and 1557 is unclear, but in the latter year at the battle of Saint-Quentin in August, 1557, he received further forceful proof of their usefulness in battle.[14] Philip II's forces had several thousand pistolers who, the accounts of the battle agree, played a major role in his victory.[15] The French gens d'armes, on the other hand, fought very poorly. They fled from the battlefield soon after the confrontation began, leaving Philip's cavalry, both lancers and pistolers, free to devastate the French infantry.[16] Since the battle was largely a pursuit of the panicked French forces, the *reîtres*' speed was of particular advantage to the enemy. It was a pistol shot that killed Jean d'Enghien, the most prominent casualty of the battle and the most promising member of his generation of Bourbons.

Henry II clearly was made well-informed of the conduct of the battle, for he was reported as determined to rebuild his shattered forces with a large contingent of *reîtres*:

> He wished . . . to assure himself of his manpower, especially German, and above all reîtres and pistolers because the greatest force that his enemy had and which was thought to give him the most advantage over himself was by means of these reîtres . . . all of which are found loaded with pistols and seemed to have been

[12]Rabutin, *Commentaires*, 1: 148-54.

[13]Ibid., 257. H. Susane, *Histoire de la cavalerie française*, 3 vols., (Paris: J. Hetzel, 1874), 1:47-48, accepted the figure of six thousand *reîtres* given by *Mémoires de Vielleville* in C. Petitot, *Collection complète des memoires relatifs à l'histoire de France* (Paris, 1823), 27: 388-89, for the review of the army before Metz in March 1552; but that number, as with nearly all of the figures given in the memoirs, is badly exaggerated.

[14]Of the seven reports of French strength before the battle, only two mention the presence of pistolers. A Spanish source noted three squadrons of *reîtres*. Rabutin, *Commentaires*, 2:110-15; Lot, *Armées françaises*, 158-67.

[15]For the Battle of Saint-Quentin, see Rabutin, *Commentaires* 2: 124-31; Gaspard de Coligny, "Discours sur le siège de Saint-Quentin, in Petitot, *Mémoires* 32: 417-67; *Calendar of State Papers, Venice*, 6/2: 1243-48; Rabutin, *Armées françaises*, 163-66; Emmanuel Lemaire, et al., *La Guerre de 1557 en Picardie* (Saint-Quentin, 1896), xli-xlvi. C. W. Oman, *A History of the Art of War in the Sixteenth Century* (New York: Dutton, 1971, reprint), 254-66.

[16]It must be noted that the two to three hundred *reîtres* in the French army sent to guard the key ford across the Somme were easily routed, allowing the enemy cavalry to cross unmolested and catch the main French forces by surprise.

invented for the stunning and breaking up of the French men-at-arms.

In order to draw them away from his enemy and take them into his own service and to teach the French to use such arms, Henry sent agents into Germany to raise a vast levy through promises of high pay.[17]

Reîtres did not appear in large numbers in the next major French enterprise, the taking of Calais in early January, 1558, probably because it occurred so soon after the battle of Saint-Quentin but perhaps also because the encounter was expected to be a long siege. Some eight hundred are reported as present. In the following June, however, the army that François de Guise led to Thionville, south of Luxembourg, included between four and five thousand *reîtres*,[18] although the successful storming of the fortress depended little on them.

At virtually the same time, Paul de Termes led a French force north from Calais to raid the prosperous cities of western Flanders. His army also included several thousand *reîtres* as did the army that Count Egmont assembled to oppose him. Egmont's forces surprised de Termes's as the latter were returning along the coast to Calais. Egmont's *reîtres* used their speed to cut off the retreat of the French; that, with the poor showing of the French gens d'armes, assured the French defeat in the battle of Gravelines. De Termes wrote in his report that the gens d'armes collapsed under the *reîtres'* assault much more quickly than he had thought possible. Rabutin, albeit in a second-hand report, was even more critical of the lancers: de Termes was poorly supported by his gens de'armes, and some of their captains and companies were accused of "d'avoir fait mauvais devoir."[19]

Two months later, in August of 1558, Henry II held his last major review of his forces at Pierreport in Picardy. Rabutin placed the number of *reîtres* present at 8,200 and the gens d'armes at 1,750; a second source has 7,800 and 1,550; and a third, probably less reliable, document has 9,000 and 1,650.[20] Clearly by late 1558 Henry had succeeded in recruiting a vast number of German pistolers but not in obtaining his goal of training a native French force.

---

[17]Rabutin, *Commentaires* 2:195. For a similar statement see BN, Fonds français 4738, fol. 27r.

[18]BN, Collection cinq cens de Colbert 26, fol. 111v; Rabutin, 2:199.

[19]On the defeat at Gravelines see De Termes, "Discours du voyage de Dunquerque" in Boyuin du Villars, *Mémoires*, vols. 29-31 of Petitot, *Collection complète* 3:176-85; Rabutin, *Commentaires*, in Petitot, 32: 196-203 (the Taurines edition I have been citing excised Rabutin's material on Gravelines). See also Oman, *Art of War*, 274-81.

[20]Rabutin, *Commentaires* (Taurines ed.) 2: 224-30; Lot, *Armées françaises*, 176-85. see also Monluc, *Commentaires*, 455. All the sources for the royal review noted the presence of French light cavalry such as fifteen hundred *harquebusiers à cheval*.

With Henry so determined to move his mounted troops in the direction of carrying pistols, the manner of his death dealt another major blow to the traditional mounted lancer. The French defeats at Saint-Quentin and Gravelines had been balanced by victories at Calais and Thionville, and in April, 1559 Henry and Philip agreed to the Peace of Cateau-Cambrésis. It called for the marriages of Henry's daughter to Philip and his sister to the Duke of Savoy. In June Savoy and the Duke of Alba, serving as Philip's proxy both for the wedding and for swearing the peace, arrived in Paris. Henry was still enough of a traditionalist not to let such an occasion pass without a grand tournament. On June 30, Henry himself took to the lists. After defeating two opponents, the king was given a sharp blow by a young opponent, Gabriel de Montgommery, captain of the Scots Guards, which almost unhorsed him. Henry was determined to make a better showing and ordered Montgommery to run against him again despite the rule that permitted only three jousts a day. On the second run Henry's powerful but inexperienced opponent gave him such a solid blow on his breastplate that it shattered the lance. Instead of dropping the lance immediately, Montgommery brought the lance up, catching Henry in the face of his helmet with the shattered end and driving a large splinter through the eye opening. After ten days' agony the king died on July 10, 1559.

There was a sharp reaction against the whole mystique of jousting and the romance upon Henry's death. It can be rightly called the true end of the popularity of the medieval romance; as *Amadis of Gaul* abruptly disappeared, and the appeal of other romances to the upper and middle classes declined sharply.[21] Henry's widow, Catherine de Medici, outlawed jousting at the court and abandoned the Palace of Tournelles with its broad jousting grounds, where the accident had occurred. Compounding the impact of the king's death was the death of twelve-year-old Henry de Bourbon-Montpensier, son of the Prince of Roche-sur-Yon, in early 1561, as he practiced using a lance with other boys his age.[22]

With the virtual cessation of tournaments, the style of fighting for which they provided practice declined rapidly as well. Certainly other factors contributed greatly to the dwindling numbers of the traditional armored lancers on the battlefield: their vulnerability to gunfire, their expense at a time of increasing economic trouble, the difficulty of breeding horses strong enough to carry the heavy plate armor; but the tournaments and the romances had

[21]Etienne Pasquier, cited by H. J. Martin, in W. Gundersheimer, ed., *French Humanism 1470-1600* (New York: Harper & Row, 1969), 138-39. Martin also argues that while romances continued to be sold in good numbers, it was to the "less sophisticated public in the country and small towns.".

[22]*Calendar of State Papers, Reign of Elizabeth*, 3: 490-91. The English ambassador reported that the boy had been "shocked off his horse."

served to emphasize the traditional values and skills of the traditional knight. With knightly combat in disfavor, without the opportunity to practice their skills in tournaments and impress the noble ladies, and without the romances to fire their imaginations, the nobles let the old style of combat die out. In the rest of Europe many of these developments in the military had already occurred, but it was in France, the birthplace of the feudal system, the knight, the romance, that the system and the code of medieval warfare had lasted the longest.

In the Wars of Religion that followed Henry's completely unnecessary death and were its direct consequence, mounted troops were the most important arm, in large part because neither side could afford to hire the vast numbers of mercenary infantry that had been the foundation of the French military under Francis I and Henry.[23] *Reîtres*, however, were present in relatively large numbers. Early in the civil war they were employed largely by the Huguenots, since most were Lutherans. Fighting at Dreux in 1562, the pistolers in the Protestant army executed the cavalry tactic known as the caracole for the first time for which there is clear evidence.[24] The caracole, in which each rank of *reîtres* rode close to the enemy, fired their pistols, and wheeled away to reload, was a more effective use of the pistoler and enhanced his appeal. Marshal Tavannes, who was present at Dreux and by 1568 had become de facto commander of the royal-Catholic forces, ordered the formation of French pistoler companies because he found that those lancers still present in the French army were largely ineffective. The increasing amount of armor they were wearing tired both man and horse alike and greatly reduced their effectiveness. Tavannes was probably responsible for the order of October, 1568, that the men of each company of mounted troops were to march together in the formation they would take on the battlefield so that they would become accustomed to holding their positions, a clear statement of the change from the knight to the cavalryman.[25] When Henry of Navarre led the Huguenot forces in the 1580s, few of his men were lancers, while the Catholic forces remained somewhat more loyal to tradition. After Henry took control of the realm in 1594, the pistolers effectively replaced the lancers, although he insisted that they be prepared to charge the enemy with their swords after discharging their pistols but in ranks five or six deep rather than *en haie*.[26]

[23]A muster roll of the royal army in 1562 reveals the drastic decline in the number of men after Henry II's death. Only twelve hundred *reîtres* are noted as present. Lot, *Armées françaises*, 190-92.

[24] Jean de Saulx de Tavannes, *Mémoires*, ed. J. Buchon, (Paris: A. Desrez, 1836), 291; Delbrück, *Art of War*, 123.

[25]Tavannes, 203, 328. See also Monluc, *Commentaires*, 388; Choppin, *Cavalerie française*, 22. After 1568 it becomes difficult to tell in the sources whether the term *reîtres* refers to German or French horsemen unless the name of the captain is given.

[26]Oman, *Art of War*, 463-65; John Lynn, "Tactical Evolution in the French Army, 1560-1660," *French Historical Studies* 14 (1981): 176-91.

The transformation of the French mounted force from knight to cavalry-man was a long-term event, and the developments of Henry II's reign were both the culmination of changes begun earlier and the beginning of changes completed only decades later. Together, however, they vastly changed the nature of warfare and largely ended the lingering medieval traditions and practices. Certainly the final demise of medieval warfare would have occurred rather soon anyway, for the trends were irreversible, but the decisions made by Henry II and the manner of his death clearly accelerated them.

Institute for Research in the Humanities

The Millennium that Survived the Fifth Monarchy Men

Robert G. Clouse
Indiana State University

Recent studies suggest that millennialism, rather than fading into oblivion after the Restoration, was characteristic of all seventeenth-century English groups, including Royalists, Anglicans, Presbyterians, sectarians, and republicans. One historian has demonstrated that millenarian views account for the Puritan interest in science. An understanding of seventeenth-century typology of premillennialism and postmillennialism is necessary to see how Biblical prophecy was tied to current events by a distinguished line of seventeenth- and eighteenth-century English scholars, including Isaac Newton, William Whiston, Joseph Priestley, and others.

ONE OF THE PROBLEMS INVOLVED IN RECONSTRUCTING the world of thought of seventeenth-century England has been millennialism.[1] Until quite recently most of the participants in the debates on this subject assumed that this belief faded into oblivion after the Restoration. Hugh Trevor-Roper has put it plainly: "Instead of a spiritual union for the overthrow of Antichrist, the new society would be so deliberately neutral in religion that it could even be accused of a plan to 'reduce England unto popery.'"[2] Not having experienced the tensions and disasters of the 1620s the new generation in the 1680s was "exempt from its peculiar metaphysics: they would not waste their time on the Millennium, the Messiah or the number of the Beast."[3] Writing in the same vein, Christopher Hill has tied the decline of millennialism after 1660 with the demise of antichrist in the following statement: "The dramatic happenings of the early forties transformed the battle against Antichrist from defensive to offensive, raising utopian hopes, especially in the classes hitherto excluded from politics. The disappointment of these hopes, the social decline of interest in locating Antichrist, the dangers of Fifth Monarchist revolution against him, led the respectable to abandon the search for him altogether. . . ."[4]

---

[1]Helpful information on millennialism is available in the following works: Robert G. Clouse, ed. *The Meaning of the Millennium: Four Views* (Downers Grove, Ill.: InterVarsity Press, 1977); Theodore Olson, *Millennialism, Utopianism, and Progress* (Toronto: University of Toronto Press, 1982); C. A. Patrides and J. Wittreich, *The Apocalypse in English Renaissance Thought and Literature* (Ithaca: Cornell University Press, 1984); and Ernest L. Tuveson, *Millennium and Utopia: A Study in the Background of the Idea of Progress* (Berkeley: University of California Press, 1949). For a general survey of literature about millennialism see Hillel Schwartz, "The End of the Beginning: Millenarian Studies, 1965-1976," *Religious Studies Review* 2 (July 1976): 1-15.

[2]Hugh Trevor-Roper, *The Crisis of the Seventeenth Century: Religion, the Reformation, and Social Change* (New York: Harper & Row, 1968), 292.

[3]Ibid., 293.

[4]Christopher Hill, *Antichrist in Seventeenth Century England* (London: Oxford University Press, 1971), 154 f.

Certain scholars—including Margaret Jacob, Michael McKeon, and Charles Webster—have disagreed with the judgment expressed by Hill and Trevor-Roper. Professor Jacob in a thoughtful work entitled *The Newtonians and the English Revolution 1689-1720* argues forcefully that the leaders of English religious thought at the end of the seventeenth century and the beginning of the eighteenth century were informed by a millennial vision.[5] Called latitudinarians, these liberal clergymen and scientists (including More, Cudworth, Boyle, and Wilkins) accepted Newtonian ideas and tried to apply Christian teaching to the market society emerging in the England of their age. The scheme which they thought would insure the coming of a golden age included the unification of Protestantism under the leadership of the Anglican Church and the spread of the gospel to other lands. As Protestant strength increased, the Roman Catholic Church would be defeated thus ending the fourth and final worldly empire. At this point history would end with the second coming of Christ, "and the saints led by the English church would reign triumphantly in the millennial paradise. Certain minor details would have to be worked out en route: the Jews and Mahometans would be converted, and those who resisted any form of religious worship, the immoral and atheistical, would be shown the error of their ways."[6]

The Churchmen who followed these ideas felt that the new science as well as the prophetic scriptures supported their plan. As Margaret Jacob states,

> There is evidence that many of the latitudinarians, quite probably including Newton himself, were millenarians. If we are surprised at their attitude it is because we have misunderstood the nature of seventeenth-century English millenarianism. We have mistakenly assumed that such views were held only by radicals or fanatics, the understandable expression of their longing for justice and economic freedom. Anglican millenarianism can be found throughout the seventeenth century, and it served the interest of its advocates just as powerfully as did the millennial dreams of the radicals. To be sure, their paradises bore little resemblance to one another and especially after the Restoration Anglican preachers appear reticent to discuss the approaching millennium in their sermons. Enough evidence is available from other sources to show that as late as the early eighteenth century millenarian speculations continued in church circles.[7]

[5]Margaret C. Jacob, *The Newtonians and the English Revolution 1689-1720* (Ithaca: Cornell University Press, 1976).

[6]Ibid., 58.

[7]Ibid., 70 f.

In a perceptive study of John Dryden's *Annus Mirabilis*, Michael McKeon gives impressive scholarly support to Jacob's idea that millennialism continued as an important aspect of English thought after the Restoration.[8] Dryden's poem states that the future holds a time of trouble for England which he terms a second Punic War after which she will lead the world into a rich and glorious Golden Age through the perfection of navigational technique. The coming millennial age would be a magnificent era of martial, commercial, and religious imperialism under the leadership of Charles II as the instrument of God on earth. A comparison of Dryden's royalist prophecy with the Fifth Monarchist dissenting views reveals that eschatological prophecy was compatible with more than one ideology. In Restoration England there was a "great mass of disparate and scattered allusions to the wonders to come in 1666, wonders for London, England, and the world. Nostradamus, Mother Shipton, and numerous more obscure and private sources of speculation were pondered over, updated, and shown to have reference to the war with the Dutch, the Great Fire, the imminent catastrophe in Turkish-Christian relations, and other extraordinary happenings...."[9] The *Annus Mirabilis* rather than condemning millennial prophecy demonstrates that such views are characteristic of all seventeenth-century English groups including Royalists, Anglicans, Presbyterians, sectarians, and republicans. What Dryden discredits is not millennial speculation, but the dissenting policies often advocated by prophecy.

Charles Webster's recent study of seventeenth-century science also contributes to the view that millennial thought continued to be of major importance throughout the century.[10] He believes that millennialism led to the development of modern science. His work focuses on a group of Puritans—including Hartlib, John Webster, Boyle, Wallis, Oldenburg, Petty, Graunt, and Wilkins—who were followers of Bacon's philosophy. Although their contributions have been either ignored or undervalued, once they are given due weight, scholars will understand that the first phase of scientific advancement occurred during the Puritan Revolution and not after the Stuart Restoration. Thus the political upheavals of the 1640s did not inhibit the progress of science but actually contributed to its growth. Since the Puritans were the dominant element in the scientific community, the triumph of their cause meant that English science benefited from the cataclysmic influences of the revolutionary intellectual situation.

Professor Webster contends that the fundamental motivation of the Puritan Baconians was provided by millennialism. According to their calculations,

[8]Michael McKeon, *Politics and Poetry in Restoration England: The Case of Dryden's Annus Mirabillis* (Cambridge: Harvard University Press, 1975).

[9]Ibid., 221 f.

[10]Charles Webster, *The Great Instauration: Science, Medicine and Reform 1626-1660* (New York: Holmes and Meier, 1975).

the millennium was at hand. They cited certain verses in Daniel which prophesied that with the approach of this period "many shall run to and fro and knowledge shall be increased" (Dan.12:4). It was clear that the kind of knowledge people could hope to gain was to be of a practical and utilitarian nature. Since the attainment of the millennium would include the restoration of the sons and daughters of Adam to a pre-fallen state, the wisdom of the end time would be similar to that of Adam, namely, how to control the environment which would lead to longer life and increased fruitfulness of the earth.

Webster believes that his analysis accounts for the Puritan interest in science. The approach of the millennium provided them with a basic motive, so that their scientific studies had a firm religious base. Millennialism, also, explains why their projects concentrated on "knowledge for use." Since the wisdom to be achieved at the millennium was expected to take the form of "dominion over nature," it was obvious that precedence should be given to schemes which offered control over the environment.

The answer to the confusion of claims for the influence of millennialism and its fate after 1660 can be found in a proper typology of millenarianism. It has been the habit to read back into time the current labels of premillennial, postmillennial, or amillennial to categorize eschatological options. These categories are used despite the fact that in a sense they are misleading, for the distinction involves much more than merely whether Christ returns before or after the millennium. The kingdom expected by the postmillennialist is quite different from that anticipated by the premillennialist, not only with respect to the time and manner with which it will be established but also with regard to the nature of the kingdom and the way Christ exercises his control over it. The postmillenarian believes that the kingdom of God is extended through Christian preaching and teaching as a result of which the world will be Christianized and will enjoy a long period of peace and righteousness. This new age will not be essentially different from the present and it emerges gradually as an ever larger share of the world's population is converted to Christianity. Evil is not eliminated but is reduced to a minimum as the moral and spiritual influence of Christianity is heightened. During this age the church assumes a greater importance, and many social, economic, and educational problems are solved. The period closes with the second coming of Christ, the resurrection of the dead, and the final judgment.[11]

In contrast to the above view, the amillennialist believes that the Bible does not predict a period of universal peace and righteousness before the end of the world. Instead, good and evil will both continue until the second coming of Christ when the dead are raised and the last judgment held.[12]

[11]For one of the more perceptive presentations of the postmillennial view see Loraine Boettner, *The Millennium* (Philadelphia: Presbyterian and Reformed Publishing Co., 1966).

[12]For amillennialism one should consult Anthony A. Hoekma, *The Bible and the Future* (Grand Rapids: Eerdmans, 1979).

The third major millennialist interpretation, premillennialism, affirms that the Lord's return would be followed by a period of peace and righteousness, before the end of the world, during which Christ will reign as king in person or through a select group of people. This kingdom is not to be established by the conversion of individual souls over a long period of time, but suddenly and by overwhelming power. The new age will be characterized by the conversion of the Jews and the reign of harmony in nature to such an extent that the desert will blossom like a rose and even ferocious beasts will be tame. Evil is held in check during this period by Christ who rules with a rod of iron. Despite their idyllic condition, men are not satisfied and launch one last rebellion against God and his followers. This final exposure of evil is crushed by Christ and then the last judgment is held. Many premillennialists have believed that during this golden age believers who have died will be reunited with glorified bodies to mingle freely with the rest of the inhabitants of earth. Usually, premillenarians have taught that the return of Christ will be preceded by certain signs such as the preaching of the Gospel to all nations, a great apostasy, wars, famine, earthquakes, the appearance of the Antichrist, and a great tribulation.[13]

It is necessary once more to caution those who approach the subject of millennialism that the usual classifications are not adequate. Although the terms postmillennial, amillennial, and premillennial continue to be used, one must constantly guard against a simplistic outlook because of the use of this scheme. For example, it is often stated that postmillennialism is an extremely optimistic creed that is little more than a Christian blessing on the secular teaching that men will evolve to some utopian social goal. In reality, many fervent Christians have taken a postmillennial view, believing that the Holy Spirit can bring a great revival to the world. This outlook has caused them to preach the gospel with great fervency and to encourage global evangelism and missionary work. It is even possible to be a pessimistic postmillennialist—that is, one who believes the immediate future holds a time of trouble for the church, but that God will send his Spirit in a special way to overcome these problems.[14]

Premillennialism is also a more difficult doctrine to define than it would seem at first glance. Not all premillennialists are consistent and some have decided in ages past to prepare the way for the coming of Christ, even if force was necessary. The current teaching of most premillenarians, that the Jews will be restored to their land and Jerusalem will be the center of the millennial

[13]Premillennialism is explained by Clarence Bass, *Backgrounds to Dispensationalism* (Grand Rapids: Eerdmans, 1960); Charles L. Feinberg, *Millennialism: The Two Major Views* (Winona Lake, Ind.: BMH Books, 1985); Charles Ryrie, *Dispensationalism Today* (Chicago: Moody Press, 1965); and Ernest R. Sandeen, *The Roots of Fundamentalism: British and American Millenarianism* (Chicago: University of Chicago Press, 1970).

[14]Note the cases of George Junkin and Joseph Berg in Robert G. Clouse, *Millennialism and America* (Portland: Western Baptist Press, 1977), 43-47.

state, has not been followed by all who hold to a premillennial advent. An important colonial American premillennial interpreter believed that America would be the center of Christ's kingdom.[15]

For the purpose of the present discussion, a revised version of millennial options will prove helpful. The seventeenth century witnessed the following kinds of millenarians: those who expected a literal coming of Christ and a literal reign (apocalyptic millennialists), those who looked for a literal coming and a spiritual reign (academic millennialists), and those who anticipated a spiritual coming and a spiritual reign (enlightenment millennialists). To illustrate these categories it is necessary to examine the teachings of an individual who held each view.[16]

An outstanding proponent of apocalyptic millennialism, William Sherwin (1607-87), was a minister ejected from his parish in 1662. This experience led him to turn to the study of prophecy which he presented in several books and tracts.[17] Sherwin believed that Christ would rule on earth as a new King David, aided by Christians who would be raised from the dead. When this reign is established the enemies of the church would be destroyed and Satan would be bound for a thousand years. At the close of the millennium the Savior leaves the earth and Satan is loosed. With the aid of evil men Satan attacks the saints, but Christ returns and defeats him, instituting the final judgment and the eternal state.

The millennial reign gave Sherwin a key with which to interpret Holy Scripture. The literal kingdom of God was to be the political breaking of Satan's head as prophesied in Gen. 3:15. The careers of David and Solomon were also used by Sherwin as types to explain the coming millennium. He

---

[15]Samuel Sewell, *Phaenomena quaedam Apocalyptica, or Some Few Lines Towards a Description of the New Heavens* (Boston, 1697).

[16]These categories are suggested by Bryan W. Ball in *A Great Expectation: Eschatological Thought in English Protestantism to 1660* (Leiden: Brill, 1975). Further typologies of seventeenth-century millennialism may be found in Paul Christianson, *Reformers and Babylon: English Apocalyptic Visions from the Eve of the Reformation to the Eve of the Civil War* (Toronto: University of Toronto Press, 1978); James A. De Jong, *As the Waters Cover the Sea: Millennial Expectations in the Rise of Anglo-American Missions 1640-1810* (Kampen: Kok N.V., 1970); Katherine R. Firth, *The Apocalyptic Tradition in Reformation Britain 1530-1645* (Oxford: Oxford University Press, 1979); James F. Maclear, "New England and the Fifth Monarchy: The Quest for the Millennium in Early American Puritanism," in *Puritan New England: Essays on Religion, Society, and Culture*, ed. A. T. Vaughan and F. J. Bremer (New York: St. Martin's Press, 1977), 65-89; Ian Murray, *The Puritan Hope: A Study in Revival and the Interpretation of Prophecy* (London: Banner of Truth Trust, 1971); and James West Davidson's fine book, *The Logic of Millennial Thought* (New Haven: Yale University Press, 1977). For a perceptive analysis of the main millennial views and their typologies in Tudor-Stuart times see George Kroeze, "The Variety of Millennial Hopes in the English Reformation 1650-1660," (Ph.D. dissertation, Fuller Theological Seminary, 1984).

[17]*The Times of Restitution of All Things . . . Two Tracts on Rev. XX.5 and Rev. XXI.5* (London, 1675); *the Doctrine of Christ's Glorious Kingdom . . . Now Shortly Approaching* (1672); *The Saints Rising* (1674); *The World To Come* (1671); *A Plain & Evident Discovery of the Two Personal Comings of Christ* (1670); *The Science of God's Eternal Great Designe* (1675).

found the New Testament replete with millenarian teaching ranging from statements by Jesus to those of Paul, James, Peter, and John. Sherwin spent a great deal of time in his writings answering the critics of millennialism. He also set the date for the coming of Christ as the year 1700.

As Sherwin was an example of apocalyptic millenarians who believed in a literal coming and a literal reign, so Nathaniel Homes represents the academic millenarians who taught a literal coming and a spiritual reign. Homes (1599-1678) attended Oxford University where he received the B.A., M.A., B.D., and D.D. degrees. He served as minister of an independent congregation but was forced to leave this charge in 1662. In his most popular work, *The Resurrection Revealed*, he attempts to continue the teaching of Joseph Mede.[18] Homes carefully explains that millennialism was not a new doctrine, but was believed by both ancient and modern theologians of great repute. When he outlines his scheme for the thousand years he notes that Christ will appear at the beginning and end of the period "though we cannot . . . hold forth that he shall continually be all that time personally present upon the earth." Nevertheless, he assures his readers that "the devil . . . shall be wholly, and absolutely confined and restrained, in efforts, acts, and person from the precincts of the Church."[19] After Christ establishes his kingdom the saints are to rule the earth for him. Homes elaborated his views with many glosses on the Scriptures. For example, in Matt. 24:30 the text states, "And then shall appear the sign of the Son of Man in Heaven: and then shall all the tribes of the earth mourn, and they shall see the Son of Man coming in the clouds of heaven with power and great glory." This means that people will be repentant at the time of the second coming because of the judgment of Christ. The reference to the clouds indicates that Christ will not come in an obscure fashion as he did in the incarnation, but rather in a conspicuous and glorious manner. Another sample of Homes's explanation is his exposition of Matt. 24:34, "This generation shall not pass away till all these things are fulfilled." He informs his readers that the term "generation" refers to the Jews and means that at Christ's coming they will be restored to the Holy Land as an independent nation.

To further bolster his academic millenarianism, Homes cited quotations from a wide variety of scholars to prove that the kingdom of God was coming. He divided these scholars into four groups: unbelievers, Muslims, Jews, and Christians ("whether Papist, Lutheran or Calvinists"). Although his discussions of the millennium avoids what he terms gross or carnal details, he informs his readers that the age would be characterized by the restoration of Edenic conditions to earth, by sinlessness on the part of the saints, and by the

---

[18]For Mede's ideas see Robert G. Clouse, "The Apocalyptic Interpretations of Thomas Brightman and Joseph Mede," *Journal of the Evangelical Theological Society* 11 (1968): 181-93

[19]Homes, *The Resurrection Revealed* (London, 1653), 3 ff.

absence of sorrow and death. There will also be a great outpouring of the Holy Spirit resulting in amazing answers to prayer and a great increase in understanding of the mysteries of God. The millennium would be marked by a successful ecumenical effort as indicated by Zech. 14:9, "And the Lord shall be king over all the earth: in that day shall there be one Lord and his name one." Homes indicated that the attitudes of the Papists, Lutherans, Calvinists, Presbyterians, and Independents each of which indicated that God was only in agreement with their sect would pass during the millennium. Zeph. 3:9 ("They shall serve the Lord with oneness of consent, all being of a pure language") led him to rhapsodize about the passing of sectarian division with the statement, "surely the saints union shall be as that in paradise before Adam fell. The history of dissension now is grievous to Saints; therefore on the contrary, how sweet will the mystery be in the enjoyment of Union."[20]

Homes's work also includes a compilation of various opinions concerning the time of the beginning of the millennium. He cites dates suggested by Thomas Brightman, Johann Heinrich Alsted, Joseph Mede, and Thomas Parker. Although these men do not agree as to the exact set of numbers they combine, they all believe that the later seventeenth century is a crucial time in prophetic affairs. So Homes believed he had arrived at a consensus of prophetic numbers, placing the second advent within the fifty-year period from 1660 to 1710.

In addition to the academic millenarianism of Nathaniel Homes, there was another approach to millennialism which can be identified as enlightenment millennialism. It is illustrated by the apocalyptic writings of the Cambridge Platonist, Henry More (1614-87). As a student and later a fellow of Christ's College, Cambridge, More left an impression on many bright young scholars. His millenarian views are most clearly expressed in a commentary he wrote on the Book of Revelation, *Apocalypsis Apocalypseos: or the Revelation of St. John the Divine Unveiled*. More states the position of the Cambridge Platonists in his reason for writing about the Apocalypse. The book, he believes,

> will refute those that believe neither Angel nor Spirit; for their being a deduction of things foretold from the beginning of the Church to the end of all, so natural, so solid, and so true, and every way unexceptionable to any Rational Man, this is the greatest Evidence desirable to evince a Divine Providence over the Church, and the Affairs of Mankind, and consequently the existence of a God; as also of Angels, the Ministers of his Providence, which is all along inculcated in this Book of the Apocalypse. And particularly it is asserted in the beginning of the Book that this Revelation was

[20]Ibid., 541.

made to St. John by the ministry of an Angel: And that this can be no imagination of St. John's, as the prophane Hobbians and Spinozians would be ready to suggest out of the Principles of their stupid and incredulous minds, but a real thing, the Book itself is an ample Testimony and plain demonstration, it being out of the reach of any man by his own natural wit or fore-sight, to write a Book of such comprehensive Prophecies, and so continuedly true: to say nothing of the manner of writing it, the very Wit and Artifice thereof, which seems to imply . . . the Stile and Wit is not the Stile and Wit of a man, but certainly of an Angel.[21]

More also believed that his work would refute the apocalyptic writings of Ribera and Grotius. Francisco Ribera (1537-91) was a Spanish Jesuit who published a lengthy apocalyptic commentary challenging the claim that the Roman Catholic Church was antichrist. He used a futurist interpretation which stated that most of the statements of the book would be fulfilled just before the return of Christ.[22] Hugo Grotius, the famous Dutch jurist, statesman, and theologian, presented his views in a *Commentary on Certain Texts Which Deal With Antichrist* (1640). Grotius came to believe that the perverseness that Protestants expressed in applying passages from the Apocalypse to the pope was a stumbling block to a greater understanding between Christians, so he decided to interpret these prophecies in a convincing way without showing any relationship to the papacy. He believed that the first beast of Revelation was Roman paganism; the deadly wound, the destruction of Rome; the three-and-a-half times, the persecution under Domitian; and the two-horned beast from the earth, a belief in magic. The thousand years of Rev. 20 begin with Constantine's edict of 311 and end with the rise of the Turkish empire in 1311, while the holy city represents Constantinople which fell to the Turks in 1453. The millennium was fulfilled in the church but the application of all the details of prophecy was in the spirit of the seventeenth-century millennialists with the exception that it was all safely in the past.[23]

In addition to providing an antidote to false teaching, More's commentary on the Apocalypse was designed to combat atheism, exonerate the Reformed Churches in their break with Rome, and prove the futility of Fifth Monarchist ideals for using violence to establish the millennium.

He used a verse-by-verse method to explain the book. These comments follow a prophetic history of the church, outlined by the letters to the seven churches in Rev. 2 and 3 in the following manner:

[21]Henry More, *Apocalypsis Apocalypseos* (London, 1680), "Preface to Reader," xvi f.

[22]For Ribera's position see Leroy Edwin From, *The Prophetic Faith of Our Fathers* (Washington, D.C.: Review and Herald Publishing Assoc., 1948) 2:489-94.

[23]Grotius's views are presented in Ibid., 521-24.

1. The Ephesian Church which represents the period from the foundation of the church to the tenth year of Nero's reign.

2. The church of Smyrna that extended from Nero's time to the year 324 and was characterized by great persecution.

3. The church at Pergamos signifying the era 324-1242 when the church was under the absolute sway of the superstition and idolatry of the papacy.

4. The Thyatira era which lasted from 1242 to Reformation times.

5. The church at Sardis referring to the era from the beginning of the Reformation to the last vial of Rev. 16.

6. The Philadelphian church which stands for the period from the last vial to the fourth thunder during the millennium.

7. The church of Laodicea, signifying the lukewarm Church which existed from the fourth thunder until Christ visibly appears for the last judgment at the conclusion of the millennium.

More believed that the seventeenth century would witness the pouring out of the seven vials of Rev. 16. The vials signified the destruction of Papal Rome, the defeat of Islam, and the conversion of the Jews to Christ. These events would lead to the millennial age when Satan would be bound in the sense that God will lead the rulers of the world to issue laws forbidding anti-Christian worship. The martyrs live and reign with Christ in the persons of their successors who live on earth at that time. Thus More's millennium was a paradise controlled by a properly reformed church. At the close of the golden age Satan is allowed to rebel against God once again by leading the forces of Gog and Magog against the church. Just as it seems that victory is in the devil's grasp, Christ personally intervenes and holds the last judgment, thus ending the Laodicean period. More's work is a further demonstration of the fact that millennialism continued into the later seventeenth century. He paid a conscious tribute to Joseph Mede who was followed by theologians throughout the eighteenth century as well.

The writings of Sherwin, Homes and More illustrate the fact that the apocalyptic, academic, and enlightenment strands of millennialism continued as live options during the entire seventeenth century and did not die out as a result of the collapse of the Fifth Monarchy Movement after the Interregnum. However, the number of those adhering to each view changed with most accepting the academic and enlightenment outlooks, but there remained some who followed apocalyptic millenarianism.

Millennialism continued to exercise a strange fascination over the minds of a sizeable proportion of scholars, preachers, and common people in Early Modern Europe due to the ability of commentators to tie Biblical prophecy to current events, particularly the struggles of Protestantism against its enemies. This was carried on by a distinguished line of scholars who were influential in the eighteenth century, including Isaac Newton, William Whiston, David Hartley, Moses Lowman, and Joseph Priestley. Indeed, it is true of only one kind of millennialism (apocalyptic) that it "became a harmless hobby for cranky country persons [and that] . . . the Little Horn, the Scarlet Woman, and the precise significance of 'a time, times, and half a time' were relegated to that dim twilight in which the lost tribes of Israel wander around the great pyramid."[24]

[24]Christopher Hill, *Puritanism and Revolution* (New York: Schocken Books, 1958), 336. On the other hand, there are those who would agree with Hillel Schwartz that even apocalyptic millennialism remained a popular option. As he states, "After the Restoration of Charles II to the Stuart throne in 1660, millenarianism as a creed or program of action is assumed by many to have lost its political thrust, its vitality and its wide appeal. By the time of the Glorious Revolution of 1688-89, so the tradition goes, millenarians had become introspective, or exponents of a secular notion of progress, or mildly insane. Historians fascinated by the politically active chiliasts of the mid-century—Fifth Monarchists, Levellers, Ranters, Diggers—have often neglected those millenarians of minor political engagement, such as the French Prophets, for they have been more concerned to determine the roots of political theory and action than to investigate all facets of a millenarian's world. They have focused upon political failures, not upon the social or affective continuity of a millenarian ethos. I hope to demonstrate in this book that the French Prophets appealed to an astonishing variety of people who drew upon types of millenarian ethos common to men and women of the early seventeenth century. . . . Scholars have recently discovered millenarian ideas in the papers and programs of some of the most prominent figures of later seventeenth-century English society: Robert Boyle, Thomas Hobbes, Sir Isaac Newton, and the latitudinarian bishops. The new scholarship argues that images of the world's end had lost neither their intellectual attraction nor their political thrust some forty years after the Restoration. I argue in this work that an entire millenarian way of life flourished in England between 1660 and 1740. The French Prophets were not the source but the sign of its vitality." *The French Prophets: The History of A Millenarian Group in Eighteenth-Century England* (Berkeley: University of California Press, 1980), 7 f.

The Last Judgment by Jean Cousin, 1500-1590

Possevino's Papalist Critique of French Political Writers

John Patrick Donnelly, S.J.
Marquette University

In 1592 at the urging of Innocent IX Antonio Possevino, the much travelled Jesuit diplomat and scholar, published *Iudicium de Nuae militis Galli, Ioannis Bodini, Philippi Mornaei, et Nicolai Machiavelli quibusdam scriptis.* The volume is a criticism of the French political thinkers Gentillet, La Noue, Bodin, and Mornay from a strongly papalist viewpoint. An abbreviated version of the *Iudicium* was included in Possevino's influential *Bibliotheca selecta.* The Jesuit attacked Innocent Gentillet's interpretation of the St. Bartholomew's Massacre as an Italian-Catholic plot based on Machiavelli's recommendations. He criticized Bodin for being too sympathetic to Huguenots, for Judaizing tendencies, for allowing duelling, and for suggesting that the papacy be made hereditary. Possevino found grave doctrinal error behind Mornay's efforts at an ecumenical piety. He developed a sustained attack on La Noue's plea that Catholics and Protestants put aside their differences and combine forces in a crusade against the Turks: La Noue's call for toleration ignores the enormous doctrinal differences between Catholics and Protestants and among various groups of Protestants. In the past such toleration has led only to sedition and civil war. Years later Possevino read Jacques Auguste de Thou's *Historia sui temporis* (Volume I, 1604) with great interest. In an attempt to influence de Thou's second volume in a more Catholic direction he sent de Thou personal reminiscences of his years (1560-72) in France. De Thou resisted Possevino's attempt to influence him. Possevino's reading of the French political writers suggests how contemporaries often miss the main contribution of innovative thinkers such as Machiavelli and Bodin and become bogged down in detail.

AT TWENTY-SEVEN ANTONIO POSSEVINO (1533-1611) threw over a promising career as a humanist and entered the Jesuits. Within a year he was debating theology with the Waldensians and founding colleges in Savoy. There followed 28 years of incessant activity in France, Italy, Sweden, Muscovy, Poland, and Transylvania; along the way he helped found seven colleges or seminaries and negotiated a peace between Poland and Ivan the Terrible. He also incurred the displeasure of Sixtus V, of the Jesuit General Claudio Aquaviva, and of the House of Habsburg so that in 1587 he found himself exiled to the Jesuit college at Padua. *Otium* followed *negotium*, but Possevino's *otioum* was not very restful. In 1591 he was back in Rome with a giant manuscript to be shepherded through the Vatican Press, his *Bibliotheca selecta.* Its thousand folio pages provided a bibliographic guide to most areas of Renaissance thought. It was the most important of Possevino's forty books and established his reputation as a polymath—*Italorum omnium doctissimus* according to one writer.[1]

While at Padua Possevino developed close links with the Venetian Inquisitor, at whose urging he prepared a list of the errors in the works of Machiavelli, Jean Bodin, and Phillippe de Mornay to be given as an antidote to those who asked the Inquisitor for permission to read these prohibited authors.[2] The Inquisitor also forwarded a copy of Possevino's notes to Cardinal della Rovere of the Congregation of the Index, and Possevino circulated his notes to friends for their comments. When he returned to Rome in 1591 with the manuscript of the *Bibliotheca selecta*, Cesare Baronio, the great church historian, brought Possevino to see an old mutual friend, Gian Antonio Facchinetti, who had just become Innocent IX. Their conversation turned to Possevino's notes, which the Pope encouraged him to publish in both Latin and Italian—in the event there never was an Italian edition. The day previous to his conversation with Innocent IX Possevino received a letter from another old acquaintance, Duke William of Bavaria, who urged him to take up his pen against Machiavelli. Possevino saw this coincidence as providential and got down to work.[3] In 1592 the Vatican Press issued his *Iudicium de Nuae militis Galli, Ioannis Bodini, Philippe Mornaei, et Nicolai Machiavelli quibusdam scriptis.* The next year a pirate edition appeared at Lyons.[4] Possevino included an abbreviated version of his *Iudicium* in the *Bibliotheca selecta*, issued by the Vatican Press in 1593 with a prefatory letter from still another old friend, the new pope Clement VIII.[5]

---

[1]Hugo Hurter, *Nomeclator Literarius Theologiae Catholicae* (Innsbruck: Wagner, 1907), 2:466. The secondary literature on Possevino is very large. I am presently working on a biography. Among the most valuable contributions are Liisi Karttunen, *Antonio Possevino: un diplomate pontifical au XVIe siècle* (Lausanne, 1908); Stanislas Polcin, *Une tentative d'Union au XVIe siècle: La mission religieuse du Père Antoine Possevino S.J. en Moscovie* (Rome: Pont. Institutum Orientalium Studiorum, 1957); Oskar Garstein, *Rome and the Counter-Reformation in Scandinavia*, Vols. 1 and 2 (Oslo: Universitetsforlaget, 1963, 1980).

[2]On 19 November 1588 Monsignore Minuccio Minucci wrote Possevino a letter discussing his manuscript comments on Bodin: see Mario D'Addio, "Les six livres de la republique e il pensiero cattolico in una lettera del Mons. Minuccio Minucci al Possevino" in *Medioevo e rinascimento: Studi in onore di Bruno Nardi* (Florence: Sansoni, 1955), 1: 127-44.

[3]Possevino described the circumstances behind his *Iudicium* in a letter to Achille Gagliardi, 13 July 1597; Archivum Romanum Societatis Iesu, *Opp. NN.* 333, ff. 29v, 30r. This letter to his friend Gagliardi together with its tone and content make it clear that Possevino was the author of the *Iudicium*, contrary to the suggestion of Silvio Barbi that Possevino may have used Giovan Battista Strozzi as a ghostwriter. Barbi's other suggestion that Possevino had Strozzi translate the section of the *Iudicium* against La Noue into Latin is more probable. S. A. Barbi, *Un accademico mecenate e poeta: Giovan Battista Strozzi il Giovane* (Florence: Sansoni, 1900), 43.

[4]For this essay I have used the Lyons edition: (Lyon: Buysson, 1593). This edition also prints Possevino's judgment on the Augsburg Confession, on Erasmus, and on the "secta Picardica" as well as another attack on La Noue by Pierre Coret.

[5]The arrangement and material in the *Iudicium* and the *Bibliotheca selecta* differ somewhat; the *Bibliotheca* adds an introduction but radically shortens the section on La Noue.

There were later editions of the *Bibliotheca selecta* at Venice and Cologne. Obviously Possevino's *Iudicium* came with high official approbation.[6] So much for the external background of Possevino's critique of the French political writers. What of the internal—Possevino's own viewpoint? It was militant papalist Catholicism.[7] The common thread uniting the political writers that Possevino attacked was precisely their opposition to militant Catholicism; otherwise they were rather diverse since three of them were Huguenots and two were at least nominally Catholic. Possevino can be seen as an almost stereotypical counter-reformer, but he was also eloquent, observant, and clever. His learning was very broad, though often not very deep.

Possevino's critique of Machiavelli has already been studied elsewhere.[8] The brevity of his remarks on Machiavelli suggests that he was less interested in Machiavelli, who had been answered by others, than in refuting the French political writers he was dealing with. He devotes as much space to refuting the *Anti-Machiavel*, which we now know was written by the Huguenot Innocent Gentillet, as he does to Machiavelli himself.[9] Possevino did not know the author's identity, but he considered Gentillet's Calvinist comments as evil as the blasphemies of Machiavelli.[10] Gentillet's argument that the St. Bartholomew's Massacre was an Italian-Catholic application of Machiavelli was hardly a thesis likely to please Possevino, who had been personally involved in an unsuccessful attempt to save some Huguenot prisoners in the sequel to St. Bartholomew's at Lyon.

Possevino's critique of Jean Bodin took up three works: the *Methodus Historiae*, the *De Daemonomania*, and the *Six Books on the Republic*. His criticism was not synthetic but pegged to specific passages or chapters in Bodin's works,

[6]Not everybody approved. Sir Henry Wotton, who later when English ambassador at Venice made it a practice to intercept Possevino's correspondence, wrote to his superiors from Siena that Lord Darcy "Having no other way to resist or retract, bought up all the examples" of Possevino's *Iudicium*, apparently those in Tuscany. This aroused the anger of the Inquisition, but the Grand Duke supported Lord Darcy, probably to curry English favor. See the letter of Wotton to Lord Zouche, 25 November 1592, printed in Logan Pearsall Smith, *The Life and Letters of Sir Henry Wotton* (Oxford: Oxford University Press,1907), 1:291-92.

[7]Of the many evidences of Possevino's devotion to the papacy none is so striking as the will that he drew up in 1607 when he felt close to death; in it he prayed to God that whatever form of death "that I may take from this vale of tears shall be to the glory of Thy name and to the honor of the Holy Apostolic See in which Thy vicar infallibly sits": Archivum Romanum Societatis Iesu: *Opp. NN.* 333, f. 302.

[8]Antonio Panella, *Gli Antimachiavellici* (Florence: Sansoni, 1943), 54-63.

[9]Innocent Gentillet, *Discours contre Machiavel*, edited by A. D'Andrea and P. D. Stewart (Florence: Casalini Libri, 1974). Both Panella (54-55) and D'Addio (129) claim that Possevino never even read Machiavelli's own text but based his criticism entirely on Gentillet. This assertion was first made by the German polyhistor Hermann Conring (1606-1681), as Panella points out (54). They are both unaware that Conring was answered in the eighteenth century by Nicolo Ghezzi, the Italian editor-translator of Jean Dorigny's *Vita del P. Antonio Possevino* (Venice: Remondini, 1759), 2:71-72.

[10]*Bibliotheca selecta* (Rome: Typographia Apostolica Vaticana, 1593), 1:127-28.

which he noted in the margins. Much of it was nit-picking. Possevino found that Bodin's *Methodus Historiae* often relied on Calvin and the Magdeburg Centuries and that it downplayed the role of free will and divine providence. Bodin was both too skeptical in treating Christian miracles and too credulous in relying on astrology as causal explanation. Possevino censured Bodin for following Plato and Xenophon in allowing political leaders to lie for reasons of state. He also took exception to Bodin's claim that the morally good individual made a bad citizen, to his praise for the high morals of Geneva and to his criticism of the papacy.[11] The Jesuit noted the relative absence of Christian sources and the heavy dependence on rabbinical authors in Bodin's *De Daemonomania*.[12] Bodin slid over the whole Catholic liturgical and paraliturgical apparatus for dealing with the diabolical. Possevino then developed a theme which D. P. Walker has recently studied,[13] namely that Catholic controversialists stressed the ability of their rites (especially exorcism for which Protestants had little or no equivalent) to defeat diabolical intervention, which was a major interest for many contemporary writers such as Bodin. Possevino found it ironic that Bodin wanted both religious toleration and the execution of sorcerers, magicians, and witches.[14]

Possevino criticized the *Six Books of the Republic* for its reliance on the Old Testament and Jewish sources; had he known Bodin's *Colloquium Heptaplomeres*, which was not published until the nineteenth century, his suspicions of Bodin as a Judaizer would have increased.[15] Possevino claimed that the translation of the *Republic* had been doctored by a third party to make it less offensive to Catholics, but this only sugar-coated a dangerous book.[16] Possevino also pounced upon Bodin for allowing duelling and brandished against him the excommunication of the Council of Trent against those involved with duelling.[17] Possevino agreed with Bodin that Englishmen were ethnocentric and formed little introspective enclaves when abroad. He also claimed that he could always spot a Frenchman who was a Calvinist—look carefully, his downcast eyes always reveal his bad conscience! Possevino disagreed, of course, with Bodin's attack on celibacy and his arguments for special

---

[11]Ibid., 130-31.

[12]Ibid., 132-33.

[13]D. P. Walker, "Demonic Possession Used as Propaganda in the Later Sixteenth Century," in *Scienze, credenze occulte, livelli di cultura*, no editor (Florence: Olschki, 1982), 237-48. Possevino (*Iudicium*, 96) related the same story of Nicole Obry described by Walker (241-42).

[14]*Bibliotheca selecta*, 1: 136.

[15]Ibid., 134, 139. Bodin's real religious convictions are the subject of considerable dispute. Externally he claimed to be a Catholic most of his life. The Jewish tendencies are stressed by Paul Lawrence Rose, *Bodin and the Great god of Nature: the Moral and religious Universe of a Judaiser* (Geneva: Droz, 1980).

[16]*Bibliotheca selecta* 1:135.

[17]Ibid., 138.

taxes on those who do not marry and have children. He also took exception
to Bodin's arguments for hereditary versus elective leadership. To Bodin's
suggestion that the papacy be made hereditary he noted sarcastically that the
Frenchman knew better than Christ, who instituted the papacy. Possevino
answered Bodin's claim that the Venetians tended to elect second-rate men as
doge with a eulogy of six recent doges, some of whom he knew personally.[18]

Possevino's critique of Philippe de Mornay's *De la Vérité de la religion
chrétienne* was more succinct. Mornay was even more sinister than Bodin since
his book was tricked out in the garb of piety and orthodoxy until one examined it closely. Possevino objected to fourteen statements scattered through
Mornay's more than five hundred pages. He quoted Mornay briefly, citing
page numbers, and then appended a short refutation. Sometimes he objected
on philosophical grounds; thus when Mornay claimed, "We sometimes will
what we do not understand," Possevino replied with the standard scholastic
doctrine that the human will is never directed toward an unknown object.
Sometimes the objections were theological. Against Mornay's statement,
"God alone satisfied and can satisfy," Possevino cited the Council of Trent and
argued that Christ as the God-man and even human beings in grace with his
cooperation could satisfy and merit. Since Mornay's book deliberately avoided
issues that divided Catholics and Protestants, Possevino's criticism can only
strike modern readers as nit-picking.[19]

By far the largest part of Possevino's *Iudicium* was his attack on François
de la Noue's *Discours Politiques et Militaires* (1587).[20] This section was radically
shortened in the *Bibliotheca selecta*, from eighty-seven to four folio pages. La
Noue argued that French Catholics and Protestants ought to live together in
peace and toleration since what they shared religiously was more important
than their differences. Their arms should be turned against a common enemy,
the Turk. Meanwhile there should be a General Council, or at least a French
National Council, to settle religious issues. La Noue's motive was partly to end
the Wars of Religion that had been wracking France and in which he was intimately involved. Little in his discourses pleased Possevino. For Possevino the
differences between Catholic and Protestant were enormous and included not
only the usual controverted points but also differing views of Christology and

[18]Ibid., 131, 139-42.

[19]Ibid., 142-44. On Mornay's life, see E. Haag and E. Haag, *La France Protestant* (Geneva:
Slatkine Reprints, 1966), 7:512-42.

[20]There is a good modern edition, François de la Noue, *Discours politiques et militaires*, ed. F.
E. Sutcliffe (Geneva: Droz, 1967). For his life see Henri Hauser, *François de la Noue (1531-1591)*
(Paris: Hachette, 1892). More recent are James J. Supple, "François de la Noue's Plan for a
Campaign Against the Turks," *Bibliothèque d'Humanisme et Renaissance* 41 (1979): 273-91, and
William H. Huseman, "'Bayard Huguenot'? Un réexam en de la carrière de François de La Noue,
1531-1591," *Bulletin de la Société de L'Histoire du Protestantisme Français* 130 (1984): 137-73.

Trinity. Possevino was not a professional theologian, and he did not develop theological arguments; after giving a few scripture quotations, he referred readers to the Catholic controversialists Robert Bellarmine and Thomas Stapleton. He then moved on to historical arguments against religious toleration. His basic argument was that tolerating Protestants led to civil war or unrest, whereas suppression (perhaps with a few judicious executions to encourage the others) was a small price to pay for peace and harmony. He then reviewed the history of Savoy, France, Belgium, and Bavaria to prove his point. La Noue had pointed to Switzerland and Germany as countries where Catholics and Protestants were living together in peace. But, Possevino rejoined, were Catholics allowed to worship in Geneva, or Saxony, or England?[21]

Possevino next posed a host of difficulties to La Noue's proposals for a General or French National Council. What would be the criterion of truth? The Word of God? Of course, but there would be no agreement on its interpretation. Luther and Calvin contradicted each other. Suppose the Augsburg Confession were accepted as a basis—but there were different versions of the *Augustana*. If Catholics allowed Lutherans and Calvinists to vote at such a Council, votes should logically be given to Anabaptists and Antitrinitarians—in some areas such as Transylvania they outnumbered Lutherans and Calvinists. And what about the Eastern Orthodox? What about the Copts, Georgians, Armenians, and the St. Thomas Christians of India? What about votes for women, who shared the same baptism and grace with men?[22] What about procedural difficulties—who should settle disputes, set agendas, promulgate and enforce decrees? The Emperor? But he was a good Catholic and denied that he had such authority. Possevino also developed arguments against a more simple accord involving only Catholics and Calvinists. He then contrasted Catholic unity with Protestant diversity in a way that foreshadowed Bossuet's *Histoire des variations des églises protestantes*.[23] So much for a General Council. What about a French National Synod? After a few pages on the glories of the French church and its past synods, Possevino reviewed the history of Catholic-Lutheran-Calvinist colloquies at Worms, Luneberg, Maulbronn, Altemberg, and Dresden. All these failed because Protestants lacked a principle of unity in a strong visible magisterium. Even the Frankfurt book fairs divided their religious offerings into three divisions: Catholic, Lutheran, and Calvinist.[24] Possevino next turned to problems of religious unity in Eastern Europe, where he had expert knowledge. His conclusion was

[21]*Iudicium*, 1-14.
[22]ibid., 14-26.
[23]Ibid., 26-34.
[24]Ibid., 34-40.

predictable—in Eastern Europe heresy was not just a seven-headed hydra but a hundred-headed hydra that poisoned kingdoms and destroyed unity.[25]

La Noue's appeal was mainly to *politiques*, many of whom felt that harmony was possible if each side could give a little ground. But, Possevino retorted, this attitude ignored the fact that Christ built his church on rock. The Church was a given. The *politiques* felt that they could independently negotiate away the articles of faith, a power that neither the papacy nor an ecumenical council had ever claimed. Even popes and councils were not masters of the faith but only dispensers of its mysteries.[26]

Was religious peace in France obtainable? Yes, replied Possevino, but only on the basis of integral Catholic restoration. He tried to show that two faiths and two peoples could not live together in harmony. He opposed even such minor concessions as communion under both species: that compromise failed when it was tried with the Hussites in Bohemia, Moravia, and Silesia and with the Lutherans in Bavaria.[27] In fact Possevino knew that there was little hope that his Catholic integralism would be tried. He admitted that a cure for heresy was unlikely, but at least French Catholics should hold on to the fullness of faith. Then health might return to others with less danger. Possevino tried to show with selected examples from French history how the past glories of France rested on the Catholic faith. His tour of the horizon of French history put great stress on the role of the king.[28] When Possevino was writing in 1592 civil war was still raging in France. Although a zealot, Possevino was careful not to align himself with the Catholic League. He said nothing directly against Henry of Navarre. Indeed Possevino was called from retirement in 1593 by Clement VIII for negotiations dealing with Henry's absolution. In describing kingship Possevino uses the most glorious of images, the sun, now obscured by an eclipse. But the eclipse would soon pass, "ut clarissime micet potestas futuri regis."[29] But he said nothing about who was the rightful king: "let him who will be the legitimate king in France know that he must keep his own heart and that of others from evil."[30]

Possevino closed his treatment of La Noue by attacking his proposed Catholic-Calvinist crusade against the Turks, which would have two columns, one Catholic under the Duke of Lorraine, the other Protestant, presumably under Henry of Navarre. One might expect that Possevino would be sympathetic to this proposal since much of his own diplomatic career was

[25]Ibid., 41-45.
[26]Ibid., 45-47.
[27]Ibid., 51-60.
[28]Ibid., 69-79.
[29]Ibid., 72.
[30]Ibid., 78.

devoted to building an alliance of Poland, Russia, Venice, and the Emperor against the Turk. In fact Possevino opposed La Noue's crusade. God did not favor mixed forces, and such mixed forces had rarely been successful. The Protestant army would hurt relations with the Eastern Orthodox. The added numbers that the Protestants would provide were not needed—with God's help a small but devout army was enough against the Muslims as had been shown by Scanderbeg's victories in the Balkans, by the Portuguese accomplishments in the Indian Ocean, and by the recent defense of Malta by the Knights of Rhodes.[31] Although La Noue's proposals for toleration and an anti-Turkish crusade must have been attractive to Frenchmen wearied by civil war, his arguments concealed a host of unexamined presuppositions and practical difficulties that Possevino skillfully exposed and exploited.

Possevino's dealings with the last of the French political writers had a different character. In 1604 Jacques Auguste de Thou published the first part of his *Historia sui temporis* covering the years up to 1560. Possevino wrote de Thou an extremely long letter, which covers sixty quarto pages of fine print.[32] Possevino told de Thou how fascinating and learned his work was and promised to plug it in two of his own forthcoming books. Possevino, however, gently reproved de Thou for relying on such Protestant writers as Philip Melanchthon, John Sleidan, and Isaac Casaubon.

De Thou's second volume was to cover the years 1560 to 1572, the period of Possevino's work in France. He tried to influence the projected volume by supplying de Thou with documents, mostly correspondence, and his reflections on personalities with whom he had had first-hand contact, for instance Gregory XIII, Sixtus V, Innocent IX, Clement VIII, Emmanuel Philibert of Savoy, Michel de l'Hopital, and Pierre Viret. Some of his confidences were those of a garrulous old man—Possevino was then in his seventies. Some were grossly unfair. To give the worst example, he related how after a public debate with Pierre Viret he managed to get the Protestant patriarch aside and begged him to repent of his heresy. Viret put him off with, "C'est tout un," which Possevino took in a sense Viret could hardly have meant, namely that religious dogmas do not matter. Possevino was aghast—the man he thought was merely a heretic turned out an atheist.[33] Possevino concluded his letter by urging de Thou to revise his works in a more Catholic direction, not very subtly suggesting the example of St. Augustine's *Retractationes* and the more recent retraction of Joseph Scaliger. Indeed he even sent a copy of Scaliger's *Elenchus* along with his letter. In the event de Thou retracted nothing.[34] On the contrary, his second volume (1608) drew so much Catholic fire that it was put on the *Index*.

[31]Ibid., 80-86.

[32]Francesco Antonio Zaccharia published the letter in his *Iter Litterarium per Italiam* (Venice: Sebastiano Coleti, 1762), 264-324.   [33]Ibid., 308.   [34]Ibid., 323-24.

We have traced Possevino's criticism of five French political writers, Gentillet, Bodin, Mornay, La Noue, and de Thou. In one respect the results are disappointing: Possevino was content to attack specific statements rather than delve deeper issues. The criterion he measured these writers against was always his own Counter-Reformation orthodoxy without trying to understand them on their own grounds. His was an era of change in which political thinkers played a major role, the Machiavellian Moment of J. G. A. Pocock. Values that Possevino cherished—stability, universality, hierarchy, and authority—were being replaced by a world and a world view increasingly dominated by progress, nationalism, relativism, and secularism. Possevino would not have liked the brave new world that was foreshadowed by writers such as Machiavelli and Bodin. When we come to Possevino after reading Pocock's *The Machiavellian Moment* or Julian Franklin's *Jean Bodin and the Sixteenth-Century Revolution in the Methodology of Law and History* we are disappointed that Possevino has missed or at least passed over what was most profound and momentous in these authors. And yet Possevino was an intelligent observer with wide learning and practical experience. He far surpassed the Frenchmen he was criticizing in the experience of lands and peoples; nor was he a man of narrow intellectual horizons. In some sections of the *Bibliotheca selecta* Possevino developed sweeping visions for cultural hegemony and world evangelization which illustrated his ability to build concrete plans of action from his erudition.[35] When we look back over the developments of the last four centuries we have the advantage of hindsight and can see how the books of Machiavelli and Bodin carried the seeds of the future and how other ideas that Possevino was attacking, such as La Noue's scheme for a joint Catholic-Protestant crusade against the Turk, had no future; but we know which seeds were destined for good soil and which were to fall on rocky ground. Contemporaries could not see that. We should be grateful when they tell us what they see, for we can learn nearly as much from their blind spots as from their clairvoyance.

[35] Albano Biondi, "La *Bibliotheca selecta* di Antonio Possevino. Un progetto di egemonia culturale," in *La "Ratio Studiorum": Modelli culturali e pratiche educative dei Gesuiti in Italia tra Cinque e Seicento*, ed. G. P. Brizzi (Rome: Bulzoni editore, 1981), 43-75.

Telescope in the Old Observatory

The Spiritualist Paradigm
An Essay on the Ideological Foundations
of the German Revolution

Jerome Friedman
Kent State University

Few major religious upheavals were more inextricably bound up with political theory than the sixteenth-century German revolution of the Protestant Reformation. Indeed, it is often difficult to differentiate political from religious ideas and the political or social use of religious concepts developed to facilitate new political realities. This very short essay will attempt to demonstrate the existence of a conceptual mechanism which permitted the creation of the first ideologies of revolution expressed in a religious idiom but predicated upon considerations of pragmatic power. The conceptual mechanism which could adapt itself to a wide variety of political and confessional settings and characterized so much sixteenth-century religious/social thought is the spiritualist paradigm. Traditional divisions such as Magisterial and Radical Reformations, and concentration upon such limiting and possibly artificial confessional terms such as "Erasmian," "Lutheran," "Calvinist," or "Anabaptist" only obscures those more general intellectual tendencies, like the spiritualist paradigm, which cut through all such ideologies of change.

Dualistic spiritualism was the primary intellectual engine and conceptual framework for a spectrum of sixteenth-century ideologies seeking religious and institutional change. Already in the previous century it had become a significant intellectual vehicle for popular social change conceived in a religious idiom. The Bohemian Taborites, the Spanish Alumbrado Illuminists, and Savanarola's Florence demonstrated how large numbers of rural peasants, urban activists, and Christian *conversos*, might employ spiritualistic religion as a function of social alienation. After 1500 spiritualism was no longer the escape of mystical individuals, small dissenting groups, or even alienated urban or rural classes, but an ideological mechanism with broad-based public appeal. Brief examinations of Erasmian, Lutheran, and Radical social religious thought demonstrate how this mechanism would achieve near universal acceptance as the intellectual format of choice for social, political, or religious change in the German Revolution.

FEW MAJOR RELIGIOUS UPHEAVALS WERE MORE INEXTRICABLY bound up with political theory than the Reformation. Indeed, it is often difficult to differentiate political from religious ideas and the political or social use of religious concepts developed to facilitate new political realities. This very short essay will attempt to demonstrate the existence of a conceptual mechanism which permitted the creation of the first ideologies of revolution expressed in a religious idiom but predicated upon considerations of pragmatic power.

41

The conceptual mechanism which could adapt itself to a wide variety of political and confessional settings and characterized so much sixteenth-century religious/social thought is the spiritualist paradigm.

Spiritualism looks numerically and historically insignificant from the conventional view that distinguishes between the Magisterial and Radical Reformations. This popular distinction, however, is predicated upon ecclesiastical institutions and confessional ideas that were the subsequent developments of the Reformation. While this confessional approach is useful for church historians and others whose interest is primarily doctrinal or ecclesiastical, it is not satisfactory for secular historians wishing to understand how and why change comes about. Should we place the horse before the cart and seek those intellectual frameworks which initiated and facilitated the sixteenth-century German Revolution, we will find that dualistic spiritualism was the primary intellectual engine and conceptual framework for a spectrum of sixteenth-century ideologies seeking religious and institutional change. Moreover, already in the previous century it had become a significant intellectual vehicle for popular social change conceived in a religious idiom.

Medieval orthodox religion postulated the virtue of practical piety and the efficacy of a church-sanctioned ritual within a God-created world. Spiritualism, however, detested the world and its institutions and believed the eternal conflict between spirit and matter originated in the contest between God and Satan. Rather than further ensnaring the believer in a web of worldly and materialistic ritual, spiritualists sought the soul's repose without external trappings. But if truth resides outside the satanic-material world while orthodoxy taught a religion of the world, those who possess the truth are bound to experience alienation from the larger orthodox community of men. Consequently, both psychologically and socially, spiritualism is an affirmation of the believer's individuality and value against the collective community. In its political dimension, spiritualism argues that the temporal present is immutably corrupt and must be transcended. This appraisal meant that the world, and the fate of alienated seekers after truth, could not change because matter and spirit, like God and the devil, must remain eternally opposed. Religious rituals and political institutions were only the corrupt extensions of a material world and subject to an inner-light antinomianism, an acid-bath concept which makes organized religion, ritual, clergy, and a Bible irrelevant parodies of truth. Hence, spiritualistic belief is the intellectual vision of unfettered existence, of absolute freedom and total liberty. The worldly call this system of thought anarchy.

This strident dualism left little hope for improvement in the world and perhaps for this reason medieval spiritualists lived as hermits or sought to avoid the world in the spiritual serenity of the isolated monastery. As monasteries themselves became politically significant, indeed, a potent force in forming social policy, a new Joachite spiritualism emerged which was able to conceive of and provide for change in disregard of the social limitations imposed by the dichotomy of matter and spirit, original sin, or the evident need to wait for the second coming. By dividing time into a materialistic age of the Father, a ritualistic age of the Son, and a future transcendent age of the Spirit, Joachite spiritualism assumed that human tradition constituted the essence of that which is obsolete and evil. This pattern could still accommodate the older dualism's alienation from the material world, but, unlike earlier systems, Joachism provided a measure of hope and pointed to a new age in which the alienated few, as saints, would inherit a spiritual world cleansed of contemporary religious and political institutions. Some believed it possible to rush the onset of this new age through political activity. This new spiritualism could couple the common feeling of sad personal isolation with an acceptable medieval avenue of personal dissent–the mystical journey inward–and convert both into a social program involving the demise of temporal political or social institutions. In sum, spiritualist dualism separated matter from spirit and the flesh from the soul but it also differentiated saint from sinner socially, psychologically, and politically, and that which is from that which will be. While it could lead to quietism, pietism, and other traditional forms of spiritual withdrawal from the world, the new spiritualism might also lead committed saints to the violent destruction of this earthly nest of the Antichrist. In short, the new spiritualism could convert personal alienation and spiritual values into temporal and political imperatives.

Before the fifteenth century, dualistic spiritual religion was the province of lone dissenting individuals or small groups of social misfits such as the Beghards and the Brethren of the Free Spirit. It could also thrive in Franciscan monasteries or other institutions philosophically alienated from the outside world. This heretical orientation left the monastery when the collapse of feudal land tenure and guild protections, coupled with a new trade-based and capital-efficient economy, created a large mass of socially alienated people without the traditional security accorded peasants, workers, and townsmen. A new more secular and social spiritualism, most clearly reflected in the three very different phenomena, the Bohemian Taborites, the Spanish Alumbrado Illuminists, and Savanarola's Florence, demonstrated how large numbers of rural peasants, urban activists, and Christian *conversos* might employ spiritualistic religion as a function of social alienation.

Neither Taborite nor Alumbrado ideas had a lasting impact because it was easy for established authority to destroy these socially extraneous and politically deficient individuals. Their religious ideas would prove more durable, however, should societal conditions further decay and cut across class lines. Indeed, Savonarola's program posed this danger for he appealed to all classes and all cultural groups. In short, after 1500 spiritualism was no longer the escape of mystical individuals, small dissenting groups or even alienated urban or rural classes, but an ideological mechanism with broad-based public appeal.

This mechanism would achieve near universal acceptance as the intellectual format of choice for social, political, or religious change in the Protestant Reformation.

The many crises occasioning the German Reformation provided rich soil for new spiritualist growth much as the crises of previous centuries facilitated the initial transition of spiritualism from the monastery to the secular milieu. The long-festering conflict between the territorial princes and the emperor aggravated Germany's unfortunate fiscal position as the milk cow of the church. There were problems with the French to the west and difficulties with the powerful Turks in Eastern Europe. The injection of Spanish gold caused a terrible inflation which proved unsettling to those classes tied to contracted feudal obligations as well as to the unprotected urban lower classes. While knights and peasants rebelled and merchants' fortunes rose or fell, many southern German towns abolished their guilds, leaving workers and others unprotected in a market increasingly dominated by strong inter-city competition. It is within this context of universal discontent and social alienation that most classes and population groups sought social redress and discovered in the spiritual paradigm both a solvent for their unhappy present and a mechanism for developing ideologies of change. For this reason, the spiritualist paradigm cut through almost all sixteenth-century ideals of change from the most conservative to the most radical.

As an example, Erasmus's personal sense of alienation from the "worldly church" is well known. A priest's bastard and possibly a homosexual, Erasmus vented his acid against his own past and the monasticism and structured religiosity which he believed limited his spirit. His *Enchiridion*, a virtual handbook of dualist spiritualism, rejected the rituals and institutions that stifled spiritual creativity and sought instead an interiorized Christianity where the soul could find adequate expression. These views were easily predicated upon the spiritualist's traditional admiration of Paul and strong dislike of Moses. Erasmus further obviated original sin, the traditional stumbling block to human spiritual integrity, by explaining that it was a state of confusion experienced by the believer caught between the material body and the spiritual soul. More than any other literary figure of any class in any country, Erasmus popularized a spiritualist religious orientation that sapped the inner strength of the institutions he detested. Shrewdly, Erasmus never converted his dualism into a social program with political overtones. And yet, had he been less witty or less successful in supporting himself by cultivating the largess of the rich and famous, historians might have concluded that Erasmus lived the life of a wandering spiritualist Beghard.

Luther certainly looked spiritualistic. He scoffed at Erasmus and other humanists extolling human potential but his own program was simple; Luther wished to liberate the Christian spirit from the dead man-made rituals of an evil institution representing the worst influences of Satan. Like Erasmus,

Luther suffered from emotional alienation and had much to destroy in a personal past that led him to believe that God hated him. If Erasmus would undo a hated monasticism, Luther would undo the entire hated church. Indeed, in the spirit of alienation he even embraced the Jews and congratulated them for not having converted to the Catholic Church. For the young Luther, the Jew, too, stood as a rejection of "the past," and Luther actually wrote that he would prefer to be a Jew than a Catholic. Luther was soon rejected by the institution he sought to reject, and went through an "anarchistic" free phase in which institutions were considered unnecessary.

Like so many spiritualists before and after him, Luther was indebted to Paul to explain how and why the rituals of the past were no longer applicable. Much as Paul liberated earlier Christians from Old Testament ethnic Hebrew practices dating from the "killing" age of the Law, Luther would relieve all of the burdens of a corrupted medieval ritualistic Catholicism. Luther argued that the worst attributes of Pharisaic Judaism and the obsolete Law had been re-incorporated into the age of the Gospel since the ninth century when the church fell. Luther would service his age as Paul served his, and yet, Luther's updated Pauline dichotomy of Law and Gospel was also a more orthodox version of the Joachite dichotomy of an obsolete ritualistic age of the Father and the present age of the Spirit. Both systems enabled one to transcend a corrupt present as a remnant of an obsolete past. Pauline Erasmus, too, continually complained about those Pharisaic and Judaistic elements of Catholicism which impaired the spirit but, unlike Erasmus, Luther did convert his spiritualism into a social program. Where Erasmus sought inner piety, Luther, like the Minor Brethren, desired the destruction of a spiritually irrelevant but Satanic institution

Translating the Pauline-Lutheran dichotomy of Law and Gospel into temporal political terms was necessary because one could only bring about religious change by politically dislodging "spiritual usurpers." This task did not prove difficult and Luther's revolutionary notion of the priesthood of all believers did much to undermine the most fundamental premises of traditional ecclesiastical governance. Calvinism would go even further and argue that religious calling might provide an adequate justification for the killing of temporal [i.e. Catholic] tyrants. The early Luther wrote about many other traditional revolutionary spiritualist themes which helped sap ecclesiastical institutions of their religious validity. He wrote of the "liberty of the Christian" and the "freedom of conscience" and the need to persuade rather than coerce. He appealed to every commoner's desire to see his country free of burdensome papal taxation. Best of all, this program of change might be justified as the triumph of Paul's spiritual Gospel over Rome's worldly Law.

Luther's life looked as revolutionary as the views justifying his life were spiritualistic. When he laughingly waved the writ of his excommunication over the bonfire in Wittenburg and cried out that within two years time the church itself would be in flames, we are reminded less of conservative princes and magistrates than of Thomas Müntzer. If it is difficult to conceive of Luther as a law-breaking-spiritualist-outlaw, we might remember why Luther went into hiding. Hence, it was not surprising that the Zwickau prophets came to Wittenburg in search of kindred spirits at this same time. Their initial reception would indicate they understood something about the well-springs of this reform movement. Like the people from Zwickau and other radicals, Luther believed there was little need to worry about reforming decadent religious institutions; a central problem of Catholicism was that it had institutions at all. He consoled that the soul needed no sacramental institutions or agencies of this world to facilitate its growth. Reform did not matter because the early Luther, and the folks from Zwickau too, believed the second coming close at hand. Some historians of the German reform movement have dismissed the Zwickau prophets as crazy men but some Lutherans were of another mind.

Andreas Carlstadt, Rector of the University of Wittenburg, knew Luther well and while he was slower to arrive at Luther's radicalism, he quickly surpassed his mentor. Luther the spiritualist attacked the intellectual vanity of humanism, the arrogance of church tradition, and demanded a Scripture-true religion. Carlstadt, the middle-aged, stodgy, stuffy, and conservative University of Wittenberg rector, threw position aside to become a humble pastor to a community of peasants attempting to live in an apostolic community of shared goods. To an extent, Carlstadt demonstrated the social spiritualistic potential latent within Lutheranism, and was a good example of where some radical Lutherans thought the Reformer himself was heading. Like Luther, Carlstadt disapproved of the actual Peasants' Rebellion but thought the social issues worth addressing. His attempts to mediate for peasants failed, and, with Luther's complicity, Carlstadt was eventually banished from his spiritualist parish to accept a teaching position at the University of Basel.

It is not hard to appreciate Luther's dilemma in the mid-1520s. Luther's Spiritualist bubble had burst and he presented a new thermidorean face for new times and conditions that found the spiritualist solvent uncomfortable. His golden-cage protection by the Elector of Saxony taught him the limitations of the spirit and the necessity of having worldly protectors. One could chase the Zwickau Prophets away, force Carlstadt into exile, condemn Erasmus as a dangerous skeptic, and he would soon write against the peasants in words more violent and harsh than those used against the Roman Church. But Luther had already demonstrated the applicability of spiritualism to the political setting, and there were others for whom the revolutionary kernel of dualistic spiritualism remained the foundation for an open-ended ideology of change. Erasmus was passè.

Thomas Müntzer had been an early Lutheran but he, Gaismair, Bunderlin, and others with peasant links are called "revolutionary Spiritualists" rather than "magisterial reformers" and when three hundred thousand peasants exercised their own Christian liberty and justified it in Luther's name, the reformer was beside himself. Confessional apologists have consoled themselves that these peasant leaders misunderstood Luther's call for Christian liberty to apply to them when in fact it was the Christian prince Luther had in mind. But Christian liberty was not a concept for Luther alone to define but was part of a much larger spiritualist tradition. In this same tradition, Erasmus had sought to free himself from stultifying rituals, and Luther liberated himself by rejecting the satanic ecclesiastical institutions sponsoring these same stultifying rituals. The peasants conceived of themselves as part of this larger movement and saw Luther in messianic terms as the Drummer of Niklashausen once again coming to lead them to their liberty. Iconoclastic peasants smashed church windows and set altars ablaze and sought to free themselves from the evil prince who defended the satanic church sponsoring stultifyng rituals.

Some historians argue that Luther, unlike Müntzer and the others, respected legitimate authority. The princes he invited to provide Christian liberty, one reads, were not rebelling against "legitimate authority," something Luther would never condone, but against "abusive, satanic, and anti-Christian corruption." One finds Müntzer expressing similar sentiments. Luther noted that the princes he invited to rebel were already magistrates and hence might oppose other magistrates. In fact this was just another way of observing that he already had the support of inferior magistrates and that he needed an agency possessing at least some measure of power to topple those with greater power. Understanding who has power and who has not does not make one magisterial, radical, or spiritual—merely sensible. Each reformer was sensible, though not equally successful. Luther appealed to the small group of politically separatist princes with grievances against the emperor while Thomas Müntzer competed for princely attention, had little to offer them, and in the absence of other power bases, was forced to suffice with the peasants. Luther won and was able to institutionalize his ideas into a Magisterial Reformation. Luther's appeal to German princes provided the Elector of Saxony with a rationale for taking political matters into his own hands against the wishes of Emperor Charles V. Similarly, the Elector's support of the Saxon monk made Luther's program legitimate rather than revolutionary. This marriage was surely made in heaven and perhaps for this reason rebelling princes, with the support of the new religion, found it possible to confiscate church wealth and monastic property. Müntzer lost and his supporters were left with small voluntary "gathered churches" because, in the end, what else was left for them? Historians have noted that Müntzer loved "the peasantry" and merely detested each individual peasant. Clearly, it was easier to love successful princes.

Thomas Müntzer and Andreas Carlstadt both lacked an adequate power base for durable social change and this pragmatic political deficiency, and not their ideas or beliefs, separated them from Luther and accounted for the success of one and the failure of the others. Other spiritualists were more politically well-situated. Among these one finds Rothman and the spiritualist leaders and popular heroes of the "crazy phase" of the Münster revolution who were the very Lutherans also responsible for the earlier "sane and sanitary" Lutheran phase of the Reformation. That Rothman, too, had been a Lutheran minister may not seem impressive but one should consider that Müntzer and his peasants were Lutheran and so was Carlstadt. But, we must finally wonder whether it was really "Lutheranism" they shared or whether all of them, plus Erasmus, were spokesmen for alternate wings in a German revolution which sought varied degrees of change and found in the same spiritualism a universal solvent and an open-ended ideology to dissolve the past and justify the changes they sought.

Münster city was a case in point of what could happen if Radical Reformation-spiritualism succeeded in making a revolution. And yet, the history of this Westphalian city is typical of ecclesiastical seats accepting Magisterial Reformation-Lutheranism. Here as elsewhere, the role and power of the merchant-dominated Town Council increased with the destruction of Catholicism. Property and power changed hands when a Protestant ideology enabled merchants and others with the informal economic power of the age of the Gospel to triumph against those with formal ecclesiastical authority of the age of the Catholic Law. Unlike other cities, however, Münster retained its powerful guild organizations and after a Lutheran revolution, we see a continuing revolution of those without property seeking to implement the freedom from property of the age of the Spirit. Spiritualists justified this continuing revolution by arguing that there was little need to protect status, property, or other conventions of the obsolete Old Testament age of the Father or the religious rituals of the New Testament age of the Son in this age of the Spirit. Or, from the Lutheran perspective, much as there was no need to retain those religious observances originating from Hebrew ethnic practices under the Law or the Law-like corruptions introduced by Rome, the social-economic relationships characterizing the restrictions of the Law were similarly unnecessary in the age of the Everlasting Gospel. For Rothman, the spiritualist's age of the Spirit and the Lutheran age of the Gospel were the same; social-economic conventions, and not merely the religious habits of the past, must be obliterated.

Whether one believes this revolution of the spirit to have succeeded depends largely upon one's orientation. Policies in Münster included polygamy, the communization of goods and the creation of a community of saints. Hence, the revolution succeeded in destroying established norms for morality, governance, religion, and property ownership deemed obsolete or unnecessary in this age of the Spirit. In all this, the revolution did precisely what its creators desired. Most contemporary observers were shocked by these reforms, and yet

Münster was the culmination of a tradition which included Erasmus, Luther, Müntzer, and many others but which found its historical feet in the Taborites, the Alumbrados, and Savanorola and others before that. In other words, Münster was what might have happened had Thomas Müntzer succeeded a decade earlier and taken control of some specific territory; or, had Luther not been wedded to landed princes and instead proved more pragmatic about institutionalizing the revolution; or, had Erasmus entertained and popularized ideas about the division of the social classes equivalent to those describing the dichotomy of flesh and spirit and had chosen to oppose the political power of the flesh as well as the monastic religion of the flesh. Münster demonstrated that revolutionary spiritualism, the same conceptual solvent and mechanism employed by Luther, Carlstadt, Müntzer, and others yet earlier, was still a viable intellectual option for all those who sought continued open-ended radical change.

We have dealt with four spiritualistic strains. Each accommodated different demands for varying amounts of change with a religious ideology suited to its needs. In each case, spiritualism provided an open-ended dualistic ideology to explain how personal alienation from existing social or religious institutions might be converted into a social program to go from some temporal "here" to some spiritual "there," however variously both conditions were understood. In each case, each thinker tailored his religious ideas–from essentially similarly functioning spiritualist concepts–to the degree of personal or social change desired.

Erasmus was clearly the most conservative and wished to limit change to the individual spirit. He did not need Luther's institutional change to justify remaining personally free of the monastery. Luther sought to change the church's institutional relationship with society and because he doubted that bishops and cardinals would voluntarily abdicate their power, he catered to those princes already set against the Catholic emperor to facilitate change. Lutheranism may have proven appealing to princes for no other reason than Luther asked the princes to make a revolution. If it is doubtful that German princes required a monk's blessing to grab church land and oppose their emperor, it is equally doubtful these princes would have supported Luther without a religious imprimatur for doing precisely this. After all, these same princes had opposed the emperor long before Luther did.

Had Luther's primary support come from urban centers we would find him developing a very different attitude regarding ecclesiastical authority and the rights of princes. Geneva, for instance, had just asserted its independence by overthrowing princely power, and the town council needed no additional princes or religious theories justifying their authority. Since the prince was no longer God's agent, Calvinism appealed to merchants by providing an ecclesiastical constitution institutionalizing deacons, elders, and others drawn from the business community. What Genevan merchants lacked from the Lutheran perspective of established and legitimate princely authority, they soon acquired in Calvinist predestined election. Upholding one's local prince or town council as a measure of legitimacy *after* the revolution does not constitute belief in the concept of magisterial legitimacy; it is only a self-serving justification for successful revolution. Müntzer too would have supported right-thinking princes and Münster actually created a revolutionary king.

Who can blame Thomas Müntzer for appealing to the peasants? It was the peasant who suffered at the hands of landed Catholic "tradition" and a mercantile Protestant scripturalism which legitimized the confiscation of church property but not the economic grievances of the poor. What if Luther, like Müntzer, had been able to attract only the wretched peasants? This indeed had been poor Carlstadt's fate and he was forced to become a university professor, in Basel. Thomas Müntzer wished to alter the political foundations of society and needed to destroy that much more before he could reconstruct social institutions. Müntzer should not be differentiated from Luther other than to wonder if he provided an adequate intellectual and religious basis for continued change much as thoughtful historians should analyze Luther from the perspective of whether his ideas could justify the change he sought. Hence, who can blame Müntzer for spiritualizing the text? Catholicism had the built-in pliancy of the four-fold tradition of interpretation through which almost anything was justified and Lutheranism, though it claimed the letter of the law, was equally pliant. We think of Luther as a literalist and not as an allegorical spiritualist but it was Lefevre, Luther's source, who explained about literalism; "We call the literal sense that which agrees with the spirit and which is revealed by the Holy Spirit . . . and is infused by the Holy Spirit." Perhaps it was through the spirit that Luther was able to translate the Old Testament since he knew very little Hebrew. It was certainly not the literal text that called for the revolution which instituted Lutheranism but denied Caesar Charles V his due. Of course, it was necessary for Protestantism to argue for the literal scripture since actual law, political theory, and tradition all favored Catholic legitimacy. Radicals, seemingly forever one step behind, were left with demonstrating that neither the pliant Catholic four-fold tradition nor the equally pliant Protestant spiritual-literalism expressed the good intentions or true *Spirit* of the gospel.

Rothman and his associates wished to wipe the slate clean and needed a far more radical ideological base. Hence where Catholicism interpreted the Bible four different ways and chose the most comfortable and Luther interpreted the literal test *with* the Spirit, and Müntzer *followed* the spirit, Münster's strange leader's *were* the spirit. Münster's radicals attempted to arrive at that most perfect spiritualist state where all has been destroyed and the spirit can repose in freedom because there is nothing left to provide restriction. The spirit is free because it has transcended churches, princes, economic systems, and human relationships. Though ideologically the most radical, and conceptually the most spiritualistic, Münster's urban revolution was also the most dangerous precisely because this Radical Reformation was a Magisterial Reformation from its very inception. Religion and institutions of power went hand in hand in Münster much as the princes settled for Luther and Genevan burghers finally made do with Calvin. Had they proved a little more enduring, the peasants, too, like Luther and Calvin, would have found it possible to rely upon opportunistic "friendly princes" much as the somber madmen in Münster, once they consolidated power, succeeded in finding businessmen and guild leaders to support their program. Had they been successful, Müntzer's peasants would have created institutions as "magisterial" as any created by Luther or Calvin. Indeed, this was precisely Carlstadt's intention. Had he not been banished, his community might well have created a model of magisterial Anabaptism much as Münster city re-created monarchy in the form of King John of Leiden. It is possible that some radical rural programs would have managed without some specific prince, much like Genevan Calvinism, or without an emperor, much like Saxon Lutheranism. And had Erasmus been influential, this community might even have done nicely without a church.

Münster's radicals, like Calvin and Luther, must also demonstrate how easy it was to provide, after the fact, an adequate religious and scriptural basis to justify that which had already occurred and then promptly call a halt to change. When change adequate for their needs had been brought about, Erasmus, Luther, Münster and the rest re-corked and re-shelved the spiritual bottle. All spoke in the name freeing the human spirit from usurping and obsolete institutions but, in the end, all worshiped power. Erasmus worshiped anyone who could support him; Luther created Erastian ecclesiastical superintendents; Calvinism created the consistory; and Münster created a new tyrannical monarchy. The same phenomenon would occur a century later when English parliamentary rebels would decry Stuart oppression and replace royal and Episcopal tyranny with a worse Presbyterian tyranny. In turn, the semi-spiritualist Cromwell would marshal the antinomian New Model Army to destroy both a tyrannical Parliament as well as a tyrannical state church only to rule through a military dictatorship thereafter.

If we look at sixteenth-century thought from the vantage point of each denomination's ability to provide for change already in the process of occurring, most did so by expressing themselves in terms of essential dualistic spiritualism to accommodate the required degree of change and then justified themselves in the text. Indeed, an investigation into comparative exegesis would find that each, in his own way, fully justified his spiritualist views in scripture. If Luther justified change by holding the Church's feet to the fire of the literal text and Müntzer spiritualized the Word (as did Erasmus) while Münster's theoreticians allegorized the Bible into a nose of wax, it only demonstrates how sufficiently ingenious these thinkers were to develop the necessary religious and scriptural arguments to justify and rationalize their various programs of radical change. *Sola scriptura* was a vehicle for them all, but the goal of none.

Confessional Reformation history draws artificial distinctions between denominations but whether an ideology of change is drawn from the point of scripture, from majesty of God, double supralapsarianism, or the peregrinations of the free spirit becomes less important when we realize that every revolutionary agency will surely find an adequate ideological base to justify its purpose. Similarly, we need not pause too long on essentially confessional distinctions such as the precise rituals used to celebrate the mass, the Lord's Supper, how the priest/minister should dress, whether penance was a public or private sacrament, how many sacraments there were and whether baptism was practiced at one specific age or another, by sprinkling or submerging. Such distinctions may have been important to a vocal minority at the time and may even continue to be important to those for whom the sixteenth-century is more a source of truth than a source of understanding. Yet, these technical details were secondary to the extent that Luther, Calvin, Müntzer and others all joined revolutions already in progress and the same political events and social changes would have occurred with or without this or that baptismal ritual or priestly garb. Surely none studying the development of the Vietnamese revolution would find importance in the varying formulae used to bless rice by different local Buddhist priests in the Mekong Delta or the rituals of religious initiation employed by Buddhists or Christians in North and South Vietnam. Even those admiring the Ayatollah of Iran would hasten to explain the Immam's rise to power through factors other than his specific understanding of scripture or ecclesiastical concepts. The same is true of the sixteenth-century German Revolution and concentrating upon the totality of expressions of similar ideas in a similar conceptual framework permits us to see the continuous flow of the revolution.

Despite the formal differences that distinguish one thinker from another, or one confession from another, Lutheranism, Calvinism, radicalism, and even humanism presented variants on possible spiritualist ideologies. Taken together, these diverse reformers facilitated a continuum of change and provided their various constituencies of German intellectuals, princes, burghers, or peasants with justifications, explanations, and rationalizations for changes they desired but might not have been able to understand or accept as good traditional Roman Catholics. In all cases spiritualism provided the universal solvent dissolving the experiences of a nasty human past in favor of a divine future and provided the intellectual basis upon which, depending upon which class, institution, or agency was available, an opportunistic revolutionary future would be built and justified. Personal, social, and institutional problems could be identified with "the past" and might be laid to rest for it was now possible to build the *New* Jerusalem. Tomorrow would be better, more Godly, and, whatever developed, more scriptural.

The Religion of the
First Scottish Settlers in Ulster

W. Fred Graham
Michigan State University

Although historians of Northern Ireland usually assume that the Scots who came to Ulster in the plantation of James VI/I were Presbyterians, because they arrived some half-century after the Reformation in Scotland, the evidence seems to show that they arrived with little or no religion of any kind. It seems clear that most of the early settlers from Scotland came from the Border region. That region had been in constant turmoil since the end of the thirteenth century, and efforts on both sides to pacify border "reiving" met with little success, especially after the depredations of Henry VIII's "rough wooing" of the Scots in the 1540s. And the records of the Kirk of Scotland are full of lament about lack of church planting in the region, as well as abortive attempts to secure the funds, refurbish "demollishit" kirks, and draft ministers for the job. It appears that a large area had no formal religious practice when its inhabitants were given the choice of death or becoming tenant farmers in Ireland.

PRESBYTERIANS IN NORTHERN IRELAND constitute the majority of Protestants in that part of Great Britain. Among their numbers most trace their ancestry across the Irish Sea to Scotland. Their oppostiion to Roman Catholicism is strong—nearly legendary. A Belfast pastor friend of mine was censored by the Presbytery of Armagh for speaking in the Roman Catholic Cathedral in that city. It did not matter *what* he said there, so far as the presbytery was concerned, it was *that* he had spoken there, where sits the papist archbishop of all Ireland.

It is generally understood that the Scots in Ulster were always Presbyterian—at least that was my understanding. After all, when James began his Plantation there in 1610, Scotland had been Protestant for a half a century. And while it is true that bishops had been re-introduced into the Scots Kirk in 1597 and Parliament had given them diocesan rule again in 1606, still the presbyteries continued to plant kirks, and train and appoint ministers, and see to discipline during that period of plantation until the death of James in 1625. John Harrison expressed this view succinctly:

> Perhaps it is one of the most remarkable and most striking features of this Scottish colony in Ulster, that it was from the first, and has remained even through many persecutions, so consistently and strongly Presbyterian.[1]

[1] John Harrison, *The Scot in Ulster* (Edinburgh: William Blackwood and Sons, 1888), 21.

53

Constantine Fitzgibbon takes the same position, but believes few if any of the first settlers survived the native Irish rebellion of 1642.[2] And James Leyburn takes issue with the judgment of Robert Blair, fiery Presbyterian minister from Scotland, who came to Bangor in 1623 and characterized most of the early settlers as having no care for planting religion. He also rejects the Reverend Andrew Stewart's verdict that the settlers were "the scum of both nations," i.e. Scotland and England. In summing up his disagreement with the judgments of these early Presbyterian ministers, Leyburn argues:

> First, the colonists who were married brought with them their wives and families; next, within two years these very Scots had, by their industry made such a success of the enterprise that thousands of their countrymen now followed them over to Ireland; and finally, as soon as ministers came to Ulster, the settlers welcomed them with open arms and shortly made their churches a replica of the strict moral environment that had now become normal in Scotland.[3]

It would never have occurred to me to question the generally high level of belief on the part of the earliest Scottish emigrants had I not read George MacDonald Fraser's *The Steel Bonnets* a few years ago.[4] His account of the life among the Border people of Scotland and England is devoid of any interest in religion, but as I read the horrible account of three centuries of social distress and economic upset, it became clear that religion could hardly have been alive on the Border in the late sixteenth and early seventeenth centuries. And if it was the Scot on the Border who was the chief emigrant to Ireland—a contention I half-remembered reading in Perceval-Maxwell's work some years before—then how could that poor, cattle-stealing wight have any of the fear of God or of kirk session within his soul?[5] I had no idea of doing research when I began my study of a couple of years ago. I only wanted to read someone else's work in order better to understand the contemporary stand-off between Catholic and Protestant in Northern Ireland. My real interest, then, was existential: I was going to Northern Ireland to stay there for a month, and I wanted to know more of the history of the embattled province.

I have found it a curiously hard history to get a hold on. In order to try for that hold I shall outline my material in the following way. First, we shall try to ascertain whether the bulk of early settlers in Ulster were from the Scots

[2]Constantine Fitzgibbon, *Red Hand: The Ulster Colony* (London: Michael Joseph, 1971).

[3]James G. Leyburn, *The Scotch-Irish: A Social History* (Chapel Hill: University of North Carolina Press, 1962), 108-10.

[4]George MacDonald Fraser, *The Steel Bonnets* (New York: Knopf, 1972).

[5]Michael Perceval-Maxwell, *The Scottish Migration to Ulster in the Reign of James I* (London: Routledge & Kegan Paul, 1973).

side of the Border. Second, we shall look very briefly at life in the Border region at the time of the Ulster Plantation and the generation or so before that time. Finally, we shall ask what religious life in that region was like at the time of the Plantation.

Where Did the Planted Come From?

So far as I know, the only study of James's scheme of plantation is the one by Perceval-Maxwell. Unlike the memory I carried around from having read his book, he does not say unequivocally that the majority of Scots who came to Ulster under James were Borderers. What he does, instead, is show that the region provided many people who were no longer welcome in their own land. As will be seen in the next section, the constant depredations of Border "reivers," the scarcity of justice, and the conniving of appointed and hereditary officials in constant and continual criminality on the Borders had persuaded James VI, long before he became James VI/I, that order had to be forced on that unhappy land by draconic means. Perceval-Maxwell notes this and observes that "the social upheaval brought about by the firm policy seems to have had the greatest impact in creating a reserve of potential emigrants."[6] The firm policy came about when James was able to unite the separate Border wardens on both sides into one commission in March, 1605. Immediately, hangings and expulsion became the order of the day, and the message was clear: too many lawless and largely landless peole lived on the Scottish side, and the Borders must be depopulated.

But he does not argue that Ulster became a penal colony. True, most of those who were criminals and either volunteered to leave, like the Grahams of Eskdale, or were forced to do so, were from the Borders. And it was also true that in 1622 the Irish council proclamation deplored "the extraordinary resort of people of the meaner sort of the Kingdome of Scotland into this Kingdome, much more abounding here of late than of in former times."[7] At most he says that opening up Ulster helped the Scottish government establish order in the middle shires (i.e. the Borders):

> It is true that the plantation encouraged cattle thefts and supplied criminals with a convenient sanctuary. Yet this was a small price to pay for the departure of a very large number of Borderers who would otherwise have had little else to do but create disorder at home.[8]

Nevertheless, when he examines the lists of names that survive the early years, it is clear that Border names predominated. In Fermanagh the 1630 Ulster muster role shows that the most frequent names were Johnston,

[6]Ibid., 22.   [7]Ibid., 283.   [8]Ibid., 312.

Armstrong, Elliot, and Beatty—all Border names. In the same 1630 records from County Tyrone, Elliott, Armstrong, and Scot share with Stewart, a non-Border name, the most-common designation, while Bell, Graham, and Johnston share with Hamilton, a non-Border name, the palm for second most common. But in Antrim and Down Counties, both partially settled just before James's Plantation but during his reign, names from the Borders are less in evidence. In Down, after the names Montgomery and Hamilton (also the names of the chief landowners) came Johnston, Scot, Bell, Maxwell, and Gibson—all names from the Borders. The same, says Maxwell, is true of Antrim, where the most common names were Stewart, Boyd, and Hamilton, with Borderers mixed in with the less common ones that follow.[9] This suggests, he concludes, "that the 14,000 or so adult Scots who populated Ulster during the Jacobean plantation came largely from the eight counties which lay either along the Border with England, or up the west coast to Argyllshire."[10]

Godfrey Watson, in his study, *The Border Reivers*, concurs, pointing to the exiling of Grahams to Roscommon and Connaught (though neither is, of course, in Ulster) and the Armstrongs to Ulster. He argues that gradually the violence of the Borderers became, after James's pacification, absorbed in the religious fervor of the Covenanters.[11] But neither his nor Fraser's more complete study really searches through the records to see what became of the pacified Borderer. Probably Perceval-Maxwell's study is the best we have or are likely to get, unless we find documentation he did not explore.

It leaves us, then, with the clear likelihood that many, perhaps a majority, of the Scots in Ulster after James's planting were from the Borders. But it amounts to less than full proof.

What Was the Border Region Like?

It is not easy to inscribe a line around the Scottish side of the frontier with England and say with confidence that one has included south and east of that line to the Border itself all that in the sixteenth century was called the Borders. A map shows that the borderline meanders in a northeasterly direction from the Solway Firth at Gretna Green until it finds the Tweed River and follows that lovely stream almost to the North Sea. Berwick lies at the Tweedmouth and geographically surely belongs on the Scottish side. But ancient conquest—Edward I is supposed to have put all its seventeen thousand inhabitants to death on a Good Friday in 1295—has made it English, and so the Tweed is abandoned in its last few miles by the border line. Nithsdale, with

[9]Ibid., 286-89. See the map in Raymond Gillespie, *Colonial Ulster: The Settlement of East Ulster, 1600-1641* (Cork: Cork University Press,1985), 32.

[10]Perceval-Maxwell, *The Scottish Migration to Ulster*, 289.

[11]Godfrey Watson, *The Border Reivers* (London: Robert Hale, 1974), 196.

Dumfries to the south and Drumlanrig Castle to the north, should probably be counted the Border's western limit, although modern Scots living in Dumfriesshire do not consider themselves Borderers. Next, to the east, is the valley of the Annan, which like the Nith, runs south into the Solway Firth. At the very top of the Annan one can stand on the edge of the Devil's Beef Tub, where thieving reivers drove their stolen cattle into a deep depression to hide them from the "hot trod" mounted by the English Wardens of the March. Finally, the River Esk is the last stream in Dumfriesshire to create a dale for Border folk to follow till it joins the Ewes Water,and together they flow to Liddel Water and immediately into the firth. Liddesdale, haunt of Armstrong and Elliot, was part of the Debateable Land, so called because the actual Border there was always in dispute.

North of the Ettrick Forest and not far from the source of the Annan, the Tweed begins its flow, first north and then east, past Peebles and Galashiels, beside the ruined abbeys of Melrose, Dryburgh, and Kelso, until it becomes the border between the two countries. All of that region, in olden times called Tweeddale—spelling uncertain— is Borders, with Peebles perhaps the northern outpost, only twenty or so miles from Edinburgh. Between the Tweed and the actual border a number of streams run eastward from the hills. The major one is the Teviot River, which emerges from the hills in numerous streams, but is one river at Hawick when joined by Slitrig Water. It joins the Tweed after flowing past Roxburgh, but not before it has given its name to the middle of the Scots Borders, Teviotdale.

Before 1606 the two kingdoms had divided the surveillance of the Borders into three Marches on either side, so there were six administrative districts, the East, Middle, and West Marches, either Scotland's or England's. The Scottish East March, which included mostly a low, agricultural area known as the Merse (until 1972 Berwickshire) was the easiest of the Marches to govern, as it was by the Home family. The Middle March comprised most of Roxburghshire—Teviotdale and Tweeddale—and was very difficult to govern. Peebleshire and Selkirkshire are mostly Middle March lands. Hawick, Jedburgh, and Kelso were the principal towns, but the high craggy hills of the southern uplands of Scotland and the Cheviot Hills of England made passage across the Borders easy and raiding difficult to stop. The Kerrs were often the Wardens of the Middle March on the Scottish side, but just as often they were the reivers as well. The West March included the three valleys running south, whose waters eventually wound up in the Solway Firth, Nithsdale, Annandale, and Eskdale (or Eskadale). Liddesdale, on the Borders, is so forbidding that Sir Walter Scott is supposed to have been the first person to take a wheeled vehicle into it two centuries later. Technically part of the Middle March, it contained such a lawless pack that it had its special administrator called the Keeper of Liddesdale. The rest of the West March usually was administered by Maxwells or Johnstons, who often were at "deidly feid" with each other, and the intra-Scottish reiving and feuding seems to have been almost worse than the thieving raids back and forth across the frontier. Grahams and Armstrongs also inhabited the West March, comprising two of the worst surnames among the Borderers, and the Debateable Land, including Liddesdale, was mostly in the West March. Modern Dumfriesshire is the West March Land, if you cut Galloway out of it.

Enough has been written to indicate that lawlessness was the chief characteristic of life on the Borders. On the Scottish side except for the Merse to the east, the land was hilly and stream-cut—difficult to farm and hard to administer. Cattle, horses, and sheep were its main sources of wealth, and the Border reiver (=robber, thief, raider, cf. "bereave") on both sides of the frontier was the main object of justice. According to Thomas I. Rae, part of the difficulty of administration lay in the fact that there were three overlapping social organizations in the land.[12] First, there was the feudal order, led by barons with names like Hume, Maxwell, Ker of Cessford, Scott, and the like. Next, there were the Border kinship groups known as "surnames," which were similar to highland clans, and in many cases the surnames were found on both sides of the Border. This was particularly true for the Middle and West marches where Halls, Robsons, Ainslies, Olivers, Battsons, Littles, Irvings, Grahams, Bells, Croziers, Nixons, Hendersons, Armstrongs, Elliots, and Johnstons would raid on either side and sometimes protect their foreign surnames from the law. Then, third, there were clans of thieves, "coupled in felowshippis be occassioun of their surnames or neir duellingis togidder or throw keping societie in thift."[13] So the brigand gangs were united by blood ties, but also by geography.

It might happen, then, that a feudal baron, united with blood ties to his surnames, would raid a neighboring landowner, thus bringing on a deadly feud compounded of feudalism, kinship, and brigandage. Social struggle created landlessness and landlessness bred lawlessness. All of this was complicated by intermarriage across the frontier, by hereditary sheriffs who would not arrest anyone of their own surname and weren't trusted by those of another. Further, judicial competence was confused, because many private persons—usually barons—had judgeship right of several kinds. These tended to overlap with sheriffdoms. And the Scottish wardens, although appointed by the government, were sometimes also sheriffs, almost always barons, and (of course) of one surname or another. Justice was an iffy prospect on the Borders, and it is not surprising that cattle raids, followed by "hot trod" reprisals—either private or led by wardens on the other side—led to feuds, strained relations between Elizabeth and James, re-call and re-appointment of Wardens.

Raids were common and often led to capture of criminals, quick court trials, with consequent hangings, drownings, banishment, and prison

---

[12]Thomas I. Rae, *The Administration of the Scottish Frontier, 1513-1603* (Edinburgh: University Press, 1966), chap. 1.

[13]Ibid., 7, from *Acts of the Parliaments of Scotland*, 3:218.

sentences. Some of the great Border ballads tell of the exploits of a Kinmont Willie (Armstrong) or other malefactor, hated by the law but understood and admired by the Borderers, even those who suffered the outrages of reiver criminality. Rae counts forty-eight raids by Scottish sheriffs and other administrative officers from 1560 to 1603. James VI took pacification of the Borders seriously, for from 1587 to 1602, he personally led fourteen such expeditions. He knew the area well, suffered a great deal of personal inconvenience because of outlaws, and it is not surprising that he put a quick end to a wicked way of life when he became king of both realms.

If Edward I's massacre at Berwick near the end of the thirteenth century began the Border strife, Henry VIII's "rough wooing" to secure a royal wife for his son Edward in the 1540s destroyed all semblance of civilization on the Borders. The wars and the great battles are known to many—Bannockburn and Flodden to mention only the first and last—and through it all the Borders were never really at peace. The people became almost nomadic during the most difficult times. Fraser says that the people could live on the move, cut crop subsistence to the minimum, rely on meat they could drive in front of them. They could build a house in a few hours, and have no qualms about abandoning it.

> All these things they were forced to do while English and Scottish armies marched and burned and plundered what was left of their countryside.... Unfortunately, to the ordinary people, war and peace were not very different.... There was no future for the Borderer in trying to lead a settled existence, even in so-called peace-time. Why till crops when they might be burned before harvest? Why build a house well, when it might be a ruin next week? Why teach children the trades of peace when the society they grew up in depended for its existence on spoiling and raiding?

But it was Henry's incursion that destroyed the Borders so far as community was concerned. The five months' warfare of July through November 1544, and the atrocities of the previous September 1543 to March 1544, destroyed 312 hamlets, towers, and other structures on the Scots side.

> But no figures can begin to suggest the smouldering horror that was left in the Scottish Border country when the last raiders clattered away, laden with plunder, and the terrified fugitives crept out of the woods and gullies to look at the ruin of homes and fields, and search out their relatives among the dead.[14]

[14]Fraser, *Steel Bonnets*, 255-56.

All of that, together with the ruination of the four Border abbeys, meant an end to official warfare, but a half-centry where "the phenomenon of Border reiving flourished more strongly than ever without warlike excuse and without military direction."[15]

The Church on the Border

Historians of the Borders tend to ignore the kirks; church historians tend to ignore the Borders. Thus a silence surrounds Liddesdale and Annandale which is not conspiratorial, but springs from the scarcity of church organization and thus of church records. When, in *The Scottish Reformation*, Ian Cowan discusses the kirks there at all, he waffles a bit, and sometimes is simply wrong. For example, he maintains that in Peeblesshire "almost the whole county was served by a reformed ministry by 1563 . . . [but] other parts of the Borders were not so well served."[16] He seems unaware that as late as 1589 Peebles Presbytery had only three ministers and was a presbytery in name only. He correctly notes that parts of Dumfriesshire were destitute of ministry for many years after the Reformation. Eskdale, for instance, had no Protestant ministry until the seventeenth century, Annandale was devoid of ministry east of the river, and by 1608 twenty-eight charges were said to be vacant. He thinks the fact that eight priests conformed to the Reformation on the Dumfries side of the Nith helped it get quickly established, but then cites a 1608 General Assembly record that as late as that year "no fewer than 17 charges in Nithdale were still vacant."[17]

Margaret Sanderson's work on the disposition of church lands after the Reformation is an important one.[18] Presbytery and General Assembly records are filled with laments from church leaders about the alienated lands, and the poverty that starves the kirk because of the careless and greedy giveaway of its resources. Indeed, the nobility's support for James and their turning against his son Charles was primarily due to their perception that Charles might begin to return to the kirk the lands that had been alienated.[19] But little in her work touches the Borders, except for the great abbeys that Henry VIII destroyed, and whose lands have fallen into the hands of lairds and merchants. Of those abbey lands it is unsurprising to find that feuars were not occupying the lands of Jedburgh and Kelso. Only Melrose Abbey lands fit the national average, two-thirds of that land feued (long-term rents) to occupants, mostly resident farmers. Probably only those lands were safe enough from reivers to make farming attractive.

[15]Ibid., 276.

[16]Ian B. Cowan, *The Scottish Reformation: Church and Society in Sixteenth-Century Scotland* (London: Widenfeld and Nicolson, 1982), 176.   [17]Ibid., 177-79.

[18]Margaret H. B. Sanderson, *Scottish Rural Society in the Sixteenth Century* (Edinburgh: John Donald, 1982).

[19]See, for example, Walter Makey, *The Church of the Covenants, 1637-1651* (Edinburgh: John Donald, 1979).

If church historians neglect the Border region, historians of the Borders are scant in their discussion of kirks. From Fraser one would not suppose there had ever been religious observance on the Borders. Perhaps his one notation serves notice on the whole subject. He describes a pre-Reformation visitor to Liddesdale, in the Debateable Land, who, finding no churches, demanded, "Are there no Christians here?" He received the reply, "No, we's a' Elliots and Armstrangs"![20] Rae notes that in the 1596 treaty between Scotland and England there is a provision that the two realms should encourage the expansion of the reformed religion in the Border area by the provision of ministers. Six years later it was noted that inhabitants of the West March were "voide of the feir and knawledge of God and consequentlie of that dew reverence and obedience quhilk they aucht to his majestie and lawis." The warden was ordered to cause the kirks in twelve parishes within his march to be 'reedefeit and biggit up."[21] Such slight attention to religious life is consonant with this writer's hypothesis that there simply was none, at least until James pacified the Borders after 1606, largely through sending its most obstreperous denizens to Ulster.

If modern historians give us few details about the Borders, contemporary records reveal it as a region without religion. Records of the General Assembly are the most fruitful source of information, but let us look briefly at the diary of James Melville, pastor at Kilrennie in Fife, nephew of Andrew Melville whose ardent presbyterianism caused uncle and nephew to be exiled by King James.

For the most part the Border area is important in Melville's work because of its absence. By that, it is meant that Melville talks a great deal about kirks, ministers, and church-noble conflicts all over Scotland. Only the Highlands and the Borders are absent. When he does mention either, it is usually to say that there is no religion in either. For example, two years after his "Uncle Andro" returned from Geneva he had persuaded the General Assembly to agree that all pastors were bishops, and the Assembly sent representatives around the country to persuade kirks everywhere. Such theological evangelists were sent to the West country, Lothian, Fife, Merns, and Angus, Aberdeen, but none were sent to the Highlands or to the Borders.[22]

When he is exiled and is living in England, he writes a document for the Earl of Angus for the mending of abuses. In it he laments that reforming the finances of the Kirk "with Judges, Lawers, Lords and all" infected by an acquisitive sickness is so hopeless, "sa that the remead falles amang impossibilities, lyk the Heiland or Bordour theift."[23] In 1597, in response to James's

[20]Fraser, *Steel Bonnets*, 46.

[21]Rae, *The Administration of the Scottish Frontier*, 67. He is quoting from *Leges Marchiarum or Border Laws*, assembled by William Nicolson in 1705.

[22]*The Autobiography and Diary of James Melvill*, ed. Robert Pitcairn (Edinburgh: The Wodrow Society, 1842), 55.   [23]Ibid., 190.

inquiry as to why the pastors haven't condemned "Bordour and Hieland thieffs" as strongly as they have the men who have taken church lands for their own and refuse to share with the ministry, the response in that "Gif the Hiland and Bordour Kirks war planted, there wald be less thift."[24] And he quotes the 1608 General Assembly as finding an increase of Jesuits and other papists, which increase is laid to several causes, especially kirks without "persones, to witt, fitt Pastoris, togider with great disorders, especially in Caitnes and Sudderland, in the Merse, and the rest of the Daillis [by which he means Teviotdale, Tweeddale, Eskdale, Liddisdale, Annandale, and Nithdale] annexit to that Synod."[25]

So the Borders is a symbol of Scotland's want of planted kirks for Melville. And the Borders becomes a metaphor for a national Kirk that is poorly ordered: writing to the ministers who subscribed to James's episcopal policy, Melville writes that bishops and the Court were as likely to bring good order to the Kirk as "Martin elwod and will Kinmont Armstrong with stealing on the Bordours"![26]

But General Assembly records are the most fruitful source. Meeting regularly from 1560, the agonies of the reformed Kirk are spread on its pages. At the first Assembly in 1560 idolaters who cause mass to be said are located in Nithsdale, as well as other places in the realm.[27] Two years later the superintendents of the Scots Kirk attended, but none were working in an area where supervising kirks in the Borders would be likely. But at that Assembly ministers or commissioners (lay elders in later parlance) came from both Jedburgh and Melrose.[28] At the same Assembly three ministers were "appointed to teach in the unplanted kirks of the Merce, thair month by course."[29] Later that year there were two names proposed for the superintendentship of Jedburgh, with John Knox among others appointed to inaugurate the one elected. The task was "planting of kirks in the Shirefdomes of Dumfries, Galloway, and Nithisdaill, and the rest of the West Daills."[30] Unfortunately, this will be but the first of a long list of attempts to get things going in the Borders in the way of kirk planting. Indeed, less than six months later that same superintendentship was vacant, and a note to that effect was published again,

[24]Ibid., 400.

[25]Ibid., 758.

[26]Ibid., 262.

[27]*The Buik of the Universal Kirk: Acts and Proceedings of the General Assemblies of the Kirk of Scotland, from the Year 1560*, 3 vols. (Edinburgh: Bannatyne and Maitland Clubs, 1839-1845), 1: 4-6. Scholars always abbreviate this simply *BUK*.

[28]*BUK*, 1:13.

[29]*BUK*, 1:18.

[30]*BUK*, 1:28.

twelve months later.[31] And eighteen months later, on 28 December 1565, Knox himself was appointed "to visite, preach, and plant kirks in the south, where there was not a superintendent and to remain so long as occasion might suffer."[32] Indeed, there is no evidence that a superintendent was ever found for the region, and when bishops were re-introduced in 1597 and 1606 by Parliament, the General Assembly acquiesing in 1610, there is still no evidence of any episcopal oversight in the southlands. (This could be checked in works on the Covenanters, where it might turn out that covenanting was so strong in the region by 1638 partly because presbyteries had a free hand in governance.)

One evidence for paucity of religious life in the Middle March might be that for a number of Assemblies in the late 1560s and 1570s the lay commissioner from Teviotdale is one Andrew Ker of Fadounside. Fadounside is technically in the Borders, but it lies in the Merse, only a few miles into Scotland from Berwick, a relatively peaceful area. Were there no representatives to be taken from the Middle March, or were the churches so scarce that the Merse was considered within the same jurisdiction? In 1572 John Brand, minister at Edinburgh's Hollyroodhouse, was given the commission to visit Teviotdale, Tweeddale, and Forrest (i.e. Ettrick Forrest) until the next General Assembly and then to report to that Assembly, presumably on his success at planting kirks. But he protested that he could not go until someone was appointed to take care of his own charge.[33] Two years later, it appears that either he did not go or he had no success, for several noblemen in the region caused a letter to be presented which lamented that for three years no superintendents or vistors had come so that people were "altogether forgetfull of their duty toward God." Indeed only one Peter Watson had done any visiting at all, and the Lords Maxwell and Herries wanted the Assembly to commission Watson to visit the bounds of Nithsdale and Annandale until the next Assembly.[34] Fortunately, a 1574 list of kirks, ministers, and readers, extracted from the *Book of Assignations of Stipends, 1574*, shows us clearly the paucity of kirks and pastors in the dales of the Middle and West Marches. The gaps will be explored below, in connection with the 1586 list. From that time on, Watson and Andrew Clayhill are listed as commissioners of Nithsdale and Teviotdale. In the 1576 Assembly, as Andrew Melville and others are urging greater order and discipline in the Scottish Kirk, lists are drawn up for the whole country. Watson and four other ministers are listed as responsible for oversight in Nithsdale and Annandale, Clayhill and a layman, Andrew Ker, the Laird of Fawdounside, for Teviotdale, and John Brand and the Laird of Traquair for Tweeddale. Later in the same Assembly the names are adjusted somewhat, and only the three chief

[31]*BUK*, 1:32, 53.
[32]*BUK*, 1:73.
[33]*BUK*, 1:290.
[34]*BUK*, 1:315.

ministers remain on the list. No explanation is given for this change, but it appears that the Borders are going to get scant discipline! Perhaps it should come as no surprise that at Sanquhar (Sanchar) a minister, James Blackwood, could not go there for fear of his life. The brethren told him to do his work at another place, apparently in another region, but to keep trying to serve his charge.[35]

Volume 2 of the General Assembly records (1578-1592) shows a general desire to plant kirks in the Borders, but except for notable towns, it is pretty clear that little gets done. Even in the Merse the minister John Clapperton had to admit in 1579 that he had done no visitation, excusing himself because "he found no concurrence in the Countrey; be reason of the ruine of kirks which he could not get repaird, albeit he had letters to that effect, because he durst not execut the same; thirdly, *Nemo in sui patria propheta*, therefor a stranger would doe more good in these places nor he being native in these bounds."[36] Peter Watson admitted that he only visited within six miles of Dumfries, the rest of the country being destitute of ministers.[37] It is possible that kirks in Nithsdale served by readers in 1574 were destitute, for former monks, as were most readers, were being pensioned off as unfit for ministry. The Assembly of 1581 abolished the office.

During this period visitors for kirk planting were often appointed, but it is not clear that they had much success. But a rational planting was planned. A poll was taken of all kirks in the realm, and 924 were counted, although many were very small and many "demolishit."[38] A model was set up which would divide the Borders among Jedburgh Diocese (four presbyteries), Peblis Diocese (three presbyteries), with some of Dumfries's four presbyteries in our region. However, when actual presbyteries with churches appended are listed, only one of the presbyteries in this model actually exists, that of Chirnsyde Presbytery, which was projected to be in Jedburgh diocese. Chirnside, of course, is in the Merse, perhaps the only area really tame enough for presbytery erection. But by 1582, Tweeddale Presbytery had been erected.[39] Teviotdale was a presbytery in name, but scarcity of ministers meant no "presbytery can be had," so the kirks in the area were requested to report to the Synodall Assemblie of Lothian.[40] In 1586 another listing of presbyteries is made, but it is evident again that most of them are only paper administrative units, except for the real presbytery called Chirnsyde and the one in Tweeddale with Peebles its center. Visitors for planting are regularly appointed to the various dales, but it appears certain that they accomplished little during this period.

[35]*BUK*, 1:359.

[36]*BUK*, 2:429. 7 July 1579.

[37]*BUK*, 2:429.

[38]*BUK*, 2:480. 24 April 1581.   [39]*BUK*, 2:566.   [40]*BUK*, 2:588.

Finally, in 1586, as James Melville and others are being excommunicated for the first time for their oppostion to his majesty's episcopal policy, a full list of presbyteries and kirks is given. This is most helpful, for it lists the putative places where kirks either are or are expected to be planted sometime and can be compared to the 1574 list. It also makes clear that for the West and Middle Marches there are still no presbyteries. "Merce, Teviotdaill, Tweddale" are bracketed with about seventy kirks listed within their bounds, whereas real presbyteries are simply listed without brackets. Similarly, Dumfries is listed as a putative presbytery in brackets, and various plans to make presbyteries out of Nithsdale, or Annandale, for instance, are abandoned in this listing, and those are simply listed among the seventy or so under the "Dumfries" heading.[41] Three years later a Peebles Presbytery exists, but because ministers from outside the presbytery are appointed to lead the trials to determine competent and incompetent ministers, whereas other presbyteries in the Midlands, West counties, Fife, and the Northeast are competent to conduct their own trials, it is evident that its existence is tenuous. Indeed *The Records of the Synod of Lothian and Tweeddale* for 1589 show only three ministers "able to function" for seventy kirks![42]

When we take the 1574 list from the *Book of the Assignation of Stipends*[43] and the 1586 General Assembly list and locate the kirks on a map, we discover that not only is most of the Middle and West March region bereft of clergy, they are not even projected to have kirks. The Merse of East March has significant gaps, but in the Middle March all the kirks cluster around Kelso, Jedburgh, Melrose, Selkirk, and Hawick. Everything between those places and the actual Border are empty of kirks—planted with ministers or not—and the great area west, northwest, and southwest of those safer towns are unmentioned: Ettrick Forrest, Eskdale, Ewesdale, Liddlesdale, all the lands to the Annan river are bereft of any church life whatsoever. And those are the lands of the Elliots, Armstrongs, Maxwells, Johnstons, Grahams, and many other surnames, the people we will find as "loyal Presbyterian" tenants in Ulster. Two thousand square miles of folk who have no religion—in 1574 and 1586.

Furthermore, surrounding that region, mostly on the west toward Dumfries, the two lists find thirty-eight kirks, but only one has a pastor, James Maxwell at Lochmaben, which lies on the Annan. So in these small communities we can assume that the kirks are shells, probably empty of ministry long

[41]*BUK*, 2:668-684.

[42]*Records of the Synod of Lothian and Tweeddale, 1589-1596, 1640-1649*, ed. James Kirk (Edinburgh: The Stair Society, 1977), 14.

[43]"Register of Ministers and Readers in the Kirk of Scotland," *Wodrow Miscellany*, Vol. 1, ed. David Laing (Edinburgh: The Wodrow Society, 1844), 329f.

before the Reformation of 1560. To make matters worse, later General Assembly laments in 1595, 1600, 1601, 1602, 1606, and 1608 make clear that the situation had not changed.

Volume 3 of the General Assembly records (1595-1618) covers the period of the Ulster Plantation. By 1618 James had his way with the Kirk of Scotland; General Assemblies were abolished by his express command, bishops were active, but presbyteries still kept up the work of kirk planting and discipline. But until the Assemblies cease, we read of visitors appointed, usually to plant kirks, sometimes to try ministers to see if their qualifications are sound. Many protestations are made to the king about the alienation of tithes (teinds), the inability to plant ministers in kirks, assertions that "the most part of the parish kirks of Scotland are altogether destituted of all exercises of religion."[44]Intimations are made that papists and Jesuits abound wherever no kirks are planted, and several of the nobles who are indicted for papistry are Borders men of the West March—the Lords Home, Herries, and Maxwell.

Finally, the king himself has decided to do something about poor Annandale. In the year before he becomes king in both realms, and after he has himself led raids against the raiders in that region, the General Assembly is pleased to announce the King's Majestie's declarations and to append to his intention its own intention to find ministers to enter a field the Assembly is confident will soon be ripe for missionary work. On 11 November 1602, it is recorded:

> Anent the planting of the kirks within the bounds of Annandaill, quhilk hes bein desolat continuallie, sen the reformation of the religioun within this countrey: After that the Kings Majestie had made declaratioun of his godlie intent ther anent, how that his Majestie was myndit to cause the barrones and gentlemen of Annandaill, at their compeiring befor his Hienes, quhilk wil be shortlie, find sufficient catioun and sovertie for provisioun of reasonable and competent livings to every ane of the kirks within the bounds of Annandaill; and therefor desyreand that ane number of qualified men may be provydit for to enter in the Ministrie at the kirks within the saids bounds: The Assemblie ordaines every ane of the Commissioners present to give up the names of such persons quho are vacand within thair Presbitries, and willing to entir in the Ministrie, to the effect they may be exhortit and earnestlie dealt with the Commissioners of the Generall Assemblie, quho sall plant them in places they think most meit, for to accept upon them the cure of the saids kirks, how soone sufficient provisioun may be found out for them, and securitie for themselves: And in cace that

[44]*BUK*, 3:878. 15 March 1595.

after all the discretioun be usit with them, they then refuse to accept the saids callings upon them, the Assemblie declares that they salbe countit uncapable of the function of the Ministrie, ay and quhill they meine themselbes to the said Commissioners, whose calling and directioun they refused, and be content to be employed in any part they sall think expedient; and if they be already actuall Ministers, and craves transportatioun, if they refuse to be transportit to any of the saids vackand kirks, the Assemblie finds, that the libertie of transportatioun salbe denyed to them, so that they sall remaine at the saids kirks, fra the quhilk they craveit to be transportit.[45]

And that is just about all we can find in those records. In 1608, we are told, the major cause of "mess-sayers in the land" is lack of preachers; in one unnamed province (but probably in the Highlands) there were thirty-one vacancies, seventeen in Nithsdale, twenty-eight in Annandale. So six years made small difference, it appears. In that same Assembly the final word is given:

And in respect of the Kirks of Annerdaill, Ewisdaill, and Eskdaile, and the rest of the Kirks of the Daills quhilk are altogether unplantit, as lykeways of the Kirks of Cathnes and Ros, in quhilks it is regraitit that in many of them the holie communioun was never celebrate.[46]

There is much more work that needs to be done on the old records before it can be said that the Border Scots who became tenant farmers in James's Ulster plantation had no religion when they went to Ireland after 1610. But this preliminary explanation tends to support the hypothesis that there were no Christians, certainly not Presbyterians, but only Johnstons, Maxwells, Elliots, Grahams, and Armstrongs: reivers on the way to becoming the Protestants of Northern Ireland and the eighteenth-century Scotch-Irish immigrants to America.

As a footnote, Annandale finally had enough kirks to form a presbytery in 1625. Thirteen years later it ws the citizens of the dales who fled to the hills and inscribed their names in blood on the National League and Covenant of 1638. It may well be, as one writer surmises, that covenanting absorbed the energies once given over to reiving. Certainly, the reign of terror on the Borders that created the emigration to Ireland under James rebounded on the

[45]*BUK*, 3:997.
[46]BUK, 3: 1061.

House of Stewart and helped cause its collapse. As one Cleland, a Covenanter, writes:

> For instance lately on the Borders
> Where there was nought but theft and murders;
> Now rebels prevail more with words
> Than dragons [dragoons] do with guns and swords.[47]

[47]Watson, *The Border Reivers*, 196.

Repressing "A Mischief that Groweth Every Day": James I's Campaign Against Duelling 1613-25

Rudolph W. Heinze
Oakhill College

James I issued royal proclamations designed to end duelling in 1613 and 1614. They were part of a major effort to correct what Francis Bacon described as "a mischief that groweth every day" and which was initiated by the king and supported by Bacon and the Earl of Northampton. The proclamations were intended as temporary legislation; however, when Parliament failed to enact statutory legislation, the government had to rely on the proclamations and the Court of Star Chamber. Although the proclamations were stringently enforced initially the king did not seem to have had the determination to continue it after Northampton died in 1614 and Yelverton replaced Bacon as Attorney General in 1617. Neither Yelverton nor Coventry seem to have been very active in bringing prosecutions, and the king regularly pardoned offenders. Although the duelling proclamations were specifically cited in at least 146 Star Chamber bills between 1614 and 1625 the vast majority were submitted by individuals who used the proclamations to bring private actions into the Court of Star Chamber. In the end the campaign against duelling failed despite some initial success. The major impact of the royal proclamations seems to have been that it provided another weapon for the king's litigious subjects to use in order to bring their quarrels before the Court of Star Chamber.

JAMES I ISSUED ROYAL PROCLAMATIONS DESIGNED TO END DUELLING on October 15, 1613 and February 4,1614. A lengthy treatise written by the Earl of Northampton, in the king's name, accompanied the second proclamation. The proclamations and the treatise were part of a major effort to correct what Francis Bacon described as "a mischief that groweth every day."[1] It was motivated by what seems to have been a growing problem and there is little doubt that the king and his two chief ministers were seriously committed to eliminating this social evil. Less than three years after the campaign had begun the king claimed "we have by the severitie of Our Edict, (proceeding from Our owne pen, and by exemplar censure and Decrees of our Court of Starre-Chamber) put downe, and in good part mastered that audacious custom of

[1]James Spedding, ed., *The Letters and the Life of Francis Bacon*, 7 vols. (London: Longmans Green, Reader and Dyer, 1861-74), 4: 399. James L. Larkin and Paul L. Hughes, *Stuart Royal Proclamations*, 2 vols. (Oxford: Clarendon, 1973), Vol. 1, nos. 132 and 136 (hereafter *SRP*). Northampton's treatise was entitled "A Publication of His Majesty's Edict and Severe Censure Against Private Combatants," STC 8498.

Duelles and Challenges."[2] Although James probably exaggerated the degree of success, he was not overstating the role of royal edicts and the Court of Star Chamber in the campaign. The proclamations and the accompanying treatise were the instruments which the government used for its legislation against duelling and in the period 1614-25 at least 146 cases citing one of the proclamations were brought before the court. This was the most extensive and sustained use of the Court of Star Camber for the enforcement of royal proclamations in the reign. Consequently, the campaign against duelling provides a valuable case study both of the way in which James I used royal proclamations as well as their effectiveness as instruments of social control.

Duelling appeared in England in the reign of Elizabeth after having first become popular in Italy and France in the middle of the sixteenth century. While the use of weapons such as the rapier heightened the potential for loss of life, the duel did at least introduce some rules designed to bring some fair play and a code of honor to the unregulated violence of the affray. However, despite these more positive features, as duels became more common they took a serious toll from the class which provided the crown with its most valued servants. James's well-known abhorrence of violence as well as his desire to end a practice which he considered an offense against God and harmful to the crown led him to introduce a series of measures designed to end duelling and to begin a vigorous campaign of enforcement.[3]

The royal proclamations and Northampton's treatise were the result of a carefully devised program against duelling made more urgent by a series of duels that occurred between 1609 and 1613 some of which resulted in deaths of courtiers. In 1608 Elizabethan regulations designed to keep the peace in the royal household were reissued. Meanwhile, Northampton investigated the laws on duelling. In 1609 he asked the Lord Chief Justice, Edward Coke, to write a treatise on that subject. He also consulted others and sought information on foreign laws.[4] In addition the king sought Bacon's advice. He recommended that temporary measures against duelling be introduced by royal proclamations until Parliament could enact more permanent legislation, and suggested that offenders be prosecuted in the Star Chamber "without respect of persons, be the offender never so great; and that the fine set be irremissible."[5]

[2]*SRP*, no. 160. Linda Peck, *Northampton: Patronage and Policy at the Court of James I* (London: George Allen & Unwin, 1982), 161 maintains Northampton was the "author" of the campaign against duelling and its "most active propagandist until his death."

[3]Lawrence Stone, *The Crisis of the Aristocracy 1558-1641* (Oxford: Clarendon, 1965), 242-50; G. P. V. Akrigg, *Jacobean Pageant* (London: Hamish Hamilton, 1962), 147-58.

[4]Peck, *Northampton*, 160-61; PRO LS 13/280/78; Edward Coke, "A Discourse Touching the Unlawfulness of Private Combats" in *Collectanea Curiosa*, 2 vols. (Oxford: Clarendon, 1781), 1: 9-12.

[5]Spedding, *Letters*, 4: 397.

The first royal proclamation, issued on 15 October 1613, followed Bacon's advice in part but it was very limited in its prohibitions. It simply banned provocative publications on duels by those planning a duel or who had fought a duel and provided that offenders should be prosecuted in the Star Chamber "at the discretion and censure of that Court for their high contempt against Us" by being banished from court for seven years.[6]

The campaign began in earnest on January 16, 1614 when Francis Bacon, the king's new attorney general, on instructions from James, gave a charge to the Court of Star Chamber on a case which involved two obscure individuals, William Priest, who had sent a challenge, and Richard Wright, who delivered it. Although Priest maintained he had sent the challenge in a moment of anger which he quickly regretted and that he had already been fined at the quarter sessions, he was fined £500 and Wright 500 marks. Both were also imprisoned in the Fleet and ordered to make public admission of guilt. In his address to the Court Bacon attacked duelling, discussed the existing law on the subject, and defended the government's approach to the problem. He also made it clear that the severity of the punishment was intended as a "warning to all young noblemen and gentlemen, that they should not expect the like connivance or toleration as formerly have been." The charge and the decree were published and the Court ordered that the decree be read by justices of assize "in all the places and sittings of their several circuits" so that all would know the Court's opinion and the resolve of the king and the Court to punish other offenders.[7]

Eight days after the decree James published a long and somewhat confusing proclamation filled with laments about the harmfulness and lawlessness of duelling as well as exhortations and threats. The only specific prohibition simply forbade sending or accepting challenges or seeking "satisfaction by any other meanes than those, which are made good either by the Lawes of the Kingdome, or the Court of Honour." The remainder of the proclamation outlined and defended a twofold campaign against duelling which it was argued would "appease the wrath of God and stay the current manslaughters among men." These included stringent enforcement of the regulations against duelling in which "no jot of that severity which is set down" would be remitted, and providing an alternative means of satisfaction. A "more large discourse" was annexed since, the proclamation stated, it would be difficult to cover all the details of this policy "within the bulke of an ordinary Proclamation."[8]

---

[6]*SRP*, no. 132.
[7]Spedding, *Letters*, 4: 415, 416; PRO STAC 8/19/2,3.
[8]*SRP*, no. 136.

James was not exaggerating about a "more large discourse." The annexed treatise, written by Northampton, was 119 pages long. Although a good deal of it was devoted to rhetoric, it outlined in detail and in considerably clearer fashion than the king's proclamation the government's twofold approach. It first encouraged those who were victims of "all kinds of offenses that touch honour in the least degree" to bring their complaints to the commissioners for the earl marshallship or the lord lieutenants and their deputies, who would provide for fitting punishments. It secondly tried to deter people through fear "of sharpe punishment." The punishments were designed to leave no doubt that duelling was neither honorable nor tolerable. If a person killed another in a duel, he was to be treated as a common murderer. The justices of assize were ordered to enforce the law strictly and to impress on subjects "our unchangable resolution" not to pardon offenders. Those sending challenges or accepting them were to be imprisoned and banished from the court and the presence of the royal family for seven years. All grants "depending merely on Our pleasure" were to be recalled and the offenders would not be used or employed in any government service during those seven years nor given any grants "in land, lease, pension or by letter commendatorie; to their advantage in the least degree." They would finally be deprived of their "birth-right to wear swords and daggers." Those fighting duels abroad were to be judged by the constable and earl marshal and could be executed. The treatise ended by repeating the provisions of the first proclamation. The use of proclamations was justified with the argument that many might be killed "before the parliament have time and opportunity to amend these errors."[9]

Northampton's treatise completed the government's legislative campaign against duelling. It was a well-planned campaign designed to correct a social evil using both the positive approach of offering an alternative remedy as well as the threat of severe punishments for offenders. The punishments were designed to strike at the very core of the problem that provoked duels—the nobility's sense of honor. By threatening offenders with penalties that involved a loss of honor the cure seemed ideally suited to the malady. The penalties, although seemingly severe enough to deter offenders, if they were stringently applied, were not unreasonable. Although the legislation was based on the prerogative rather than parliamentary authority, it primarily dealt with penalties rather than making new law.

Duelling was clearly illegal before 1613. If a man killed his opponent in a duel, he was guilty of murder at the Common Law. What was less clear in the law was whether preparations for a duel such as the sending and receiving of challenges were illegal. In its decree in the case of Priest and Wright the Court of Star Chamber accepted Bacon's arguments and agreed that it could punish sending and receiving challenges even though no duel took place. It

[9]"A Publication of His Majesty's Edict. . . ," 17, 18, 82, 89, 90, 92, 14-15.

also accepted the Elizabethan precedents which Bacon offered and agreed that the attorney general's actions against Priest and Wright were "proceeding according to former precedents of the Court, although he purposed to follow it more thoroughly than had been done ever heretofore, because the times did more and more require it." The Court concluded unanimously "that by the ancient law of the land, all inceptions, preparations, and combinations to execute unlawful acts . . . are punishable as misdemeanors and contempts."[10] In his treatise on the Court of Star Chamber, Hudson later maintained that "it is most sure that a challenge to single combat hath been ever punishable," and he cited two precedents which he pointed out occurred "before any proclamation."[11]

Although it seems clear that James was not introducing new laws by his proclamation, but simply decreeing specific and severe penalties for what had long been an illegal act, he followed Bacon's advice and sought parliamentary legislation. Among the list of bills noted "to be drawn by his Majesties most gracious direction for the general good of the commonwealth" for the 1614 Parliament was "an act for the repressing of duels and challenges and the trial of such duels as shall be performed beyond the seas." In his speech at the opening of Parliament, James clearly defended the proclamations on duelling as temporary measures:

> And whereas it is given out that my proclamacions are in steade of lawes because of makinge my longe proclamacion against duells, [it] was not that they should be as lawes but to expresse my self against fightinge and massacringe one another vntill such tyme as a statute coulde be made against it, which I conceived to be a godly action.[12]

The criticism which probably motivated this remark suggests that the fears expressed by the Commons' Petition in 1610 that proclamations would "by degrees grow up and increase to the strength and nature of laws" had been renewed by the duelling proclamations. Although they did not initiate new law and James sought statutory legislation at the first opportunity, the sensitive nature of the subject, involving as it did the honor of the nobility, combined with the threat of penalties that further impinged on that honor may have led some to raise again the specter of legislation by decree. After the debacle of the "Addled Parliament" James may have again sought parliamen-

---

[10]Spedding, *Letters*, 4: 414.

[11]William Hudson, "A Treatise of the Court of Star Chamber" in *Collectanea Juridica*, Francis Hargrave, ed., 2 vols. (London: W. Clarke & Sons, 1791-92), 2:87.

[12]*HMC Hastings Manuscripts*, 4: 233; Spedding, *Letters, 5: 16.*

tary legislation in 1621, when a bill "for the preventing of private combats" was introduced.[13]

Since Parliament would or could not take action the government had to rely on the proclamations and the Court of Star Chamber. Although plaintiffs had at times included "challenges" among the list of crimes charged in Star Chamber bills before 1614, as indicated by Table 1, the number of bills in which a challenge was alleged more than doubled in 1614. More significantly, the average number of cases per year alleging a challenge increased more than

TABLE 1
Star Chamber Cases in the Reign of James I
Including a Challenge to Fight as
One of the Crimes Charged

Year	Total Cases	Cases Citing Proclamation	Year	Total Cases	Cases Citing Proclamation
1603	1	0	1615	12	10
1604	1	0	1616	11	8
1605	3	0	1617	18	17
1606	3	0	1618	11	10
1607	2	0	1619	15	13
1608	3	0	1620	18	14
1609	5	0	1621	29	24
1610	6	0	1622	17	15
1611	4	0	1623	11	9
1612	4	0	1624	15	15
1613	5	0	1625	3	2
1614	13	9			

Avg. No. Cases Per Year: 1606-13:   3.36
1614-25: 14.58

[13]PRO SP 14/119/133; Conrad Russell, *Parliament and English Politics, 1621-29* (Oxfor. Clarendon, 1979), 47 doubts if it was a government bill because "no member of James's government in the Commons helped it on even to the point of a first reading." The Commons petition of 1610 and James's attitude towards proclamations is discussed in R. W. Heinze, "Proclamations and Parliamentary Protest, 1539-1610," *Tudor Rule and Revolution*, D. J. Guth and J. W. McKenna, eds. (Cambridge: Cambridge University Press, 1982), 237 ff.

tenfold in the period when the proclamations were in effect and the proclamations were specifically cited, often in great detail, in almost 85 percent of those cases.[14]

Although there was a massive increase in the number of cases, the actual degree of persistent government involvement in the enforcement campaign and its success are more difficult to determine. There is no question that in 1614 the government was very serious about enforcing the regulations on duelling. This is illustrated in part by one of the few surviving Star Chamber decrees on a duelling offense. The case involved John Lord Darcy, who accused Gervase Markham of challenging him to a duel. Although the bill has not survived, Markham's answer reveals that he claimed he had sent the letter containing the supposed challenge before the proclamation was published. Furthermore, the letter does not seem to have specifically challenged Darcy to a duel. This created a dilemma for the Court. On November 20, 1616 a letter was written to the king informing him that the verdict would be delayed because "wee were divided in opinion whether the case of Markham might fall within the compasse of a challenge (for the punishment of which kind of insolency your Majestie did expressly commaund our attendance) as well because the wordes of the letters are not a direct challenge," and because it was sent "before the proclamation could come to his knowledge." A week later the decision revealed that even what seemed a reasonable defense did not save Markham from a rather severe punishment. Even though the Court accepted that the letter was not a direct challenge but rather "a step and *primus gradus* to a challenge" and it had been sent before the proclamation Markham was fined £500 and imprisoned at the discretion of the Court. Bacon explained that the penalty had been mitigated in view of the nature and date of the letter and "had this case been after the edict and proclamation, I should have weighed down the offence in greater proportion than now I shall and set a fine ratably."[15]

Although in most cases the Court's verdict is difficult to find because of the disappearance of its Order and Decree Books, another conviction in the first year of the campaign can be established through fines recorded in the Exchequer. Bacon brought the action "Pro Rege" against John Bryan and Samuel Neast. Both parties were convicted and fined £30 each. The small

---

[14]Thomas Barnes, *List and Index to the Proceedings in the Star Chamber for the Reign of James I (1603-25) in the Public Record Office* (Chicago: American Bar Foundation, 1975) was indispensable for locating the duelling cases, but there are some differences between his figures and mine, because many of the cases which cited proclamations were not listed under his category "Proclamation Contemned." In addition I have included *Ore Tenus* cases in my totals.

[15]Spedding, *Letters*, 4: 113; J. R. Dasant et al, eds. *Acts of the Privy Council of England 1542-1625*, 21 vols. (London: HMSO, 1890-1934), (1616-1617), 71-72; PRO STAC 8/127/4; Markham tried to help his case by bringing a cross suit against the retainers of Lord Darcy for challenging him to a duel. PRO STAC 8/212/2.

fines are somewhat surprising, but they actually seem to have been collected.[16] In contrast, Thomas Bellingham and Brice Christmas were sentenced to very heavy fines in 1617, but these were remitted shortly afterwards. Bellingham and Christmas were convicted *Ore Tenus*, upon their confession of violating the duelling regulations. In order to make an example of them the king came to the Court on February 13, 1617 to deliver the verdict. He used the occasion both to state his determination to maintain peace and to claim success for the campaign against duelling maintaining that since the proclamation "there had bene but 3 challenges." Bellingham and Christmas were sentenced to suffer the full penalties threatened in the proclamations. Both were fined £1,000 and ordered imprisoned in the Tower. In addition, they were forbidden to wear weapons and banished from court. However, the severity of the sentence was quickly mitigated by a pardon and release from prison a week later. Although the king did not remit the rest of the sentence and warned that "the clemency which wee shall now use cannot be drawne in example in other cases" the example can hardly have served as much of a deterrent.[17]

Even if the king's statement on the number of challenges is accepted as accurate clearly whatever success was achieved initially was undermined by the end of 1617. Three duels or planned duels were reported between May and December of 1617 alone and one of them resulted in a death. Even though the survivor was captured and it was thought he would "hardlye escape the rigor of the law, the Kinge being a professed enemie to duels," he was pardoned in March 1618.[18] Another death was reported in the same year and in January 1619 even the captain of the guard, Sir Henry Rich, had to be restrained from fighting a duel. Needless to say, the king was particularly distressed that the captain of the guard who "was to see the peace of hys household" was prepared to violate that peace. He compared it "if hys Chiefe Justice shold violate hys laws, who shold know them best." However, despite the king's anger Rich was only punished temporarily by being restricted to his chamber. Throughout the remainder of the reign there were continual reports of duels and planned duels and little indication that the severity of punishment threatened in the proclamations was ever applied.[19]

The failure of the campaign can partly be explained by the difficulty of eradicating a practice that involved the honor of the nobility and the king's readiness to pardon offenders, but much of it may also be attributed to the lack of a really serious enforcement campaign after the initially vigorous beginning

[16]PRO E159/450 Trinity, 104; E401/2307/M1616; 2309/M1617/ PRO STAC 8/20/6; for a list of fines and a discussion of the sources see Thomas Barnes, *Fines in Star Chamber 1596-1641* (Chicago: American Bar Foundation, 1971).

[17]PRO SP 39/7/63. SP 14/90/65; SP 14/95/22; SP 14/90/81.

[18]PRO SP 14/95/22; SP 39/9/5; SP 14/94/52; SP 14/92/25; SP 14/93/24.

[19]PRO SP 14/105/8,9; SP 14/111/25; SP 14/112/82; SP 14/113/59; SP 14/115/7; SP 14/116/32; SP 14/141/289; SP 14/148/126; SP 14/149/17.

in 1614. A closer look at the actual government prosecutions reveals that very few of the 146 cases alleging violation of the proclamation were initiated by the government. Only three of the cases were prosecuted "Pro Rege" and all were initiated by Bacon. Other attorney general prosecutions were brought "on relation" from the offended parties, a procedure which closely resembled private plaintiff bills and in which the interests of the plaintiff rather than those of the state were the motivating factor.[20]

Even these cases were relatively rare when compared with the involvement of the attorney general in enforcing other proclamations. Yelverton and Coventry, who were most active overall in enforcing proclamations, paid comparatively little attention to duelling proclamations while bringing at least 17 actions "Pro Rege" for violations of other proclamations. Although this does not take into consideration the *Ore Tenus* cases, they do not seem to have been very numerous. In most instances where duels or planned duels are reported after 1617 the king was more interested in stopping the duel than in punishing the offenders. Furthermore, he clearly failed to carry out his own threat that "no jot of that severity which is set down" would be remitted.

TABLE 2
Cases Alleging Violation of A Proclamation
Prosecuted by the Attorney General
1614-1625

Attorney General	Dates	Duelling Proclamations		Other Proclamations	
		Pro Rege	On Rel	Pro Rege	On Rel
Bacon	Oct. 1613–March 1617	3	4	0	2
Yelverton	March 1617–Jan. 1621	0	4	8	4
Coventry	Jan. 1621–March 1625	0	5	9	12

If, then, there does not seem to have been a sustained and vigorous governmental campaign of enforcement, what accounts for the 146 cases which cited violations of the duelling proclamations? Most of them did not even involve the types of challenges the king had in mind in the proclamations. Rather, they were cases initiated by private litigants who used the proclamations to bring actions into the Star Chamber. Barnes points out:

[20]Thomas G. Barnes, "Star Chamber Litigants and Their Counsell 1596-1641," *Legal Records and the Historian*, J. H. Baker, ed. (London: Royal Historical Society, 1978), 9.

The private litigant may have had little or no interest in maintaining the King's peace; but he did find that pressing home a criminal charge in the Star Chamber might gain him collateral advantages in a civil–usually propriertal–action brought elsewhere. . . . If nothing else, his Star Chamber case had nuisance value and it would put his adversary to more costs–indeed, some prosecutions appear to have been motivated only by a desire for attrition.[21]

There are numerous examples of precisely this use of the duelling proclamations. Defendants often accused plaintiffs of bringing the suit to harass them or to aid them in a suit in another court. Richard Barbor, for example, answered the bill brought against him by Thomas Digby by claiming that the suit was designed "to impoverish this defendent to the end" that he would not be able to pursue a suit for debt at the Common Law. In this case Digby even used the attorney general to pursue his suit. He initiated his action by private bill on February 20, 1617 but on July 2, 1617 the same charge was incorporated in an information brought by Yelverton on relation from Thomas Digby. Digby does not seem to have been successful in either action, but he may well have achieved his real purpose of harassing his opponent and delaying an action against him in another court.[22]

Cross suits were a common method of delaying or complicating an action even in the same court. In 1614 Bacon acting "on relation" from Peter Geringe accused the vicar of Winterton, John Kynde, of challenging him to a duel. Four months later Kynde accused Geringe of the same offense. Geringe responded that the suit was intended "to take awaye their true testimony and depositions" of his witnesses in the earlier suit which was still unsettled. The plaintiff in a similar action in 1617 was accused of bringing a cross suit on the advice of his solicitor and stating that "he would keepe hym from a day of hearing these five years" and that he would "weary out this defendant before he should bring his cause to hearing." He further charged that the suit was "to take awaie the benfitt of this defendants proofe of the said bill by making all his witnesses deffendens in the saide newe crosse bille."[23]

The extensive use of the duelling proclamations by litigants to pursue private causes occurred because the proclamations were easy to use for purposes that the king had never intended. Although they were meant to deal with challenges to duels fought in single combat according to the duelling code of honor, it was easy to add a charge of challenge to fight to the common charge of riot, assault, and unlawful assembly. Although the charge was used

[21]Thomas G. Barnes, "Star Chamber and the Sophistication of the Criminal Law, *Criminal Law Review* (May 1977): 320.

[22]PRO STAC 8/24/8; STAC 8/118/7.

[23]PRO STAC 8/301/8; STAC 8/55/25; STAC 8/20/27; STAC 8/192/6.

at times before the proclamations, they encouraged both a substantial increase in the number of actions as well as making it possible to add violation of the king's command in his proclamation to the standard statement that the offenses were a breach of the king's peace and against the laws and statutes.

The proclamations were part of a well-devised campaign against duelling in which they were used as temporary legislation to meet an immediate need until Parliament could act. When Parliament did not act, the government was forced to rely on the Court of Star Chamber in its enforcement effort. That could well have been an advantage, and at least one contemporary commentator believed that "the Star Chamber . . . is like to prove a better course to cut off duells than any that hath been yet thought on."[24] As long as Bacon was attorney general and Northampton was at the king's side to encourage him the campaign had some hope of success. But, after Northampton died in June 1614 and Yelverton replaced Bacon as attorney general in March 1617, the king does not seem to have had the determination to continue the campaign with the same vigor. The weak efforts to enforce the proclamations after 1617 contrast dramatically with the thoroughness of the initial effort and the king's readiness to pardon offenders suggest a loss of his original resolve. In the end the proclamations did not stop nor probably even seriously curb duelling, but they did provide the king's litigious subjects with another weapon to use in what Barnes describes as "a sport of the gentry hardly less universal than coursing."[25] The king had hoped that he could persuade his subjects to settle their differences in the earl marshal's court rather than on the field of honor. Although that effort does not seem to have been successful,[26] James unintentionally helped litigants to bring their quarrels to the Court of Star Chamber. Whether or not that aided the campaign against duelling is doubtful, but it certainly contributed to the sport of the gentry.

[24]PRO SP 14/75/44.

[25]Thomas G. Barnes, "Due Process and Slow Process in the Late Elizabethan - Early Stuart Star Chamber," *American Journal of Legal History* 6 (1962): 337.

[26]G. D. Squibb, *The High Court of Chivalry: A Study of the Civil Law in England* (Oxford: Clarendon, 1959), 57.

JAMES I.

Montaigne's Doubts
on the Miraculous and the Demonic
in Cases of His Own Day

Maryanne Cline Horowitz
Occidental College and Visiting Scholar, UCLA

This historical analysis of "Des Boyteux" emphasizes the breadth of Montaigne's questioning of sixteenth-century popular and erudite "mentalités." For example, a discussion of Paré on monstrous births and of Agrippa on numerology helps to recapture a sixteenth-century reading of Montaigne's Book III, chapter 11. Montaigne's journal accounts of the cured cripple Michel Marteau and of his own brief experience as a cripple before his 1588 imprisonment give insight into the experiential importance of "crippling" for Montaigne. Montaigne's topical reference to Jean de Coras's account of the trial of Martin Guerre broadens to a questioning of the wisdom of heresy trials; significantly, Montaigne in his stand in the Bodin-Wier controversy on witchcraft suggests departure from the *Malleus Malificarum* definition of witchcraft as heresy. Witches awaiting trial are thus symbolic of the many people awaiting trial for alleged "heresy" in the age of Religious Wars. Doubting evidence of both demonic and miraculous phenomena as presented in legal courts of his day, Montaigne innovated in the literary recommendation of Pyrrhonian non-sentencing: "The court understands nothing of the matter."

MICHEL DE MONTAIGNE'S ESSAY "DES BOYTEUX" ("On Cripples," III: 11) highlights his doubts about the alleged involvement of the demonic, as well as the divine, in events of his day.[1] He applied his skepticism to contemporary court cases: several imprisoned witches, a few villagers imprisoned for speaking the voices of spirits, and Coras's judgment of the case of Martin Guerre. Together the examples form a study of impostering–human rather than demonic–and a questioning of scholarly accentuation of popular credibility.

In Montaigne's usage, "miracle," which arouses admiration in the observer, is closely related to the term "monstre," which arouses repulsion. In the *Essays* both apply to an extraordinary phenomenon which the observer views with astonishment.[2] One of the ironic twists of scholarship is that the

---

[1]Michel de Montaigne, *Oeuvres complètes* (Paris: Gallimard, 1962) (referred to hereafter as OC). *The Complete Works of Montaigne*, trans. Donald M. Frame (Stanford: Stanford University Press, 1965) (referred to hereafter as S). My text cites book: chapter; OC page, and S page when translation accepted.

[2]Jean Céard, *La Nature et Les Prodiges: L'insolite au XVIe siècle en France* (Geneva: Droz, 1977), 421.

title "On Cripples" appears more bewildering to modern critics than it might have seemed to his contemporaries.[3] A result has been the trend to view the title as a disguise for discussion of witchcraft. While appreciating the viewpoint that Montaigne's liberal stance against execution of alleged witches is "the real core of the essay," which is one of "the most radically subversive essays,"[4] I would like to add further evidence to the recent trend in Montaigne scholarship which emphasizes the breadth of his criticism of the "mentalité" of his times.[5] In particular, what follows is a juxtaposition of Montaigne's Book III, chapter 11 with the medical literature on monstrous births and an exploration of the implications of his placement of this essay as a chapter eleven through examination of sixteenth-century numerology on the number eleven. Moving on to contemporary accounts of priestly cures, we shall relate the essay to Montaigne's journal accounts of the cured cripple Michel Marteau and of his own brief experience as a cripple in the poignant moments before his imprisonment. With a renewed sense of the occult and experiential dimensions of this essay, we shall explore the ways in which Montaigne's discussion of Jean de Coras's account of the trial of Martin Guerre broadens to a questioning of the wisdom of heresy trials; significantly, Montaigne in his stand in the Bodin-Wier controversy on witchcraft suggests departure from the *Malleus Malificarum* definition of witchcraft as heresy. Witches awaiting trial are thus symbolic of the many people awaiting trial for alleged "heresy" in the age of religious wars. Despite Montaigne's own hesitancies about writing "history," his analyses of the interplay of popular imagination with medical and legal cases of his own day mark Montaigne as a particularly valuable early historian of sixteenth-century popular culture.[6]

The title "On Cripples" played off an entire genre of popular literature of his day; for example, the most casual perusal of Amboise Parés' *Des Monstres et Prodiges* would have familiarized a reader with illustrations of deformed children, comparable to the deformed Siamese twins described in Montaigne's essay "Of a monstrous child" (II:30). While Montaigne concludes in a post-1588 addition to that essay "We call contrary to nature what happens contrary

---

[3]Gwendolyn Bryant, "Montaigne et les boiteux: 'à propos ou hors de propos'"? *Symboles de la Renaissance*, Vol. 2, ed. C. Giarda, E. H. Gombrich, and M. Shapiro (Paris: Presses de l'École normale Supérieure, 1985), 125-30, has questioned the tradition exemplified by Henry E. Gentz, "The Relationship of Title to Content in Montaigne's Essay, 'Des Boyteux,'" *Bibliothèque d'Humanisme et Renaissance* 28 (1966): 633-35. See Nakam, notes 5, 32.

[4]Richard Sayce, *The Essays of Montaigne: a Critical Exploration* (Great Britain: Northwestern University Press, 1972), 248, 329.

[5]Géralde Nakam, *Les Essais de Montaigne: Miroir et Procès de Leur Temps* (Paris: Librairie A.-G. Nizet, 1984), 392-94.

[6]See also Maryanne C. Horowitz, "Montaigne's Stoic Insights into Peasant Death," *Renaissance Studies: Intertext and Context*, ed. M. Horowitz with A. Cruz and W. Furman (Urbana: University of Illinois, forthcoming).

to custom; nothing is anything but according to nature, whatever it may be" (OC 691, S 539), Paré's Preface labels *monstre*, such as a child born with only one arm, as beyond the course of nature" (*outre le cours de Nature*) as distinguished from *prodiges,* such as a dog born of a woman, as "against Nature" (*contre Nature*). Also "against nature" are the "mutilated," such as the blind or the crippled, *boiteux*. Paré discusses "imposters," that is demons inhabiting human beings, and the diabolical arts of witches and magicians. Paré is one of the more rational medical writers of the time in that he adds natural causation to traditional supernatural explanations, thus multiplying the causes; thus he attributes the birth of monsters to thirteen causes. Lechery among parents sometimes arouses God's ire, and God causes the offspring to be born crippled.[7]

Montaigne asserts his task of deconstructing the popular and erudite "mentalité" of inquiring into causes of "facts" not verified.[8] Paré would be an example of a "causeur plaisant," one amusing oneself fabricating causes (OC 785). Montaigne turns backwards the cause-effect notion that lasciviousness causes crippled offspring with his merriment that "he does not know Venus in her perfect sweetness who has not lain with a cripple" (OC 1011, S 791). Lurking in the background of this passage is the limping god Vulcan. Even more conspicuous in the popular imagination, though conspicuously unmentioned in Montaigne's discussion of witches, is the lustful devil, often portrayed deformed and with animal parts—claws, tail, enlarged genitals, or horns. Imposters in this essay turn out to be more ordinary: villagers counterfeiting the voices of spirits as well as a possible "judge who will avenge himself on them for his own stupidity" (OC 1007, S 788), a crowd adding to a rumor as well as Montaigne catching himself lying, two men lying that they saw a witch flying and also the authors who "attest to the reality" of commoners' visions (OC 1008, S 788). Self-delusion is the main mark on the ten or twelve old women insanely confessing witchcraft and showing "some barely perceptible marks"; and the "tightened fist" of the dogmatist, attacked in "The Apology of Raymond Sebond," (II:12; OC 483, S 372) is the visible sign of Montaigne's associates (quite possibly cousin Del Rio or in-law Pierre de Lancre) who defend the non-named "demonology."[9]

[7]Amboise Paré, *Des Monstres et Prodiges*, ed. Jean Céard (Geneva: Droz, 1971), 3-7.

[8]Ruth Calder, "Montaigne: 'Des Boyteux' and the Question of Causality," *Bibliothèque d'Humanisme et Renaissance* 45 (1983): 445-60. Contemporary literary criticism finds in Montaigne a compatible deconstructivist text: *Oeuvres & Critiques* 8, Special Issue on Montaigne (1983): esp. Lawrence D. Kritzman, "Montaigne et l'écriture de l'histoire," 103-15.

[9]Pierre De Lancre at age 29 in 1582 became a counsellor at the Parlement of Bordeaux and in 1588 married Jehanne de Mons, the grand-niece of Montaigne. De Lancre dissociates his grand-uncle's views from Luther and Melanchthon and other heretics, with whom it had been associated by Martin Del Rio, *Disquiitionum Magicarum Libri Sex* (1599). Pierre de Lancre, *Tableau de l'inconstance des Mauvais Anges et Démons* (1612) (Paris: Éditions Aubier Montaigne, 1982), 108. See Alan Boase, "Montaigne et La Sorcellerie," *Humanisme et Renaissance* 2 (1935).

Caught in the dilemma of words giving reality to phenomena misunderstood—of a supernatural vocabulary for an effect implying a supernatural cause[10]—Montaigne's colloquial vocabulary demystifies the alleged demonic and supernatural: the foolish villagers are "poor devils" (OC 1007, S 788) and one old woman awaiting sentencing is "a real witch in ugliness and deformity," (OC 1010, S 790). Monstrosity coalesces with miracle in his naturalistic satire of Pico della Mirandola's Asclepian "what a miracle is man": "To this moment all these miracles and strange events have eluded me. I have seen no more evident monstrosity and miracle in the world than myself" (OC 1006, S 787). Human imagination peoples the world with imaginary beings and imaginary phenomena: "I have seen the birth of many miracles in my time. Even when they are smothered at birth. . . ." (S 786). Paré's fanciful illustrations of man-animal monstrous births are comparable visual imagery for the birth of the miracles-monstrosities which Montaigne satirizes.

Montaigne's placement of "On Cripples" as an eleventh chapter has implications in relationship to sixteenth-century popular numerology, particularly when a numerologically attuned reader looks for links between all three of his eleventh chapters. Agrippa von Nettesheim's *De occulta philosophia* (1531) utilized by Montaigne gives a chapter to each numeral from one to twelve except to eleven which is discussed in the chapter on twelve, for eleven transgresses ten, the number of the Decalogue, and is lacking in grace and perfection, the characteristic of the number twelve. Essentially eleven is the number for sins and penitents. Visually, while charts of correspondences appear for the other numbers one to twelve, no chart appears for the number eleven because "this number has no communication with divine things, nor with the celestial things, nor any attraction nor any ladder which leads to higher things."[11]

Montaigne signals the reader to question numeric correspondences in the first sentence of Book III, chapter 11: "It is two or three years since they shortened the year by ten days in France" (OC 1002, S 785). The discussion of the calendar reform of 1582 at the beginning of "On Cripples" highlights the uncertainty in human arrangements. Tampering with the calendar upsets the predictions of prognosticators, and chapter I:11 "On Prognostication" criticizes "divination by the stars, by spirits, bodily traits, dreams and the like" as "a notable example of the frenzied curiosity of our nature, which wastes its

[10]Stuart Clark, "The Scientific Status of Demonology," *Occult and Scientific Mentalities in the Renaissance*, ed. Brian Vickers (Cambridge: Cambridge University Press, 1984), 351-74.

[11]Agrippa von Nettesheim, *De occulta philosophia libri tres*, cited in Pierre Villey, *Les Sources d'Évolution des Essais de Montaigne* (Paris: Hachette, 1933) I:62. Agrippa von Nettesheim, *La Philosophie occulte ou la magie* (Paris: Bibliothèque Chacornac, 1910), 1: ch. 14, p. 270: "Ainsi ce nombre n'a aucune communication avec les choses divines, ni avec les choses célestes, ni aucune attraction ni d'échelle qui mène aux choses supérieures."

time anticipating future events" (OC 42, S 27). The Roman censors in March and April of 1581 had discussed with Montaigne their concern for the 1580 edition's use of the word "fortune," (OC 1229, 1240; S 955, 965); from my perspective, more significant than the word "fortune" is the fact that both Chapter I:11, which they read, and III:11, stress the role of chance and fortune in human affairs and withhold assent to contemporary claims of demonic, magical, or miraculous intervention. I:11, in significant ways prognosticates III:11, which criticizes books using occult explanations for contemporary bewildering phenomena, such as monstrous births and crippling during adulthood. Montaigne's eleventh chapters of Books I and II thus ridicule the false correspondences and powers that popular imagination attributes to prognosticators and to cripples.

Disapproving of contemporary punishment which transgresses the ordinary and natural, II:11 "On Cruelty" states: "even in justice, all that goes beyond plain death seems to me pure cruelty" (OC 410, S 157). This 1570s statement was supplemented later with specific references to his witnessing in Rome of the public quartering of an executed robber. Furthermore, his eleventh chapters of Books II and III condemn court judgments which transgress justice, raising the question whether the judge or the judged is the sinner. The Roman censors had criticized the 1580 edition for his views that any punishment beyond simple death was cruelty (OC 1229, S 955). Montaigne's further additions to II:11 emphasize his original stand, and III:11 goes even further in indicating that the death sentence itself can be cruel as it often has been applied to innocent victims.[12] Significantly, in Montaigne's memory lapse on the number of accused witches he interviewed, he suggested ten or twelve, skipping over eleven with its implication of "sinner" (OC 1010, S 790).

While sixteenth-century readers would have vivid recollections of cripples awaiting miraculous cures at holy pilgrimage churches or at the royal court for "the king's touch,"[13] it is likely that as Montaigne evoked the image of "a priest who by means of words and gestures cured all illnesses" (OC 1006, S 787), he recollected his own experiences at pilgrimage sites. Only four years before Montaigne began the essay "On Cripples" he had recorded in his travel journal of April, 1581, that he had visited the religious town of Loreto, Italy, the same week as a rich Parisian, Michel Marteau, Seigneur de la Chapelle. Marteau was returning to Loreto since he credited this shrine-filled town as the cause of the miraculous cure of one of his legs. For three years Marteau's knee had been swollen and inflamed. A month or two after a previous trip to Loreto, the following event occurred: "while sleeping, suddenly he dreams

[12]Malcolm Smith, *Montaigne and the Roman Censors* (Geneva: Droz, 1981), esp. chapter 6.

[13]Lucien Febvre, *Le problème de l'incroyance au XVIe siècle*, (Albin-Michel, 1971), IV: ch. 9. That the King's touch needed to be defended against claims it utilized demonic power, see André du Laurens, *De Mirabilit strumas sanandi vi solis Galliae Regibus Christianissimus divinitus concessa* (Paris, 1609), ch. 9. Also see Febvre, ch. 5 on Loreto.

that he is cured and he seems to see a flash of lightening; he wakes up, cries out that he is cured, calls his men, gets up, walks around, which he had never done since his malady." Since then the swelling departed and the knee mended. (OC 1250-51, S 973).

Montaigne concluded that narrative account "From his mouth and all his men that is all you can get for certain" and moves on to a more well-known miracle, the presence in Loreto of a little house which is believed to be the house in which Jesus Christ was born in Nazareth (a legend not more than a hundred years old when Montaigne visited). To Montaigne, the wonder of this phenomenon was that the people of Slavonia, where the house used to be, came often protesting to Our Lady to return it to them, and yet there it was (OC 1251, S 973). Even though he had just come from Rome, Montaigne's overall impression of the town was "There is more show of religion here than in any place I have seen" (OC 1248, S 972).

While his attitude to Michel Marteau's cure of his crippled state appears to me to be inquisitive and humor-laden,[14] Montaigne might also have been in Loreto as a pilgrim, one suffering from a painful kidney ailment. In Loreto, he did donate fifty crowns and placed a tablet containing silver figures and Latin inscriptions of Our Lady, "Michel de Montaigne, Gascon Frenchman, Knight of the Order of the King, 1581," "Françoise de La Chassaigne, his wife," and "Léonor de Montaigne, his only daughter" (OC 1248, S 971). Four years later when he wrote "On Cripples," the plaque in Loreto and his experience there with a cured cripple would give personal experiential meaning to Montaigne's choice of the title of this essay on credulity. In any case, Montaigne left out of the essay "On Cripples" any examples that were remotely as convincingly miraculous as the case of the Parisian Michel Marteau.

There is little possibility that Montaigne would have forgotten the incident, for on July 10, 1588, the year Montaigne completed "On Cripples," Michel Marteau, then provost of the merchants of Paris, was a signatory to the release of Montaigne from his imprisonment in the Bastille by the Catholic League.[15] As it happened at the time of imprisonment, Montaigne had been in bed for three days for the very first time crippled in his left leg. In his own accounts of the incident in his *Ephemeris*, it did not occur to him to treat his own temporary crippling before imprisonment as a prognostication; rather he called his condition "some sort of gout" (OC 1410-11).[16]

[14]For alternative interpretations of Montaigne's journal account, see M. Dréano, *La Religion de Montaigne* (Paris: Librairie A.-G. Nizet, 1969), 218-19, and Craig B. Brush, *Montaigne and Bayle: Variations on the Theme of Skepticism* (The Hague: Nijhoff, 1966), 140-41. They precede me in discussing the journal account of Loreto before discussing the essay III:11, but neither associates the cripple Marteau with the title "Des Boyteux."

[15]Géralde Nakam, *Montaigne et son Temps: Les Evénements et les Essais* (Paris: Libairie A. G. Nizet, 1982), 185.

[16]Donald Frame, *Montaigne: A Biography* (New York: Harcourt, Brace & World, 1965), 280-81.

While the above are private, experiential references to cripples, another unnamed cripple, whom Montaigne might have expected his contemporary readers to picture, was Martin Guerre. Montaigne declares that "in my youth I saw the trial of a strange case" (i.e., the public sentencing), but denies that he remembered much about the trial by Coras in Toulouse of two men who impersonated one another (OC 1008).[17]

Anyone who had "seen" the sentencing or had read Coras's *Arrest Memorable*[18] would be reminded by Montaigne's essay title that when the man on trial for impersonating Martin Guerre was about to be declared innocent, a crippled man claiming to be Martin Guerre entered the courtroom. This trial, made sensational in the popular imagination by Coras's book and its successors, corresponded with the commonplace "Lies come on a limping leg" and with the popular saying and emblem "Punishment arrives on a wooden leg."[19]

While teasing the reader on the names of the two men which had suffered confusion in Le Sueur's *Histoire Memorable d'Arnaud Tilye*, more importantly, he tells the reader the name of the city Toulouse and the name of the judge and author Coras. The city of Toulouse was famous for its fourteenth-century inquisition and for its sixteenth-century epidemics of secular court sentences for demonic possession; Pierre de Lancre later bragged that in Toulouse in 1577 four hundred women were burned.[20] Montaigne's mentioning of the name Coras would evoke popular memories of Jean de Coras—his Protestant sympathies, his lynching by a Catholic mob in October, 1572, following his imprisonment as a Protestant during the St. Bartholomew's massacre.[21] That crucial turning point in the French Religious Wars instigated increased militancy from both Geneva and Rome, and France was still suffering from the bloodshed.[22] While on the surface questioning Coras's judgment, Montaigne's condemnation of the legal death sentence of unnamed Arnaud du Tilh doubles back on the mob death sentence on the known and named "heretical" Judge Coras.

In fact the phraseology of Montaigne's most assertive statements concerning withholding judgment and withholding sentencing in trials echoes

[17]E. V. Telle, "Montaigne et L Procès Martin Guerre," *Bibliothèque d'Humanisme et Renaissance* 37 (1975): 387-419.

[18]Jean de Coras, *Arrest Memorable, du Parlement de Tolose* (Paris, 1561), cited in Pierre Villey, *Les Sources et L'Évolution des Essais de Montaigne* (Paris: Hachette, 1933), I:115.

[19]Natalie Zemon Davis, *The Return of Martin Guerre* (Cambridge: Harvard University Press, 1983), esp. 118-22.

[20]Robert Mandrou, *Magistrat et Sorciers en France au XVIIe Siècle* (Paris: Éditions du Seuil, 1980), 92, 189.

[21]Géralde Nakam, *Montaigne et Son Temps*, 101-2.

[22]Robert M. Kingdon, "Reactions to the St. Bartholomew Massacre in Geneva and Rome," *Church and Society in Reformation Europe* (London: Variorum Reprints, 1985), ch. 14.

protests against heresy trials of Protestants, rather than the special case of the heresy of witchcraft. "After all, it is putting a very high price on one's conjectures to have a man roasted alive because of them" (OC 1010, S 788) echoes radical ideas stated in the 1554 *De Haereticis* by French Protestant Sebastian Castellio. He doubted that one could be so completely sure of truth in religious ideas as to be justified in killing for that idea and declared, "There is no remedy against murders than to stop committing murder." As Anabaptist Sebastian Franck (1499-1542) had said, "We know in part, Socrates was right, that we know only that we do not know. We may be heretics quite as much as our opponents."[23] Montaigne's proclamation that "Wonder is the foundation of all philosophy, inquiry its progress, ignorance its end" (S 788) utilizes Socratic doubt the same way as Franck did—to inhibit prosecution. Montaigne's prescription after examining witches in prison, "I would have prescribed them rather hellebore than hemlock" (S 790) directly brings to the readers the memory of the Socrates death sentence by hemlock.[24] The image of the ugly witch bounces off the readers' familiarity with Socrates' crippled features, and one grows in awareness of the public's rashness in judging the ugly as evil. The comparison is strengthened in the next essay "On Physiognomy," which begins with a praise of the humble Socrates, and asks us to recall the trials of the previous chapter when we read, "See him plead before his judges" (OC 1015, S 793).

The accusation of heresy upon witches and upon those who refrain from prosecuting witches was at the center of the contemporary theological, judicial, medical dispute that reverberates in Montaigne's "On Cripples." Ever since the *Malleus Malificarum* had shifted the emphasis from "maleficia," spells and evil deeds, to the heresy of pact with the devil, witchcraft trials had proliferated and demonic activity increased in intensity in the popular imagination.[25] Within Montaigne's context during the French Religious Wars, a particularly problematic issue was the French demonologists of the Catholic League condemning there heresy of witchcraft along with the heresy of Protestantism as evidence of the increased role of the devil in their times, and condemning magistrates, who were incredulous and lax on executing

[23]Henry Kamen, *The Rise of Toleration* (New York: McGraw-Hill, 1967), 77, 79. Richard H. Popkin, *History of Scepticism from Erasmus to Spinoza* (Berkeley: University of California Press, 1979), 10-14. Nakam, *Les Essais de Montaigne* 358-60.

[24]A year after the 1588 publication of the *Essais* Doctor Pierre Pigray, surgeon of Henry III, recommended along with three other doctors "helebore" for fourteen presented to them for sorcery. Robert Mandrou, *Magistrats et Sorciers en France au XVIIe Siècle* (Paris: Éditions du Seuil, 1980), 159. The plant was thought to reduce madness (Isidore of Seville, in Migne, *PL* 82, col. 626.)

[25]Henry Kramer and James Sprenger, *Malleus Malificarum*, trans. Montague Summers (London: Hogarth, 1928), Part I, questions 1 and 2. On Summers's belief in the veracity of *Malleus Malificarum*, see Baroja, *The World of Witches*, 245-46.

sorcerers, as particularly dangerous.[26] The authority of Jean Bodin gave wide publicity to the view that the massacres and disorders during wars of religion evidenced divine punishment for magistrates' laxity towards sorcerers and blasphemers, as it is divine law to "exterminate the peoples who would with-hold punishment of sorcerers."[27] Cripples, which in Paré were products of God's alleged anger, are thus good symbols for the victims of the disasters striking France. Faced with a war-mongering pamphlet literature and with popular scapegoating in street riots as well as in legal courts, Montaigne with-held consent from prophetic claims to explain God's use of the demonic in the sixteenth century.

In dicussing the dangers witches receive from new authors dogmatically and presumptuously applying Holy Writ to modern events, Montaigne states, "To kill men, we should have sharp and luminous evidence; and our life is too real and essential to vouch for these supernatural and fantastic accidents. As for druggings and poisonings, I put them out of my reckoning; those are homi-cides, and of the worst sort" (OC 1009, S 789). An important point in his reference to Holy Writ is the command culled up in *Malleus Mallifacarum* and other witchcraft tracts: "Thou shalt not suffer a witch to live" (Exodus 22:18). It is upon that Biblical basis that authors, as well as the conversationists he refers to, threaten with "execrable insults" (S 789)–the worst of course, the accusation of heresy to those reluctant to prosecute. Montaigne's point about druggings and poisonings likely reflects his adoption of Johan Wier's new translation of the passage (aided by Hebrew scholar Andreas Masius) to "Thou shalt not suffer a poisoner to live."[28] Bodin had condemned Wier's untraditional translation and emphasized the pact with the devil, rather than evil deeds, as the worst crime. Even if no physical act was committed against humans or animals, the crime of sorcery must be punished by death, for a sorcery in itself is an abomination in Divine law.[29] With such utter brevity that it has received little commentary, Montaigne alludes to Wier's definition against the traditional definition of Bodin.[30] Montaigne in fact goes on to say

[26]Jonathan Pearl, "La Role Enigmatique de La *Demonomanie* dans la Chasse aux Sorciers, *Jean Bodin* (Angers: Presses de l'Université d'Angers, 1985), 403-10. Frederic J. Baumgartner, *Radical Reactionaries; the Political Thought of the French Catholic League* (Geneva: Droz, 1976).

[27]Jean Bodin, *De la Démonomanie* (Paris: Jacques du Puys, 1581), 194-96, 215-17, Preface: "Premierement la loy de Dieu, qui ne peut mentir, les a declarez, & specifiez par le menu, & menassé d'exterminer les peuples qui ne feroient punition des Sorciers." Maxime Préaud, "La Démonomanie des Sorciers Fille de la République," *Jean Bodin* (1985), 424-25.

[28]Sydney Anglo, "Melancholia and Witchcraft: The Debate between Wier, Bodin and Scot," *Folie et Déraison à la Renaissance* (Brussels: Éditions de L'Université de Bruxelles,1976), dialogue with Jean Céard, 224-25.

[29]Jean Bodin, "Refutation Des Opinions de Jean Wier" in *De la demonomanie des sorciers* (Paris, 1580), 220-23, 228.

[30]This point was defended even more forcibly in England by the Protestant Reginald Scott, *The Discovery of Witchcraft*, 1584, wherein he claimed Hebrew "Chasaph" is "Latined

that even in the case of poisonings, confessions are not always reliable "for such persons have sometimes been known to accuse themselves of having killed people who were found to be alive and healthy" (OC 1009, S 789).

Already in "On Imagination," written 1572-74, Montaigne had attributed many extraordinary claims of miracle and demonology to human imagination: "It is probable that the principal credit of miracles, visions, enchantments, and such extraordinary occurrences comes from the power of imagination, acting principally upon the minds of the common people" (I:21; OC 97, S 70). At that time, he had declared restraint from writing contemporary history: "Some urge me to write the events of my time, believing that I see them with a view less distorted by passion than another man's, and from closer, because of the access that fortune has given me to the heads of different parties. . . . If I took a subject that would lead me along, I might not be able to measure up to it; and with my freedom being so free, I might publish judgments which, even according to my own opinion and to reason, would be illegitimate and punishable" (OC 104-5, S 76). Similarly in 1572-74, he had reported giving up his boyhood disbelief in "returning spirits, prognostications of future events, enchantments, sorcery" on the grounds both of humility before the unknown and that given the troubles of the church, one must not chip away one's beliefs to one's opponents but hold firmly to the full authority of the ecclesiastical government (OC 181, S 134).[31]

When from 1585 to 1588 he took up the pen to write "On Cripples," a growing wave of erudite writers' books and judges' sentences had given intellectual approval to commoners' imaginations, and there were some who would find the questioning of the miraculous and demonic as illegitimate and punishable. Yet, there were some juristic, theological, and medical precedents on the other side as well; for example, Doctor Gavars, called in by the Bishop of Chartres in 1574 to rule on a case of demonic possession, had declared Perrine Sauceron a melancholiac to be treated by rest, and the Parlement of Dijon in 1570 had recommended in two cases that the accused be secluded in a convent for Christian education.[32] Although not following the chronological narrative style and the grand causal explanations he associated with history, Michel de Montaigne in writing the last essays of Book III did assume some of the tasks and risks of contemporary history writing. Not restricting himself

---

'Veneficium,' and is in English, poisoning, or witchcraft." One book that irritated Scott to take the most rationalist position of the day, i.e., denying the existence of serious witchcraft, was Jean Bodin's *De la Demonomanie*. Robert H. West, *Reginald Scott and Renaissance Writings on Witchcraft* (Boston: Twayne, 1971), 71.

[31]Denial of ghosts was a distinguishing trait of early Protestantism. Keith Thomas, *Religion and the Decline of Magic* (New York: Scribner's Sons, 1971), 588-90.

[32]Mandrou, *Magistrats et Sorciers en France au XVIIe Siècle*, 75-197, esp. 153-63. Nakam, *Les Essais de Montaigne*, 378-87.

to "borrowed truths" of ancient authors, he wrote about what he himself had "seen" in contrast to what his less skeptical contemporaries claimed they had "seen." His Pyrrhonian know-how in questioning the reliability of sense knowledge in "The Apology of Raymond Sebond" (II:12) served him well: by not declaring what was possible and what impossible, by studying nature and human life with awed amazement, yet withholding consent to the claims of the miracle-makers and demon-hunters of his day, Montaigne created a text that would later support both the rationalism of Armingaud and the religiosity of Dréano.[33] Amid Montaigne's doubts about evidence presented to courts and amid his doubts about astonishing phenomena, Montaigne innovated in recommending a Pyrrhonian skepticism in court non-sentencing: "The court understands nothing of the matter" (OC 1008, S 788).

While theorists of demonology in the sixteenth century were finding the punishable marks of demons in crippled offspring, in human impostering, in the conjuring of magicians and witches, and in religious acts of conscience, Montaigne asserted no theory but juxtaposed alleged minor "miracles" with alleged "monstrosity" to reveal his down-to-earth tolerant acceptance of human life in its myriad and bizarre manifestations. In his conclusion of the book of essays, he wrote of another form of crippling—walking on stilts—and reinforced his doubts about the appropriateness of miracle in his own day: "Yet there is no use our mounting on stilts, for on stilts we must still walk on our own legs. . . . The most beautiful lives, to my mind, are those that conform to the common human pattern, with order, but without miracle and without eccentricity" (III:13; OC 1096, S 857).

---

[33]Dréano, *La Religion de Montaigne* and D. Armingaud, *Oeuvres complètes de Michel de Montaigne* (Paris: Librairie Conrad, 1923).

Michel Montaigne

The Advance of Dialectic in Lutheran Theology: The Role of Johannes Wigand (1523-1587)

Robert Kolb
Concordia College, Saint Paul

A critical figure in the increased use of dialectic and in the defense of that use within German Lutheranism was the Gnesio-Lutheran, Johannes Wigand, who issued such a defense of philosophy's role in theology in 1563 and who demonstrated the contributions which dialectic could make to theological argumentation in several genres of theological writing.

A SUPERFICIAL GLANCE at the development of theological method in the Lutheran Reformation might give cause for expressing surprise that the ferocity of Luther's and Melanchthon's rejection of Aristotle so quickly gave way to Aristotle's return to prominence in the curriculum of the University of Wittenberg. Beginning students of the Reformation may wonder why the use of reason became so prominent in Lutheran Orthodox theology and why metaphysics could reclaim respectability within Lutheran academe less than three generations after Luther's evangelical breakthrough, which had roots in his sharp rejection of scholasticism.[1] This essay will focus on one element of this complex process, the integration of dialectic into the theological enterprise of the Lutheran churches of the early modern period.

The matter is not so simple, of course, as suggested above. Melanchthon did reject the dominance of Aristotelian scholasticism in his inaugural address at the University of Wittenberg in 1518,[2] and Luther stormed against the whore Reason and the pagan Aristotle. But Melanchthon's humanist abhorrence of the Aristotle of the schools did not extend to the pure work of the Stagirite, and even in 1520, as he called for the discarding of Aristotle's *Physics*, *Metaphysics*, *Concerning the Soul*, and *Ethics*, Luther "gladly agreed" to keeping the *Logic*, *Rhetoric*, and *Poetics* in the university curriculum.[3]

By 1536 Melanchthon could write explicitly of the necessary role of philosophy in the practice of theology;[4] his own example set forth a model for

---

[1] Walter Sparn, *Wiederkehr der Metaphysik, Die ontologische Frage in der lutherischen Theologie des frühen 17. Jahrhunderts* (Stuttgart: Calwer Verlag, 1976), see especially the excellent bibliographical essay 6-13.

[2] *Opera quae supersunt omnia, Corpus Reformatorum*, ed. C. G. Bretschneider and H. E. Bindseil (Halle: Schwetschke, 1834-60), 11: 15-25.

[3] "To the Christian Nobility of the German Nation," *D. Martin Luthers Werke* (Weimar: Böhlau, 1883-), 6: 457-58; *Luther's Works* (Saint Louis and Philadelphia: Concordia and Fortress, 1955-65), 44:200-2.

[4] *Corpus Reformatorum* 11: 281; cf. 12: 689-90.

the use of rational analysis in the theological enterprise. Above all, his use of the commonplace (*locus communis*) approach to teaching the faith and his use of dialectical and rhetorical tools from Aristotle, Cicero, and others came to play a large role in his own exposition of the Biblical message, beginning with his *Loci communes* of 1521. That volume expounded the content of Paul's letter to the Romans, but by the 1530s his revisions of the *Loci* had become much more: carefully organized and analyzed topics, drawn from all of Scripture, arranged and presented in a framework which Melanchthon had forged from the material of ancient philosophers, particularly Aristotle and Cicero. Whatever personal inclinations Melanchthon had toward the ancients, his use of Aristotle was also conditioned by his vocation: Aristotle provided a unitary outline and approach to all learning. As an educational reformer, a role into which circumstances had cast him, Melanchthon was charged with the improvement of learning within Lutheran circles, not with its abolition. He could not have imagined doing the tasks which he had been called to do without "philosophy," without Aristotle (or more precisely, Melanchthon's own brand of Aristotelianism, shaped by his reading of Cicero and others).[5]

Yet, among the next two generations of Lutheran clergy, there arose sharp differences over the use of "philosophy" in the university, and especially in theology. [It should be noted that "philosophy" meant a number of things in various contexts for the Wittenbergers: the academic disciplines treated by Aristotle, Aristotelian logic or dialectic, the use of that logic to twist the Biblical message. One must differentiate which of these definitions is in use in any given context.] It has been suggested that the party lines created by the disputes which broke out among Luther's and Melanchthon's students following Luther's death and the Smalcald War in 1546 account for differing attitudes toward the use of philosophy and its relationship to theology.[6] This is not true; Jaroslav Pelikan is correct when he comments, "It is interesting as well as significant that those who most strenuously opposed Melanchthonian theology [chiefly the Gnesio-Lutheran party] continued to do so in terms of Melanchthonian philosophy and Melanchthonian psychology."[7]

[5]On the development of Melanchthon's use of Aristotle, see Wilhelm Maurer, *Der junge Melanchthon, 1. Der Humanist* (Göttingen: Vandenhoeck & Ruprecht, 1967), 195-214, and Peter Petersen, *Geschichte der Aristotelischen Philosophie im protestantischen Deutschland* (Leipzig: Meiner, 1921), 19-108.

[6]Petersen, ibid., 109-12, mentions a number of Philippists but no Gnesio-Lutherans among the Melanchthonian Aristotelians. Gerhard Müller, "Die Aristoteles-Rezeption im deutschen Protestantismus," in *Wolfenbüttler Abhandlungen zur Renaissanceforschung* 1 (Hamburg, 1981): 63, identifies the Gnesio-Lutherans Matthias Flacius and Tilemann Hesshus as leaders in the battle against the use of "philosophy."

[7]Jaroslav Pelikan, *From Luther to Kierkegaard* (Saint Louis: Concordia, 1950), 26. Peter F. Barton also points out that many were "Melanchthonians in method and terminology who were not members of the Philippist party," including most Gnesio-Lutherans; see *Um Luthers Erbe, Studien und Texte zur Spätreformation, Tilemann Heshusius (1527-1550)* (Witten: Luther Verlag, 1972), 10-11.

Martin Chemnitz is often recognized as the key figure in preserving the *Loci* approach and tradition of Melanchthon, for his posthumously published *Loci* bridges the period between Melanchthon and the great seventeenth-century Lutheran dogmatic compendia.[8] Pelikan oversimplifies when he gives credit to Chemnitz "for rescuing Melanchthonianism from impending defeat" in the intra-Lutheran struggles leading to the Formula of Concord.[9] Not even so formidable a figure as Martin Chemnitz alone could have swayed the intellectual approach of all of Lutheranism.

Occupying a key role in the advance of "philosophy," specifically dialectic, in the practice of Lutheran theology was a friend of Chemnitz, Johannes Wigand.[10] Wigand attended the University of Wittenberg in 1538-41 and 1544-45. He very likely heard Melanchthon lecture on dialectic between October 1544 and June 1545.[11] He left Wittenberg to serve in his native Mansfeld in 1545, where his duties included instruction in dialectic and physics at the local school.[12] From Mansfeld he proceeded to Magdeburg in the heady days of its resistance against Charles V and his Augsburg Interim. He was caught up in the formation of that movement which came to be labeled "Gnesio-Lutheran," and he became a critic of the Philippists and all others who opposed the Gnesio-Lutherans' radical understanding of Luther's teaching. That he later split with Matthias Flacius over the definition of original sin in no way makes him less a member of the radical Lutheran party to which he, alongside Flacius, gave vital leadership. Wigand differed with Flacius in large part because he used the Aristotelian terms "substance" and "accidents" in a way which was more faithful to their Aristotelian context than Flacius thought proper and thus ignored Flacius's Biblical concerns in defining original sin.[13]

Indeed, these two had worked together extensively for more than a decade, in battling the Philippists and others who opposed their positions and in producing the first massive Protestant history of the church, the Magdeburg

---

[8]Chemnitz, *Loci communes.* . ., ed. Polycarp Leyser (Frankfurt/M, 1591-92). See, e.g., Bengt Hägglund, *History of Theology*, trans. Gene J. Lund (Saint Louis: Concordia, 1968), 273.

[9]Pelikan, *From Luther to Kierkegaard*, 43, 45.

[10]Traces of their friendship may be detected in Chemnitz's correspondence with others; see *Martin Chemnitii . . . ad Mattheam Ritterum . . . Epistolae*, ed Georg Christian Joannes (Frankfurt/M, 1712), 43, 49, 69-75, or in Konrad Schlüsselburg's *Oratio funebris, de vita et obitv reverendissimi uiri, pietate, doctrina, humanitate et constantia praestantis D. Ioannis Wigandi . . .* (Frankfurt/M: Spies, 1591), 33.

[11]Karl Hartfelder, *Philipp Melanchthon als Praeceptor Germaniae* (Berlin, 1889; Nieuwkoop: DeGraaf, 1964), 561-62.

[12]Schlüsselburg, *Oratio*, 14. No modern biography of Wigand exists; see Gustav Kawerau, *Realencykolpädie für protestantische Theologie und Kirche* 21 (Leipzig: Hinrich, 1908), 270-74.

[13]On their dispute, see Wilhelm Preger, *Matthias Flacius Illyricus*, 2 vols. (1859-61; Hildesheim: Olms, 1964), 2: 310-412.

Centuries.[14] This work was apologetic in character, and it may be that Wigand's determination to make his points in a manner which would be universally understandable in the European intellectual community of his day heightened his appreciation of the dialectic which Melanchthon had taught him. The *Centuries* was organized chronologically by centuries, and within each century by *loci*, or topics. Topic four in each century treated the doctrine of the church taught in that period. Some four years after the appearance of the first two volumes, which dealt with the first century, Wigand, together with his associate on the *Centuries* team, Matthaeus Judex, published as a separate volume its doctrinal analysis of the New Testament under the title *Syntagma*, or "structuring." At the same time Wigand and Judex also published a similar *Syntagma* of Old Testament teaching. Each volume brought together relevant passages from the New and Old Testaments respectively under topics, which were analyzed with the use of Melanchthon's Aristotelian dialectic. This work was a Biblical theology in an Aristotelian framework. It lacked the philosophical argumentation of Melanchthon's later *Loci*, but it employed the Aristotelian structure and some of the tools of analysis which Wigand had learned from his preceptor.[15]

By the year 1563 Wigand had served as pastor in Magdeburg, professor in Jena, and superintendent of the churches in Wismar. He had made his mark as a leading Lutheran intellectual of the generation which followed Melanchthon's. Perhaps it was precisely the appearance of the *Syntagma*, with its extensive use of Melanchthon's dialectic, which turned him, in 1563, to clarify the relationship between "philosophy" and theology in a brief tract "on philosophy and theology, to what extent sound philosophy may serve theology, and to what extent theology goes beyond it."[16] In good Wittenberg style Wigand laid out the Scylla and Charybdis between which he wished to navigate. A total rejection of philosophy by the theologian would produce barbarism in the church, but on the other hand the use of philosophy in formulating the articles of faith would give birth to abominable errors, which would blaspheme God and destroy consciences. Therefore, Wigand intended to show how easy it is to judge to what extent philosophy must be rejected in God's church and how theology's citadel might be fortified so that philosophy might not become its proud and impudent mistress. He argued for a clear distinction regarding the place and use of the various branches of philosophy in relation-

[14]See Ronald E. Diener, "The Magdeburg Centuries, a Bibliothecal and Historiographical Analysis," Th.D. dissertation, Harvard Divinity School, Harvard University, 1978.

[15]*Syntagma, sev corpvs doctrinae Christi, ex nouo Testamento tantum, Methodica ratione, singulari fide & diligentia congestum* (Basel: Oporinus, 1563); *Syntagma, sev corpvs doctrinae veri & omnipotentis Dei, ex ueteri Testamento . . .* (Basel: Oporinus, 1564).

[16]*De philosophia et theologia. Quatenus sana Philosophia Theologiae seruiat, & quatenus Theologia excellat* (Rostock: Myliander, 1563).

ship to theology. Philosophy is a great gift of God, and theology must relin-quish fields in which God's Word does not speak clearly (those which deal with external and worldly matters pertaining to this time and life) to human reason, the instrument by which philosophy builds knowledge. In addition, philosophy is to serve as theology's handmaiden; Wigand was convinced that without the aid of philosophy Scripture could not be studied and heretics could not be refuted.[17] Wigand clearly reflects that distinction of Luther's theology which is often described as his distinction of the two governments. He believed that God had placed temporal affairs in the realm of law and of human reason, and that reason was God's gift to aid in understanding and governing human life. It could not dominate in the spiritual realm, where God's Biblical Word had the only say, often in contradiction to human reason, but reason does guide human life in the temporal sphere.

Wigand could faithfully repeat Luther's warnings regarding the dangers of using philosophy within the theological enterprise. He insisted that theol-ogy alone possesses the articles of faith—that divine revelation which teaches human creatures to fear, love, and trust in God, and how to worship, invoke, and confess him properly. No formula produced by human reason can do this. Philosophy without theology is idolatry. Indeed, theology and philosophy clash on a number of Biblical teachings, including the Trinity, the incarna-tion, predestination, salvation by grace alone. Philosophy teaches that the human creature possesses an immortal soul but that the body will be extin-guished; theology teaches the resurrection of the body. In a polemic against the Calvinist teaching regarding the natures of Christ, Wigand noted that philosophy teaches that the finite and the infinite must be sharply separated; theology teaches that the finite is capable of bearing the infinite. Philosophy rejects as absurd the notion that a human body could be in more than one place at the same time, and theology teaches that Jesus' human body can be.[18] In other areas, such as ethics, theology gives a clearer understanding of the truth than philosophy can. For the first table of the Law, which commands fear and love of God, is the font from which the second table, which commands love for neighbor, flows; the second table is best understood when used in view of its origin in the first. Because theology exceeds and supercedes philosophy and because philosophy so easily can lead the theologian astray, he must keep theology and philosophy distinct and never to confuse the two.[19]

[17]Ibid., A3r-A4v, B4v-B5v.

[18]Ibid., (B6)r-(B8)r, C4r-C5r. See Theodor Mahlmann, *Das neue Dogma der lutherischen Christologie* (Gütersloh: Mohn, 1969).

[19]*De philosophia*, (B7)r-Cr. See similar sentiments in Wigand's *In epistolam S. Pavli ad Colossenses Annotationes* (Wittenberg: Crato, 1586), 120-23 (on Col. 2: 8). Wigand's ideas are echoed in the commentary of his friend Tilemann Hesshus, who indeed, as Müller pointed out, opposed the advance of Aristotelian metaphysics at the University of Helmstedt and shared Wigand's reservations but also shared his enthusiasm for the proper use of philosophy; see his

However, all these cautions served only as warnings against the possible abuse of the "philosophy," which Wigand regarded as, in many respects, a useful and indeed necessary tool for the theologian. He insisted that the branches of philosophy could be useful in two ways: as a means for understanding life in this world and as theology's handmaiden.

Luther had rejected philosophical ethics as a discipline which would undermine the true understanding of God's design for human life, but Wigand found this branch of philosophy of use to a limited degree. The remnants of the fallen creature's knowledge of God reveal what is right and wrong and enable human reason to distinguish the upright from the dishonorable. Ethics governs the state and the household and produces order, discipline, and peace.

Other branches of philosophy also ought to be integrated into the theologian's practice. Music, arithmetic, geometry, and geography aid the reading of Scripture. Physics supplements the meager information which Scripture gives concerning nature. God gave the natural world into the care of human reason; the Bible treats the formation of the world, but not how it works. Scripture tells that God created the human creature, but physics must describe anatomy and physiology. Physics cannot compel human understanding against Scripture, for often it reports miraculous happenings; here this branch of philosophy meets theologically imposed limits. But that does not decrease its general value.[20]

Wigand had particularly high praise for the usefulness of grammar, dialectic, and rhetoric in the theological enterprise. Next to grammar, he believed, dialectic is of most importance to theology among the branches of philosophy. It teaches how to distinguish between more general and more specific terms, between the substance and accidents of a subject, between cause and effect. It demonstrates how propositions ought to be constructed and analyzed. It sets forth the goals of the structuring which is best for teaching and learning, so that what is to be learned rests in its proper place for optimum understanding, analysis, and memorization. God is not a God of confusion but of order, and so the structuring of material for learning is godly.[21]

Furthermore, dialectic helps analyze the arguments of the heretics and put them in their proper perspective by revealing the fallacy of these arguments. Dialectic must remain captive to its author, God, but within that limitation it is a necessary and effective servant of theology.[22]

Commentarivs in epistolam Pavli ad Colossenses (Helmstedt: Lucius, 1583), 56r-60v. See also Inge Mager, "Lutherische Theologie und aristotelische Philosophie an der Universität Helmstedt im 16. Jahrhundert," *Jahrbuch der Gesellschaft für niedersächsische Kirchengeschichte* 73 (1975): 83-98.

[20]*De philosophia*, Br-B4r, (A7)v-Br.

[21]Ibid., A4v-A5v.

[22]Ibid., (A6)r-(A7)v.

Most of Wigand's Latin works demonstrate how necessary he believed the use of dialectic to be. In his formal theological works on a variety of topics Wigand followed Melanchthon in interpreting Paul's charge to Timothy to "rightly divide the word of truth" (2 Tim. 2:15) as a divine command to apply the refining art of dialectic to the Biblical message. Melanchthon had defined dialectic as a knife which divides and sorts ideas into their proper categories and establishes a "method" (*methodos*) or structure for such sorting.[23] The year after the appearance of the *Syntagma* Wigand published the "method" or "structure" for teaching the faith which he had developed for the church of Magdeburg during his brief pastorate there. That method aimed at rightly dividing the word of truth.[24]

Its preface states that while Aristotle and other philosophers must be praised for using reason to illuminate human virtue, God's Word, as comprehended in the writings of the prophets and apostles, must set forth the true, certain explanation of what it means to be human. Only from Scripture's font can the wisdom which is both useful and necessary for human living be drawn. To do this some structure or method of teaching is necessary, so that the unorganized material of the Bible can be recalled. Wigand compared the chief teachings of the Scriptures to sinews; they need to be pondered and repeated at all times. A "method" aids such consideration of these doctrines by sketching a chart of them before the eyes. Once that structure is set forth, the believer must test its propositions against Biblical standards defined by the analogy of faith so that the truth is taught and sophists and heretics are fought.[25] Wigand's *Magdeburg Method* set forth some twenty-eight *loci* or topics, essentially the same set of topics which he and Judex had employed in the *Syntagma*, the New Testament preface of which had explained its purpose in much the same terms as are found in the *Method*.[26] (Although the order of the topics differs at a few significant points, for the most part the same topics are treated in the *Syntagma* and *Method* as are treated in Melanchthon's later editions of his *Loci communes*. However, the Gnesio-Lutheran Wigand presented different content and conclusions in several key *loci*.)

The *Syntagma* reveals the extent to which Melanchthonian dialectic had permeated Wigand's thinking. The subject matter has been divided into

---

[23]In the dedicatory epistle to the 1547 edition of his *Erotemata Dialectices, Corpus Reformatorum* 6: 656-57.

[24]*Methodus doctrinae Christi sicut in ecclesia Magdeburgensi traditur* (Frankfurt/M: Brubach, 1564),)(4v. Fourteen years later, as bishop in Prussia, Wigand published a German version of this work, at a simpler level, but with essentially the same list of topics: *Corpvscvlum doctrinae, Das ist: Heuptstuecke Christlicher lehre kurtz verfasset: Fuer die Kirchen vnd Schulen im Pomezanischen Bisthumb* (Frankfurt/M: Reffler, 1578).

[25]*Methodus*,)(2r-[)(6]r.

[26]*Syntagma ex nouo Testamento*, a2r-a4r.

topics, and each topic is then analyzed in a series of defining questions which reflect the Aristotelian structure of Melanchthon's dialectic. For example, the first *locus* or topic of the *Syntagma* is "On the Word of God." In the Old Testament volume this *locus* begins with a discussion "on the terminology." It continues with examinations of "What is God's Word," "Into how many parts is God's Word divided," "What is the origin of God's Word," "On the instruments or servants of God's Word," etc. The *locus* concludes with an "Admonition to listen to God's Word."[27] Within the sub-topics of such a *locus* Wigand used Melanchthon's dialectic in probing the definition of his subject, in the *Syntagma* always by accumulating Bible passages which addressed the categories of his dialectical system. Wigand often employed the Aristotelian "*causae*" or factors which analyze a term: the formal, efficient (and its concomitant, the instrumental), material, and final "causes." He and Judex did not turn to the syllogism in the *Syntagma* volumes, but he often did in other works, where he also sharpened definitions and guided his readers' instruction of their parishioners through others of Melanchthon's dialectical tools.

The method of the *Syntagma* is found in a variety of Wigand's works. His Biblical commentaries do not rearrange the texts of the books which he treated, but at the end of each pericope he provided a list of topics, or "doctrines"—matters to be taught—which he believed the pastor who was using his commentary should be sure to catch. These topical analyses of the pericope ordered its thoughts for the reader's use in preaching and teaching in his parish.[28] Polemic also played a large role in Wigand's career, and in a series of works written against intra-Lutheran opponents and foes in other confessional camps he used the dialectical tools which Melanchthon had taught him. Under each of a series of sub-topics Wigand used syllogisms to decide between contrary opinions as he wove together his argument.[29]

Apart from Biblical teaching and antithetical systems of thought, Wigand also liked to organize his thoughts in a dialectical form: in works which addressed topics such as *The History of the Augsburg Confession*, marriage, and

---

[27] *Syntagma ex veteri Testamento*, 17-67.

[28] In addition to his *Annotationes* on Colossians (note 19 above), Wigand wrote *In XII. Prophetas Minores explicationes succinctae* (Basel, 1566); *Danielis prophetae explicatio breuis* (Jena, 1571), *In epistolam S. Pauli ad Romanos Annotationes* (Frankfurt/M, 1580), *In epistolam ad Galatas Annotationes* (Wittenberg, 1580), *In S. Pauli ad Ephesios epistolam annotationes* (Erfurt, 1581), all of which utilized the topical summary of pericopes. Wigand was one of several Wittenberg commentators to use this loci approach in treating the Biblical text.

[29] E. g., *De libero arbitrio Hominis, integro, corrupto in rebus externis, mortuo in rebus spiritualibus, renato. Doctrina solide ac Methodice ex Verbo Dei tradita & explicata* (Ursel: Heinrich, 1562), which treated "whether the free will existed before the fall in the human creature," "on terminology," "what the freedom of the will is," "the parts into which it may be divided," "its origin," "in what sort of human beings it existed and what its nature was," "on certain characteristics of this free will," "on its purpose," etc. Konrad Schlüsseburg republished most of Wigand's polemical works in his *Catalogus haereticorum* (Frankfurt/M: Saur, 1591).

persecution, for instance.[30] His use of dialectic always aimed at application of the truth to Christian lives; he did not engage in dialectical exercise as a form of intellectual gymnastics. Yet he also felt compelled to force his subject matter into the form of his Aristotelian framework, whether it fit comfortably or not. Wigand's use of Melanchthonian dialectic demonstrates that not only Philip's faithful disciples, the Philippists, but also some of the most prominent of their Gnesio-Lutheran opponents embraced their common preceptor's habits of mind. Gnesio-Lutherans and Philippists alike were Melanchthonians.

Was this particular Gnesio-Lutheran, Johannes Wigand, truly a significant figure in the advance of dialectic in Lutheran theological circles? Melanchthon had introduced the use of dialectic to the Lutheran theological enterprise. Many others followed his method. But none produced so large a body of writings which exhibited so heavy a dependence on Melanchthon's dialectic as did Wigand. Wigand's theological method must have permeated the minds of the students who heard his lectures at the universities of Jena and Königsberg, but his influence reached so widely chiefly because of his written works. David Chytraeus cited the *Centuries* and Wigand's *Method* as two reasons why Wigand deserved the doctorate at his promotion at the University of Rostock in 1563.[31] His brother-in-law, Konrad Schlüsselburg, published Wigand's polemic in his *Catalog of Heretics* in 1591,[32] and from that volume many Lutheran clergymen in the early seventeenth century learned how to analyze those whose theologies they were taught to reject. Not only did they absorb Wigand's content; they also learned a method of thinking and practicing theology, within the forms of Melanchthonian dialectic, which Wigand had learned from his own preceptor in the 1540s. Furthermore, the influence of the *Syntagma* dare not be underestimated. It was read not only in the several editions in which it was produced in the decades following its publication;[33] it also shaped the way in which the readers of the Magdeburg *Centuries* categorized the content of the New Testament. Through writings and friendships Wigand's theological method shaped the way other Lutherans practiced the discipline of theology. At a minimum it can be said that Wigand may well have influenced his friend Martin Chemnitz in his use of the dialectical patterns which they both had learned from Melanchthon.

---

[30]*Historia de Augustana Confessione* (Königsberg: Daubmann, 1574); *De coniugio doctrina* (Frankfurt/M: Reffler, 1578); *De persecutione piorvm. . . .* (Frankfurt/M: Corvinus, 1580).

[31]Diener, "The Magdeburg Centuries," 251-52.

[32]See note 29.

[33]The *Syntagma ex nouo Testamento* was reissued in at least two editions, 1575 and 1585, the *Syntagma ex veteri Testamento* in 1585.

Wigand employed Melanchthon's dialectic to defend his own theological convictions, often against Melanchthon. But he seems never to have realized that the dialectic which he used to give form to the Biblical content of his thought reshaped that content at points. Few argued more passionately than Wigand that Luther was "the prophet of Germany, whom God, in his great mercy, had raised up against the darkness of the papacy."[34] Few defended Luther's teaching so ardently as Wigand. Yet, he seems to have presumed naively that form does not influence content. He probably never realized the distance which he was opening between himself and Luther with the use of a method which rested on a different conceptual framework than that with which Luther had thought. He passed on to another generation the legacy which he had received from Luther at Wittenberg, but indeed in a significantly different form.

[34]*Historia de Augustana Confessione*, A3v.

The Early Calvinists and Martin Luther: A Study in Evangelical Solidarity

Robert D. Linder
Kansas State University

This essay shows how Martin Luther (1483-1546) was viewed by the first generation of the Reformed Church—John Calvin (1509-64), Pierre Viret (1511-71), and Theodore Beza (1519-1605)—both before, during, and after the divisive eucharistic controversy of the 1540s. Generally speaking, Calvin, Viret, and Beza all maintained a basically friendly attitude toward Luther, disagreeing with his position on the Lord's Supper but revering him as a godly man and a pioneer in the restoration of the Gospel. Calvin continued to seek Luther's advice on matters concerning the French Protestants; Viret held out hopes of concord on the grounds that the Supper was in itself a source of unity; and Beza believed synods and conferences could eventually resolve their differences.

Things changed initially after Luther's death in 1546 and even more after Calvin's death in 1564. As the Lutherans sought to achieve unity among themselves, they pulled farther away from their brothers in the Reformed camp until the Colloquy of Montbéliard in 1586 when Beza, the youngest of the three Reformed leaders, became embittered toward second-generation Lutherans and experienced an erosion of his earlier respect for Luther himself. Though fragmentation was never inevitable, it occurred in the end as a result of personalities, theological disputes, and national differences.

MANY HISTORIANS EMPHASIZE THE DIVISIVE NATURE of the Protestant Reformation and of Protestantism in general.[1] For example, noted authority Hans J. Hillerbrand points out concerning the Reformation that "its most spectacular consequence undoubtedly was the division of Western Christendom."[2] Some scholars and church leaders have considered this an inestimable tragedy, while others have lauded it as a blow for freedom, tolerance, and pluralism. In any case, many historians, especially at the textbook level, have regarded fragmentation as inherent in the Protestant movement, assuming the emergent confessionalism as virtually inevitable.[3]

[1]I am grateful to Professor Mark Noll of Wheaton College for his critical reading of this essay and to the Bureau of General Research of Kansas State University for its support of a part of the research on which it is based.

[2]Hans J. Hillerbrand, *The World of the Reformation* (New York: Scribner's, 1973), 189.

[3]The most thorough study of the history of Christian unity is still Ruth Rouse and Stephen C. Neill, eds., *A History of the Ecumenical Movement, 1517-1948*, 2d ed. (Philadelphia: Westminster, 1968). For further discussion of this topic in the context of Reformation historiography, see Barry Till, *The Churches Search for Unity* (Baltimore: Penguin Books, 1972), esp. 130, 136; and A. G. Dickens and John Tonkin, *The Reformation in Historical Thought* (Oxford: Blackwell, 1985), esp. 179-212.

The Protestant movement certainly split Western Christendom into two rival camps, but was the fragmentation of the Protestant movement itself inevitable? Did the first Protestants fail to recognize a common evangelical approach to Christianity, and were their doctrinal differences beyond composition?[4] For example, did the first-generation Calvinist leaders consider Martin Luther (1483-1546) a brother and a friend? Or had the seeds of mistrust already germinated in the warm soil of theological debate—to the point that the weeds of religious strife grew quickly and flourished with abandon in the years following Luther's death?

The purpose of this study is to enhance the historical understanding of the relationships among the early Protestant reformers to one another by means of a case study exploring the attitudes held by three first-generation leaders of the Reformed Church toward Luther and his role in the Reformation. Of particular interest are the attitudes of John Calvin (1509-64), Pierre Viret (1511-71), and Theodore Beza (1519-1605). This essay will examine the manner in which Calvin, Viret, and Beza viewed Luther, his ideas, and his place in the Reformation movement. It may serve the cause of clarity to point out the obvious at the beginning of this essay: that is, Calvin, Viret, and Beza really were not "Calvinists" but evangelical Christians who wanted one, holy, catholic church, reformed according to the teachings of the Word of God. Therefore, they preferred to be known as adherents of the Reformed Church.[5]

Interestingly, neither Calvin nor Viret nor Beza ever met Luther in person even though it would have been possible since the Calvinist leaders were all younger contemporaries. However, the difficulties of travel, financial considerations, and the excessive demands on their time kept these men from ever encountering Luther face to face. Still, Calvin's earliest sentiments about Luther are known from a letter Calvin wrote to Martin Bucer on 12 January 1538, during the negotiations which followed the adoption of the Wittenberg Concord by the Wittenbergers and South Germans in 1536.[6] In this letter, Calvin declared that he was "fully persuaded" of Luther's godliness, but went on to accuse the German Reformer of being obstinate, abusive, ignorant, and grossly deluded. Nevertheless, Calvin was deeply indebted to Luther—and knew it. A glance at the first edition of Calvin's *Institutes* of 1536 is sufficient

---

[4]For purposes of this essay, the term *evangelical* refers to those Christians of the Reformation era who stressed going back to the Biblical documents (*ad fontes*) for the sole source of authority in the Church and who emphasized the necessity of spiritual regeneration by grace through faith in Jesus Christ.

[5]The first-generation Calvinists usually referred to their movement as the *Reform* and to the institutional expression of it as the *Reformed Church*. *Calvinism* is a later term which Calvin would have deplored. See "Calvinism" and "Calvinian" in *The Oxford English Dictionary* (Oxford: Clarendon, 1933), 3: 45.

[6]*Ioannis Calvini Opera quae supersunt omnia*, ed. Guilielmus Baum, Eduardus Cunitz, and Eduardus Reuss (Brunswick: C. A. Schwetschke and Sons, 1863-80), 10: 138-39. Hereafter cited as *Calvini Opera*.

to reveal that this was true early in Calvin's theological career. It has been pointed out that Calvin modeled the structure of his first edition on Luther's Cathechisms and that he borrowed theological ideas freely from Luther.[7] For example, Calvin's basic understanding of the sacraments echoed the classic treatment in Luther's *Babylonian Captivity of the Church*. But he did not absorb Luther's ideas uncritically. In the case of the Eucharist, he accepted Luther's concept of a sacrament as a sign which confirmed the divine promise but rejected Luther's teaching on the mode of Christ's presence. Therefore, even though Calvin expressed considerable suspicion of Luther in his 1538 letter to Bucer, there is also solid evidence that the younger Reformer had already been deeply influenced by Luther's theology.[8]

In 1539, news from Wittenberg indicated that Luther held Calvin in high esteem. Young Calvin—a mere theological stripling of 30 years at the time—happily reported this news to his friend Guillaume Farel in a letter shortly thereafter. Even though he still rejected the substance of Luther's views on the Eucharist, the tone of his criticism was changed henceforth and forevermore. Luther's positive comments on Calvin had been summed up in the conclusion to his letter to Bucer at Strasbourg where Calvin was then residing: "Farewell. And will you pay my respects to Johann Sturm and John Calvin. I have read their little books with singular enjoyment."[9]

Calvin quoted this commendation of his work when he wrote Farel on 20 November 1539, and added: "Just think what I say there about the Eucharist! Consider Luther's noblemindedness! It will be easy to decide what reason they have who so obstinately disagree with him."[10] In this letter, Calvin added two further testimonies of Luther's good will toward him. The first was a statement from a letter of Philip Melanchthon's that Luther held Calvin in "great favor." The second was an incident reported orally to Calvin by Melanchthon's messenger, the substance of which was passed on to Farel in the 1539 letter:

> Certain persons, to irritate Martin, pointed out to him the apparent dislike with which he and his followers were alluded to by me. So he examined the passage in question and felt that he was there, beyond doubt, under attack. After a while, he said: "I certainly

[7]See John T. McNeill, "Introduction," in John Calvin, *Institutes of the Christian Religion*, ed. John T. McNeill, trans. Ford L. Battles (Philadelphia: Westminster, 1960), 1: xxix-lxxi.

[8]The only study in English on Calvin's view of Luther of which I am aware is Brian Gerrish, "John Calvin on Luther," in Jaroslav Pelikan, ed., *Interpreters of Luther: Essays in Honor of Wilhelm Pauck* (Philadelphia: Fortress, 1968), 67-96. This is a first-rate essay and I am indebted to Gerrish for many insights concerning Calvin and Luther.

[9]The relevant part of this letter is dated 14 October 1539, and published in *Calvini Opera* 10: 402.

[10]Ibid. 10: 432.

hope that he will one day think better of us. Still, it is right for us to be a little tolerant toward such a gifted man." We are surely made of stone if we are not overcome by such moderation.[11]

Calvin continued to hold Luther and his ideas in high regard, even through the worst days of the eucharistic controversies of the 1540s and 1550s. The same can be said of Viret's estimation of Luther and his ideas. Although not as well known as Luther and Calvin, Viret was nevertheless an important figure in first-generation Calvinism. A close friend and associate of Calvin, Viret was one of the most popular of the early Calvinist reformers. More than fifty of his books appeared in at least seven different languages in the sixteenth century, and many of these works went through numerous printings. Therefore, his view of Luther was likely to be shared by rank-and-file Reformed Protestants everywhere.

There are only a few direct references to Luther in Viret's writings and no extant letters between the two men. However, like Calvin, Viret owed a great deal to Luther, though less than he did to Ulrich Zwingli. Similarly, Viret did not accept Luther's teaching on the mode of Christ's presence in the Supper in terms of any corporeal presence.[12]

However, in his writings, Viret never criticizes his fellow Protestant believers, only their ideas. His few remarks about Lutherans are positive, and he clearly regards them as fellow believers and members of the true Church of Jesus Christ. Moreover, in 1560, in the one place where he discusses Luther at any length in his books, he praises the deceased German Reformer for his recovery of the authority of the Word of God and for magnifying the Word above the sacraments as a means of grace. He refers to Luther as "a true servant of God" and "a faithful minister of Jesus Christ" who has "rid the Church of God of idolatry and superstition." But most of all, Viret emphasizes that Luther was the pioneer who was first to call for a restoration of pure Gospel preaching in the Christian Church. Thus, even though his ideas, especially those concerning the Lord's Supper, could be criticized and even rejected,

---

[11]Ibid. Calvin also stated in this letter that he was so overcome by Luther's moderation and magnanimity that he was going to write an "apology" to include in his commentary on the book of Romans in which he would explain that he in no way had meant to attack Luther in his previous works. Even though Melanchthon persuaded Calvin to leave it out of his commentary in order to avoid any further possibility of irritating Luther or his less compromising followers, Calvin did write the apology and sent a copy to Farel for his opinion. Its content appears to reveal that the book of Calvin's which Luther had read with such enjoyment was Calvin's *Reply to Sadoleto*, published earlier in 1539. Unfortunately, the original letter from Melanchthon to Calvin has been lost. However, its contents were reported in a letter from Calvin to Farel, 10 January 1540, in A.-L. Herminjard, ed., *Correspondance des Réformateurs dans les pays de Langue Française* (Geneva: H. Georg, 1864-97), 6: 131-37,165.

[12]For example, see his *Exposition familiere sur le symbole des apostres, contenant les articles de la foy et un sommaire de la religion chrestienne* (Geneva: Jean Girard, 1557), 264-70.

Luther himself was still a sterling servant of God who benefited the entire Church by "commencing to restore the light of the Gospel. God was greatly served by his preaching and writing, to combat the Antichrist and to abolish idolatry."[13]

Beza's general view of Luther and his role in the Reformation is equally positive even though, as I will point out shortly, it tended to erode over the years, especially after the death of Calvin and Viret. Beza, the youngest of the trio of Calvinist leaders under consideration, is best known as Calvin's successor as the Moderator of the Venerable Company of Pastors of Geneva in 1564 following Calvin's death, a position which he held until 1580 when he voluntarily stepped down. Before that time, he had served as Calvin's chief emissary and Geneva's leading diplomat from 1559 to 1564, traveling all over France and Germany on behalf of the Genevan Reformation. As Calvin's successor, he became the foremost pastor and councilor of Geneva until only a few years before his death in 1605.[14]

Although he had never met Luther, Beza knew the Lutherans well and had traveled to Germany on four different occasions between 1557 and 1559 to confer with them on the possibility of drafting a common confession of faith.[15] All of Beza's known comments concerning Luther came after the German's death, and all were made following the beginning of the eucharistic controversies in the 1540s. As Calvin and Viret had, Beza assessed Luther positively in a general and personal sense. For example, over the years, Beza included Luther among his poems of admiration, upheld the validity of Luther's ordination against Roman Catholic attacks, demonstrated the essential agreement between Luther's doctrine of predestination and that of the Reformed communion, and defended Luther's view of Scripture, tradition, the church, and the ministry.[16]

But, like Viret, Beza's main emphasis when he mentioned Luther in his writings in this period was to point out his role in beginning the Reformation.

[13]*Du vray ministere de la vraye Eglise de Jesus Christ, et des vrais Sacremens d'icelle; et des faus sacremens de l'eglise de l'Antechrist, et des additions adjoustées par les hommes au sacrement du Baptesme* (Geneva: Jean Rivery, 1560), 71-75. Also see Pierre Viret, *Les cauteles et canon de la messe, ensemble la messe du corps de Jesus Christ* (Lyon: Claude Ravot, 1563), 12.

[14]Jill Raitt, "Theodore Beza," in Raitt, ed., *Shapers of Religious Traditions in Germany, Switzerland, and Poland, 1560-1600* (New Haven: Yale University Press, 1981), 89-104. For a detailed study of Beza's life, see Paul-F. Geisendorf, *Théodore de Bèze* (Geneva: Alexandre Jullien, 1967).

[15]*Calvini Opera*, 16: 620, 643, and 649. Also see Johann Wilhelm Baum, *Theodor Beza nach handschriftlichen Quellen dargestellt* (Leipzig: Weidmann'sche Buchhandlung, 1843-51), 1: 301.

[16]Theodore Beza, *Poemata*, 2d ed. (Geneva: Henri Stephanus, 1569), 83-130; Beza, *De Veris, et visibilibus ecclesiae catholicae notis, tractatio* (Geneva: Eustathium Vignon, 1579), 81-86; Beza, *De praedestinationis doctrina et vero usu tractatio absolutissima, ex Th. Bezae praelectionibus in nonum Epistolae ad Romanos caput, A Raphaelo Eglino Tigurino Theologiae studioso in schola Genevensi recens excepta* (Geneva: Eustathium Vignon, 1582); and Beza, *Response aux cinq premieres et principales demandes de Fr. Jean Hay* (Geneva: Jean le Preux, 1586).

Thus, in his *De veris et visibilibus Ecclesiae catholicae notis tractatio* of 1579, Beza lists as "the restorers of God's House in the days of our forefathers: Wycliffe, Hus, Jerome of Prague, Luther, Bucer, Oecolampadius, Zwingli, Pellican, Haller, and a great many others."[17] Most revealing is his portrait of Luther in his celebrated *Icones* of 1580. His candid thumbnail sketch of the German Reformer summarizes thirty years of dealing with Luther's ideas and disciples:

> He gradually brought the glorious light of the Gospel out of the deepest darkness, like a grand herald of God, he was a human being of outstanding compassion . . . his work resulted in the cleansing of God's sanctuary, delivering it from the clutches of the Antichrist at an opportune moment, and he used the Word of God as a means of returning it to the Lordship of Christ. . . . Neither emperors, nor kings, nor threats to silence him on the part of the highest authorities kept him from his appointed task, nor did the host of intellectuals arrayed against him strike terror into his heart, rather his work brought renewal to the church so that many generations yet unborn are in his debt, and many today already owe him much; and what is more, his reputation for moderation, knowledge, and zeal are well known because he was given divine strength. He was a man with faults and with turbulent disciples, but still a great man.[18]

Thus, like Viret, Beza sees Luther primarily as the "grand herald of God," the pioneer of the Reformation movement.

In the years following the bitter Marburg Colloquy in 1529 and the Wittenberg Concord in 1536, the eucharistic debate flared up once again with even greater intensity than before.[19] There had been no resolution of the difference between Zwingli and his Swiss, the view that the Supper was a sign and a memorial, and Luther and his Germans, that it was necessary to believe in a bodily presence of Christ in the Eucharist. Calvin hoped to find some middle ground between the two views and worked assiduously toward that end. As almost everybody knows, those in the middle of any controversy often end up alienating both extremes, so Calvin tried to be as careful as possible in proposing solutions to the eucharistic impasse.

---

[17]P. 2.

[18]*Icones* (Geneva: Ioannem Laonium, 1580), ciiij.

[19]For a discussion of Calvin's role in this controversy, see Joseph N. Tylenda, "The Ecumenical Intention of Calvin's Early Eucharistic Teaching," in Brian A. Gerrish, ed. *Reformatio Perennis: Essays on Calvin and the Reformation in Honor of Ford Lewis Battles* (Pittsburgh: Pickwick, 1981), 27-47.

Melanchthon attempted to restrain Luther, but to no avail. In 1544, after several angry incidents, Luther published his *Kurtz bekentuis D. Martin Luthers, vom heiligen Sacrament*, in which he denounced the Zwinglians in no uncertain terms.[20] Then, in January of 1546, shortly before his death, Luther summed up his sentiments in a parody of the first Psalm: "Blessed is the man who walks not in the counsel of the sacramentarians, nor stands in the way of the Zwinglians, nor sits in the seat of the Zurichers."[21] Interestingly enough, Calvin's basically friendly attitude toward Luther remained unchanged in the face of Luther's farewell tirades against the Swiss. And perhaps even more surprising, Luther seemed reluctant to include Calvin in these blasts.

Calvin's response was to intervene with Melanchthon by requesting him to cool Luther down if he could. Further, at the very height of the renewed eucharistic debate, when tempers were red hot, Calvin wrote a letter to Luther himself. This is the only known letter to pass between the two Reformers. The occasion of the communication was not the debate over the Supper, however, but the severe persecution of the Protestants in France. Calvin wanted to apprise Luther of the situation and ask for the German Reformer's frank appraisal of his own advice to the harassed French Protestants. The French believers, for their part, had opted for the so-called Nicodemite solution in which, like Nicodemus in the New Testament, they "secretly" embraced Christ as Savior and discreetly accepted the Reformation of the Church. Calvin challenged this approach in two brief works entitled *Petit traicté monstrant que c'est que doit faire un homme fidele congnoissant la verité de l'Evangile quand il est entre les papistes* in 1543 and *Excuse de Jehan Calvin à Messieurs les Nicodemites sur la complancte qu'ilz font de sa trop grand' riguer* in 1544. Barely hanging on by their fingernails, the French Nicodemites requested that Calvin consult the Germans concerning this matter, either in person or by messenger. Calvin, for various reasons, could not make the journey to Wittenberg at this time, so he translated his two treatises into Latin and sent them to Germany along with two letters, one to Melanchthon and one to Luther, requesting an opinion. Calvin sent both letters to Melanchthon and asked him to use his discretion concerning what to do with the one addressed to Luther.[22]

The letter reveals Calvin's attitude toward Luther at the height of the eucharistic debate during Luther's last days. Calvin is deferential throughout his epistle and makes it clear that he shares with his French Protestant comrades a high regard for Luther's authority. Moreover, he apologizes for

---

[20]*A Short Confession on the Holy Sacrament* in *D. Martin Luthers Werke* (Weimar: H. Böhlau, 1883-93), 54: 141-67.

[21]Ibid. 11: 264.

[22]*A Short Treatise Showing What a Faithful Man Should Do, Knowing the Truth of the Gospel, When He Is Among the Papists* and *The Apology of John Calvin to the Nicodemite Gentlemen Concerning the Complaint They Have Made That He Is Too Rigorous* in *Calvini Opera* 6: 537-614, 617-44.

taking up Luther's valuable time, explains why he has written, and requests that the older man read his two treatises to judge whether or not they are reasonable and sound. It is clearly the communication of a young professor to the seasoned scholar. Calvin concludes:

> How I wish I could fly to you there, so that I might enjoy your company but for a few hours! For I should prefer, and it would be much better, to discuss with you in person, not this question only, but others too. But since it is not granted us here on earth, it will shortly be ours, as I hope, in the kingdom of God.[23]

Unfortunately for posterity, Luther never saw the letter, so the world will never know how he would have responded to it. Melanchthon exercised his discretion and withheld it from the aging and increasingly irascible German Reformer. In any event, it is clear that Calvin hoped to seize the opportunity to assure Luther of his deep respect, even in the midst of the bitter controversy then raging over the Eucharist. This does not mean that Calvin abandoned the Zurichers and their view of the Supper. However, through the crisis, Calvin tried to maintain a balance and restraint which dictated that he refrain from simply taking the side of the Swiss against Luther. His position rested partly on the conviction that neither side had a monopoly on the truth and partly on his unwillingness to forget the debt that the Reformed movement owed to the man he so often called "that illustrious servant of God."[24]

Calvin also gave his appraisal of Luther and his views of the Supper during the 1540s in three tracts written on the subject before Luther's death.[25] In these treatises, Calvin optimistically expressed his belief that there eventually would be a full and equitable settlement of the eucharistic debate and that genuine unity would result. He refused to censure either Luther or Zwingli but rather recalled in thankfulness what the Protestants had received from

---

[23]Ibid. 12: 8.

[24]Calvin's main problem with the post-Luther Lutheran's view of the Eucharist was that it retained too much of the Roman Catholic suggestion of magic in the sacrament. His dislike of superstition is apparent in the calendars published in Geneva which commemorated not the myths of saints but historical events, such as Luther's attack on indulgences in 1517 and the death of Edward VI of England in 1553. Natalie Z. Davis, *Society and Culture in Early Modern Europe* (Stanford: Stanford University Press, 1975), 204-5; and Menna Prestwich, "Calvinism in France, 1555-1629," in Prestwich, ed., *International Calvinism, 1541-1715* (Oxford: Clarendon, 1985), 83.

[25]*Petit Traicté de la Saincte Cene de N. S. Jesus Christ*, 1541; *Defensio sanae et orthodoxae doctrinae de servitute et liberatione humani arbitrii adversus calumnias Alberti Pighii Campensis*, 1543; and *Supplex exhortio ad Caesarem Carolum Quintum*, 1544, in *Calvini Opera* 5: 429-60, and 6: 225-404 and 453-534. For the full story, see Tylenda, "The Ecumenical Intention of Calvin's Early Eucharistic Teaching," 37-40; and W. P. Stephens, *The Theology of Huldrych Zwingli* (Oxford: Clarendon, 1986), 218-59.

both.[26] Most important, he displayed a sensitive appreciation of Luther's thought and personality. He several times spoke of Luther as the man whom God raised up at the beginning of the Reformation to hold a torch over the path to salvation. This last point is best summed up in Calvin's tract against Pighius when he penned the following concerning Luther: "We regard him as a remarkable apostle of Christ, through whose work and ministry, most of all, the purity of the Gospel has been restored in our time."[27] Once again, in the midst of bitterness and acrimony, Calvin refused to forget the debt that all of the Reformers owed to Martin Luther and his pioneer work.

Viret, with a somewhat more radical view, was also drawn into the eucharistic debate of the period. He stood somewhere between Zwingli and Calvin, accepting Calvin's teaching of the true spiritual presence while de-emphasizing the role of the senses in apprehending the body and blood and stressing the significance of the Supper as a sign.[28] Viret's main concern was that the Lord's Supper serve to unite, not divide, Christians. He explained: "And this is why all of us eat the same bread and drink from the same chalice; all of us are one bread, that is, one body."[29] This emphasis, no doubt, helps explain why he never directly attacked Luther's view of the Eucharist even though he disagreed with it. It does not, however, explain why he so often and so bluntly denounced the Roman Catholic teaching of transubstantiation—except perhaps that his polemics were always directed toward the perceived enemy and not toward brothers and friends.

In any case, Viret was also the most theologically eclectic of the three Calvinist Reformers under discussion here.[30] Perhaps this is best illustrated in Viret's definition of a sacrament. It is based on the Church Fathers, especially

[26]Calvin's optimism concerning a settlement here was not so much idealistic professorial claptrap. He genuinely believed differences could be composed on this important point. After all, if, as Brian Gerrish points out, the original Calvinist view (what he calls "the high Calvinist doctrine") of the Lord's Supper was really closer to Luther than Zwingli, and the Calvinists and Zwinglans eventually drew together, then why could not the same sort of rapprochement eventually have been possible between Calvinists and Lutherans? Brian Gerrish, "The Lord's Supper in the Reformed Confessions," *Theology Today* 22 (July 1966): 224-43.

[27]*Calvini Opera*, 6: 250.

[28]*Instruction chrestienne en la doctrine de la loy et de l'Evangile; et en la vraye philosohie et theologie tant naturelle que supernaturelle des Chrestiens; et en la contemplation du temple et des images et oeuvres de la providence de Dieu en tout l'univers; et en l'histoire de la creation et cheute et reparation du genre humain* (Geneva: Jean Rivery, 1564), 1: 220; Pierre Viret, *Des clefs de l'eglise, et de l'administration de la parole de Dieu, et des Sacremens selon l'usage de l'Eglise Romaine; et de la Transsubstatiation; et de la verité du corps de Jesus Christ, et de la vraye communion d'iceluy* (Geneva: Jean Rivery, 1564), 52; and Pierre Viret, *De la vertu et usage due ministere de la parolle de Dieu et des Sacremens dependans d'icelle: et des differens qui sont en la chrestienté à cause d'iceux* (Geneva: Jean Girard, 1548), 668-70.

[29]Arthur Piaget, ed., *Les Actes de la Dispute de Lausanne, 1536* (Neuchâtel: Secrétariat de L'Université, 1928), 163.

[30]For example, see Viret, *Exposition familiere sur le symbole des apostres*, 249-50; and Robert D. Linder, *The Political Ideas of Pierre Viret* (Geneva: Droz, 1964), 143-76.

St. Augustine, but contains elements of the teachings of Luther, Zwingli, and Calvin as well:

> We mean by sacrament a visible sign, given by God to the whole church, in general, to be a testimony in our hearts of his grace and mercy toward us and therein to seal his promises, to confirm and increase our faith in them; through it, he wants us also, from our side, to give testimony to the faith we have in him. Or, if we prefer, we will say that a sacrament is a testimony of the grace of God, given by him to the whole church, consisting in a visible sign by which God confirms it in us and we give him an attestation of the faith we have in him and of the honor we owe him . . . since the sacraments contain all these things (professions, protestations, and attentions of our faith and religion; admonitions, allegories, and figures of the Christian life), we take them also as summaries of the whole of religion and of Christian doctrine.[31]

But in all of his teachings, even though he never directly attacked Luther or the Lutherans, Viret makes it clear that he rejected the Roman Catholic and the Lutheran views of the presence of Christ. Even though he consistently admitted that Jesus Christ was indeed truly present in the Supper, he also—in contrast to Luther—envisioned the true presence in terms that were not dependent upon a definition tied to the physical senses. Rather, it is a sacramental presence—doctrinally speaking—which can only be defined as spiritual —materially speaking. In the final analysis, argued Viret, the exact nature of Christ's presence was a mystery mediated by the power of the Holy Spirit. In his *Des clefs de l'eglise et de l'administration de la parole de Dieu et des sacrements* of 1564, Viret's comments represent his mature teaching on this subject. He clearly rejects the Lutheran position and yet does not quite accept that of Calvin either. It is his own view, tinged with Zwinglianism, yet close enough to Calvin to allow Viret to remain in what became the Calvinist movement:

> And, in thus considering it [the presence], we confess that we cannot perceive, with our physical senses, the spiritual thing that is represented to us in the sacrament by the physical signs, indeed, that we cannot wholly understand, with our judgment and intelligence, the manner in which Jesus Christ's body and blood are present to us and communicated spiritually in the Supper, and in what manner the church, which is the mystical body of Jesus Christ, is united and joined with its head and all its members one with the

---

[31]Viret, *De la vertu et usage du ministere de la parolle de Dieu*, 76, 495.

others, and how he gives them all spiritual life and all of the things represented to us in his holy Supper.[32]

As for Beza, he had little to say directly during the eucharistic controversy of the 1540s or during the following decade and a half immediately prior to Calvin's death and his own assumption of the leadership of the Calvinist movement. In this period, Beza's position was that the Reformed and Lutheran movements certainly formed one true church and that an understanding with the Lutherans concerning the Supper eventually could be reached by means of synods and conferences. As noted previously, Beza made four trips to Germany between 1557 and 1559 in search of an understanding on the Supper and related issues—and he did this with the backing and full support of Calvin, Viret, and other Calvinist ministers. At times hampered by internal dissensions within the Reformed churches in Switzerland, Beza nevertheless persisted in his pursuit of an understanding with the followers of Luther while maintaining a high regard for the deceased German Reformer himself.[33]

But there was a noticeable deterioration of relations between the early Calvinist Reformers, particularly Calvin and Beza, and the Lutherans following the death of Luther in 1546. In contrast to the continuing high regard which Calvin, Viret, and Beza had professed for Luther in previous years, a sourness gradually permeated relations between the two communions. For his part, Calvin continued to labor for eucharistic unity. He succeeded in reaching a mutual agreement with the Zwinglians on the sacraments in 1549 when he and Heinrich Bullinger, Zwingli's successor at Zurich, published their *Consensus Tigurinus*.

But while the Reformed churches of Switzerland were achieving unity, the Lutherans were suffering from internal divisions. In general, the German Lutherans broke up into two camps: those who emphasized Luther's more hardline policies and those who followed the more conciliatory Melanchthon, who was supposed to be Luther's chosen successor. Joachim Westphal, a minister from the hardline group, initiated a pamphlet war with Calvin on the Supper in 1558. Before this time Calvin had always been careful never to attack the Lutherans by name, and he had heretofore been reticent to speak harshly of Luther's teachings on the Supper; now Westphal's attack changed things. The eucharistic debate flared up again and Calvin's words grew proportionately heated. Referring to Westphal and the Lutherans in the 1559 edition of his *Institutes*, Calvin wrote: "And surely certain men would rather

[32]Viret, *Des clefs de l'eglise*, 55.

[33]Baum, *Theodor Beza*, 1: 275-80. For a full discussion of Beza's eucharistic theology, see Jill Raitt, *The Eucharistic Theology of Theodore Beza: Development of the Reformed Doctrine* (Chambersburg, Pa.: American Academy of Religion, 1972).

manifest their ignorance to their great shame than yield even the least particle of their error. I am not speaking of the papists, whose doctrine is more tolerable or at least more modest."[34] This faint praise of the Roman position probably indicates that Calvin was beginning to give up the idea of ever reaching an understanding with the Lutherans on the Supper and thus establishing a united Protestant church. Unless twentieth-century Christians are aware of the immense importance attached to the celebration of the Eucharist by the Medieval Church, they have difficulty understanding why the Supper could be such a divisive issue. In many ways, the sixteenth-century eucharistic debate was similar to the twentieth-century inerrancy controversy.

When Calvin died in 1564, his hope for a united Reformed movement was not only still unrealized but appeared to be fast fading from the realm of possibility. The Lutherans, fearing that internal strife would completely destroy their movement, finally pulled themselves together and adopted a conservative united front. Driven by political events in Germany, they decisively rejected Calvin's understanding of the Supper and returned to the Augsburg Confession of 1530, inserting it into their official Book of Concord in 1577. Thus, the Lutherans regained their own original unity, but at the expense of any possibility of reaching an understanding with the Reformed churches of Switzerland on the Supper and related matters.[35]

All of this provided the background for what appeared to be even more strained relations between the Calvinists and Lutherans—and, consequently, of the diminishing stature of Luther in the eyes of the Reformed community. This is reflected in Beza's view of Luther following the death of Calvin in 1564, clear as early as 1566 and 1567 in Beza's correspondence. There, in a letter to the French Protestant leader, Gaspard de Coligny, in 1565 and again in one to Calvin's former protegée, Renée de France, in 1566, Beza implied that Luther had only begun the Reformation while Calvin had brought it to fruition.[36]

There are two incidents which illustrate more than any others this degeneration of the early Calvinists' regard for Luther. Both involved Beza and both occurred some years after the deaths of Calvin and Viret. The first was the experience of Beza at the Colloquy of Montbéliard in 1586 while the second was a moment of editorial pique on the part of Beza, probably in response to this theological conference.

The Colloquy of Montbéliard had been called to discuss the Lord's Supper and the Person of Christ in order to clarify the Lutheran and Reformed positions on these two subjects so that the Duke of Württemberg, the Lutheran

[34]Calvin, *Institutes*, 2: 1402.

[35]For a discussion of the reaction of the French Calvinists to the Formula of Concord, see Robert D. Linder, "The French Calvinist Response to the Formula of Concord," *Journal of Ecumenical Studies* 19 (Winter 1982): 18-37.

[36]*Correspondence de Théodore de Bèze*, eds. Henri Meylan, et al., (Geneva: Droz, 1960-80), 6: 20, 25, and 7: 100.

ruler of Montbéliard, could make up his mind whether or not the French Protestants in this portion of his realm could be allowed to take of the Supper
according to their own rite or whether they simply would be given the choice
of conforming to the Lutheran order or moving on. In particular, the question
of whether or not the French Reformed ministers of Montbéliard should be
required to sign the Formula of Concord also arose.[37]

The colloquy was called for March of 1586 at the castle of Montbéliard.
Beza and his colleagues conferred with a delegation of Lutheran theologians
led by Jakob Andreae. Whereas Beza was willing to agree on a general statement of evangelical doctrines and leave the churches of Montbéliard free to
determine their application, Andreae held out to the end for a complete capitu-
lation on the part of the Reformed camp to the Lutheran position, especially
on the Supper. The effort to reach an understanding came to naught, and at the
end of the meeting Andreae refused Beza's "hand of brotherhood" while Beza,
in turn, declined Andreae's "hand of benevolence and humanity."[38]

Later, probably in the late 1580s or early 1590s, apparently while still
smarting from this incident, Beza took out some of his frustration with his
editor's quill while reviewing Calvin's correspondence. It occurred in relation
to the very letter to Farel cited earlier as evidence of Calvin's delight in hearing
of Luther's approbation of one of his books. Calvin, it will be recalled, had
expressed almost childlike joy in hearing from Bucer about Luther's approval
and had said generous things about the German Reformer. But Beza now carefully crossed out the phrases:

> Just think what I say there about the Eucharist! Consider Luther's
> noblemindedness! It will be easy to decide what reason they have
> who so obstinately disagree with him. . . . We are surely made of
> stone if we are not overcome by such moderation![39]

This incident is an interesting commentary on the degree of frustration and
anger which Beza apparently felt as a result of the repeated failures of the
Calvinists to come to an understanding with Luther and the Lutherans
concerning the doctrine of the Lord's Supper. It demonstrates clearly that,
even though he remained officially conciliatory in his published works, Beza
was personally irked.

---

[37]Jill Raitt, "The French Reformed Theological Response," in Lewis W. Spitz and Wenzel
Lohff, eds., *Discord, Dialogue, and Concord: Studies in the Lutheran Reformation's Formula of Concord*
(Philadelphia: Fortress, 1977), 178-90.

[38]Ibid., 182; Baum, *Theodor Beza*, 1: 275-82, 409-10; and Geisendorf, *Théodore de Bèze*,
317-79.

[39]Herminjard, *Correspondance des Réformateurs*, 6: 131 n. 53. Herminjard's examination of the
original manuscript revealed that Beza had gone through the letter and crossed out what he apparently regarded as the most compromising phrases.

In conclusion, this study reveals several things about the early Calvinists' view of Luther. First, Calvin, Viret, and Beza never appealed to Luther's ideas as though they were final or definitive. He was not placed in the same category as the Bible nor even the Church Fathers. Moreover, there is manifestly evident the high regard which all three Calvinists had for Luther as a great preacher of the Word of God. Most importantly, the early Calvinist leaders in the period before Luther's death clearly considered the German Reformer to be both their brother and friend.

However, things began to change after 1571. It is clear from the conclusion of the Colloquy of Montbéliard, for example, that the Reformed communion still considered the Lutherans brothers but not necessarily friends. Evangelical solidarity was eroding but still basically intact. Unfortunately, after the death of Beza in 1605, evangelical solidarity became more shadow than substance, and the theological divisions of the sixteenth century hardened into the confessional shapes that were to be maintained until the twentieth century.

Personalities, theological disputes, and politics aggravated by national differences played a part in the progressive disintegration of evangelical solidarity in the course of the sixteenth century. For example, Luther's strong personality gave the German Reformation cohesion while leaders like Calvin, Viret, and Beza provided dynamic leadership for the Reformed communion. While Luther, Calvin, Viret, and Beza were alive, there was real hope of evangelical solidarity being transformed into a united Protestant movement. However, when the strong leaders of first-generation Lutheranism and first-generation Calvinism passed from the scene, there was no one of equal stature to replace them.

In this regard, it is perhaps best to remember Luther, not as the sharp-tongued polemicist but as the thoughtful evangelical brother. To be sure, shortly before his death in 1546, he wrote some unkind things about his fellow Protestants in Switzerland. However, in the same period Luther also told the Wittenberg bookseller Maritz Golsch that he liked Calvin's *Petit Traicté de la Saincte Cene* and remarked, "I might have entrusted the whole affair of this controversy to him from the beginning. If my opponents had done the like, we should soon have been reconciled."[40]

Protestant fragmentation was not inevitable. Free people can reach consensus on important issues. However, it takes time, patience, and statesmanship to do so. Cannot present-day Christian believers learn a great deal from these early Calvinists and their attitude of evangelical solidarity with Luther and the first Lutherans?

---

[40]Christoph Pezel, *Ausführliche warhrhafte und bestandige Erzählung vom Sacramentstreit* (Bremen: Bernhardt Peterss., 1600), 137.

The Jesuit Emond Auger and
The Saint Bartholomew's Massacre at Bordeaux:
The Final Word?

A. Lynn Martin
The University of Adelaide

Emond Auger, the French Jesuit, earned a reputation as a celebrated preacher, author of catechisms, and militant opponent of Protestantism. This militancy has lent credence to allegations that he preached incendiary sermons which led to the Saint Bartholomew's Massacre at Bordeaux on 3 October 1572. However, Auger's activities and attitudes toward the French Huguenots reveal a notable flexibility—moderation and militancy, contempt and respect. Previous attempts to ascertain the truth of the allegations have resulted in indefinite conclusions, but historians have generally thought it probable that Auger had a role in the Massacre. Two letters recently discovered at the Jesuit Archives in Rome, although containing new evidence, do not permit a definitive conclusion.

EMOND AUGER WAS ONE OF THE MOST NOTABLE FRENCH JESUITS of the sixteenth century.[1] Born at Alleman in the diocese of Troyes in 1530, Auger entered the Society of Jesus at Rome in 1550 and died at Como in 1591. His first assignment in France was at the Jesuit college at Pamiers in 1559, and just six years later, in 1565, he became the provincial of the Jesuit province of Aquitaine. Auger's ability as a preacher earned him the sobriquet "the French Chrysostom," after the fifth-century saint renown for being an exemplary preacher. In the words of one of Auger's superiors, "I have never seen nor can I hope to see in all my life anyone similar to him; he is stupendous in every respect . . . and considered to be the first preacher of this kingdom."[2] Auger's works of controversy and his catechisms have likewise earned him another

---

[1] I first became interested in Auger as a graduate student at the University of Wisconsin in 1966, when Robert Kingdon encouraged my interest in Jesuit confessors to the kings of France. Professor Kingdon supervised my master's thesis on Auger's relationship with Henry III, and he likewise supervised my doctoral thesis, *Henry III and the Jesuit Politicians*, which was published by Droz of Geneva in 1973. My research on Auger led to the conclusion that he never was confessor to Henry, even though over one hundred books stated that he was. After making this point in *Henry III*, I was surprised to see that one reviewer of the book, Jane Crawford in *Church History* 43 (1974): 407, repeated the error.

[2] Archivum Romanum Societatis Iesu (hereafter ARSI), GAL 81. f. 232v, Oliver Manare to Francis Borgia, Paris, 22 May 1568.

sobriquet, "the French Canisius."[3] Nonetheless, Auger's modern reputation rests primarily upon his relationship with King Henry III of France, a relationship which began in 1568 when Henry was then the Duke of Anjou and which reached a climax between 1583 and 1587 when Auger was the king's indispensable spiritual director.[4] This work as spiritual director earned Auger a certain amount of notoriety, as also did his supposed role in instigating the Saint Bartholomew's Massacre at Bordeaux on 3 October 1572.

Auger's role in the Massacre at Bordeaux has been the subject of historical controversy, most notably between the Jesuit historian Henri Fouqueray and the French historian Henri Hauser. In refuting allegations that Auger incited the slaughter of Huguenots at Bordeaux, in his *Histoire de la Compagnie de Jésus en France* Fouqueray claimed, "Nous n'avons trouvé dans les papiers de la Compagnie aucun document sur le massacre à Bordeaux."[5] Hauser, on the other hand, concluded his investigation of the allegations, "Le Père Emond Auger et le massacre de Bordeaux, 1572," with the comment, "Que le P. Auger ait été l'un des fauteurs des massacres de Bordeaux, ce n'est point une vérité historiquement établie, c'est une opinion qui a pour elle, à défaut d'absolue certitude, le maximum de probabilité."[6] In 1970 I examined all the evidence relevant to this dispute I could find at the Jesuit Archives in Rome and included the information in an article entitled "Jesuits and the Massacre of St. Bartholomew's Day."[7] For want of solid documentary evidence, I concurred with Hauser's conclusion. Then in 1984, while doing research at the Jesuit Archives for a book on Jesuit accounts of the plague, I encountered further evidence regarding the allegations in a letter from Edmund Hay, the Jesuit provincial of France, to the vicar general of the Society, Jerónimo Nadal. Hay wrote the letter from Bordeaux on 11 October 1572, that is, eight days after the Massacre. I also discovered a letter written by Auger himself, similarly to Nadal from Bordeaux on 12 October. The letters' location, in a volume of letters from Germany, explains why previous research had failed to find them.[8]

An evaluation of the allegations and of the new evidence included in these two letters requires consideration of Jesuit policy toward the Huguenots and

[3]Cf. the two books by Friedrich J. Brand, *P. Emundus Augerius S. I. "Frankreichs Canisius" in seinem religioesen and socialen Wirken zur Zeit der Hugenotten* (Cleve: Druck und Verlag von Fr. Boss Wwe., 1903) and *Die Katechismen des Edmundus Augerius S. J. in historischer, dogmatisch-moralischer und katechetischer Bearbeitung* (Freiburg im Breisgau: Herdersche Verlagshandlung, 1917).

[4]Cf. my *Henry III and the Jesuit Politicians*.

[5](Paris: Alphonse Picard et Fils, 1910-25), 1: 630 note.

[6]*Société de l'histoire du protestantisme français* 60 (1911): 289-304.

[7]*Archivum Historicum Societatis Iesu* 43 (1974): 103-32.

[8]ARSI, GERM 134 II, ff. 502, 504. I wish to thank Father Edm. Lamalle, archivist of the Jesuit Archives at Rome, for providing me with microfilm of Auger's letter.

an understanding of some aspects of Auger's career. Contrary to what might be expected and to what some historians have argued, the Jesuit mission to France did not initially focus upon the struggle with Protestantism. Far from finding a Huguenot under every bush and thereby justifying their presence in France, Jesuits' perception of the development of Protestantism paralleled or even lagged behind perception in the Catholic community as a whole.[9] A very concrete indication of this is the mission of Louis Coudret to Savoy in 1558 and 1559. Despite the proximity of Calvin's Geneva, Coudret came without a papal license to read heretical books, without knowing how to refute Calvin's theory of predestination, and without any idea of how or if he should talk to heretics or even say good day to them.[10] Moreover, Protestantism was not a factor in the negotiations concerning the establishment of the first two Jesuit colleges in France, at Billom in 1556 and at Pamiers in 1559.[11] Finally, as late as 1566 Emond Auger *argued* in a letter to general Francis Borgia that the Society could make its greatest contribution "in the extirpation of heresy, as much by means of catechisms as by means of sermons, lectures, and other similar exercises."[12]

When Jesuits did confront Protestantism, they displayed an admirable flexibility, a flexibility consistent with the advice repeatedly contained in Ignatius Loyola's *Constitutions* to take account of persons, places, times, and other circumstances. No better illustration of this flexibility exists than the career of the Jesuit who had the most experience in combating Protestantism, Emond Auger. As would be expected, Auger had enormous contempt for those he considered to be the enemies of God, and the comments made in his letters win a prize for invective. The Huguenot leader Gaspard de Coligny was "that Attila Admiral,"[13] and the Huguenot pastors were "the shit of the world."[14] In an age which considered dying well extremely important, Auger's

---

[9]For the perception of heresy by the Catholic community cf. Denis Richet, "Sociocultural Aspects of Religious Conflicts in Paris during the Second Half of the Sixteenth Century," in *Ritual, Religion, and the Sacred*, ed. Robert Forster and Orest Ranum (Baltimore: The Johns Hopkins University Press, 1982), 182-212, esp. 183-90.

[10]ARSI, GAL 79, ff. 35v, 52v, 54, Coudret to Diego Lainez, Annecy, 20 April and 2 August 1559.

[11]On this point cf. Marc Venard, "Y-a-t-il une 'stratégie scolaire' des jésuites en France au XVIe siècle?" pp. 67-85 in *L'université de Pont-à-Mousson et les problèmes de son temps* (Nancy: Berger-Levrault, 1974). Venard correctly argues against the views contained in François de Dainville, *Les jésuites et l'éducation de la société française: La naissance de l'humanisme moderne* (Paris: Beauchesne et ses fils, 1940), 39, and Pierre Moissy, *Les églises des jésuites de l'ancienne assistance de France* (Rome: Institutum Historicum Societatis Iesu, 1958), 20-21.

[12]ARSI, GAL 81, f. 92, Toulouse, 20 July 1566.

[13]Ibid., 82, f. 66, Auger to Borgia, Lyon, 25 May 1569.

[14]*Polanci complementa, epistolae et commentaria P. Joannis Alphonsi de Polanco e Societate Jesu* (Madrid: Gabrielis López del Horno), 2: 264, Auger to Juan Polanco, near La Rochelle, 18 February 1573.

descriptions of Protestant death were similarly scathing. During an outbreak of the plague at Lyon, Huguenots "died for the most part mad, with horrendous invocations of the devil, to whom they once again freely offered themselves; the viscera of some burst open, and many ran here and there."[15] Jean Calvin "died in extreme desperation, eaten by worms and lice, decomposed and as dry as wood, and completely mad."[16] Yet despite the invective Auger had considerable respect for Huguenot organization and methods, as indicated by his willingness to copy them. While at Toulouse he instituted classes in catechism which were similar "to the manner of the adversaries,"[17] and, in order to counter the Huguenot singing of the Psalms in the French translations by Clément Marot, Auger suggested that France's greatest poet, Pierre Ronsard, translate the Psalms into French "for singing at home, in shops, and while traveling, against those which the adversaries go around mumbling."[18]

Another somewhat surprising aspect of the Jesuit confrontation with Protestantism was the moderation of their sermons. Jesuit superiors advocated moderation for tactical reasons, as Ignatius Loyola instructed, "Do not try to put opponents in the wrong, but concentrate on affirming and strengthening the Catholic faith."[19] Although some Jesuits sometimes observed these instructions more often in the breach, the sermons of Emond Auger, that "French Chrysostom," produce some striking examples of moderation. When Catholic authorities regained control of Lyon in 1563 after a temporarily successful Huguenot uprising, Auger helped prevent popular Catholic retaliation and won the gratitude of those responsible for maintaining order by preaching moderation. He took as his text Luke 6:36, "Be merciful, even as your Father is merciful."[20] Fifteen years later at Bordeaux Auger won the gratitude of Catherine de'Medici by preaching in support of her efforts to disband

---

[15]ARSI, GAL 80, f. 263, Auger to Lainez, Lyon, 28 September 1564.

[16]Ibid., f. 244, Auger to Polanco, Lyon, 3 August 1564.

[17]Ibid. 81, f. 58, Annibal Coudret to Borgia, Toulouse, 30 April 1566.

[18]*Lainii Monumenta, Epistolae et acta Patris Jacobi Lainii secundi praepositi generalis Societatis Jesu* (Madrid: Gabrielis López del Horno, 1912-17), 7: 475, Auger to Lainez, Lyon, 15 July 1563. Cf. Thomas D. Culley and Clement J. McNaspy, "Music and the Early Jesuits (1540-65)," *Archivum Historicum Societatis Iesu* 40 (1971): 231. Henri Busson makes a mistake on this point in his *Littérature et théologie: Montaigne, Bossuet, La Fontaine, Prévost* (Paris: Presses Universitaires de France, 1962), 77.

[19]Quoted from Piet Penning de Vries, "Protestants and other Spirituals. Ignatius' Vision and Why He Took this Position," *Archivum Historicum Societatis Iesu* 40 (1971): 476. For specific examples of superiors' instructions on this point, cf. *Lainii Monumenta* 8: 811, De Collegiis Galliae Ordinationes, ca. June 1562; ARSI, GERM 104, f. 20, Lainez to Louis Coudret, Rome, 2 July 1559; GAL 84, f. 243v, William Creichton to Nadal, Avignon, 24 September 1572.

[20]*Lainii Monumenta* 2: 627, Auger to Lainez, Lyon, 15 July 1563.

the militantly anti-Huguenot congregations.[21] These two cases suggest pandering to the authorities, and, when the authorities sought less moderate sermons, Auger obliged. In 1568, for example, at the request of the Cardinal of Lorraine, Auger helped prepare public opinion for another round of religious war by his sermons in Paris.[22] On the other hand, on occasion he delivered militant sermons at a time when the court followed a policy of moderation, as he did after the Peace of Saint-Germain in 1570.[23] The sermons of Emond Auger hence make generalizations difficult; to state that they might be an illustration of Loyola's advice to take account of persons, places, times, and other circumstances might be stretching the point, but they nonetheless indicate the flexibility of the Jesuit approach to Protestantism.

While Jesuit superiors advocated moderation in sermons for tactical reasons, Jesuit books of controversy were unabashedly belligerent in tone and content. Auger's *Catechism*, for example, rather than concentrating on "affirming and strengthening the Catholic faith," was a point by point refutation of Calvin's *Formulaire d'instruire les enfants en la chrétienté*.[24] Similarly, Auger wrote a confession of faith in refutation of Calvin's *Institutes of the Christian Religion*,[25] while he directed his book on the sacrament of marriage against the heresies of the "Calvinistes, Bezeans, Ochinistes, et Melanchthoniens" and his book on the Eucharist against the "Lutheriens, Zvingliens, et Westphaliens."[26] Auger's most belligerent book, however, was his *Pedagogue d'armes*, published in 1568 as King Charles IX was preparing to renew the religious war with the Huguenots. In it Auger called for a crusade against the turbulent and bloodthirsty enemies of God.[27]

When religious war did begin again in September of 1568, the chaplain who accompanied the royal army led by the Duke of Anjou was Emond Auger.

[21]ARSI, GAL 90, f. 199, Toussaint Roussel to Everard Mercurian, Bordeaux, 24 February 1579; *Lettres de Catherine de Médicis*, ed. Baguenault de Puchesse and Hector de la Ferrière (Paris: Imprimerie Nationale, 1880-95), 6: 40, Catherine to Henry, Bordeaux, 29 September 1578.

[22]ARSI, GAL 82, ff. 207, 247, Oliver Manare to Borgia, Paris, 11 March and 1 August 1568.

[23]Abel Desjardins, ed., *Négociations diplomatiques de la France avec la Toscane* (Paris: Imprimerie Nationale, 1859-75), 3: 642, Filippo Cavriana to Bartolomeo Concini, Paris, 12 January 1571.

[24]*Cathechisme et sommaire de la religion chrestienne*, first published in 1563 at Lyon; ARSI, GAL 80, f. 126, Auger to Lainez, Lyon, 24 September 1563. Cf. Jean-Claude Dhotel, *Les origines du catéchisme moderne* (Paris: Aubier, 1967), 77-80.

[25]It evidently was not published; Auger referred to it in a letter to Lainez, from Lyon dated 22 May 1564, in ARSI, GAL 80, f. 209v.

[26]*Discours du Sainct Sacrement de Mariage* (Paris: Gabriel Buon, 1572); *De la vraye, reale et corporelle presence de Jesus-Christ au Sainct Sacrement de L'Autel* (Paris: Pierre l'Huillier, 1563).

[27]*Le pedagogue d'armes, pour instuire un prince chretien à bien entreprendre et heuresement archever une bonne guerre, pour estre victorieux de tous les ennemis de son estat, et de l'eglise catholique* (Paris: Sebastien Nivelle, 1568).

Following the Catholic victory at Jarnac on 13 March 1569, a jubilant Auger sent details of the battle to Rome and later celebrated the mass of thanksgiving, *Te Deum Laudamus*, for the victorious leaders.[28] So notorious was Auger's reputation among the Huguenots during this period that Gaspard de Coligny reportedly wanted him murdered.[29] Five years after the battle of Jarnac, following the Saint Bartholomew's Massacre, Auger once again accompanied a royal army led by the Duke of Anjou, this time to besiege the Huguenot stronghold, La Rochelle. On this occasion the Jesuit chaplain procured an oath from the young duke not to abandon the struggle until France was free of heresy.[30] The relationship between the Jesuit Auger and the Duke of Anjou, founded as it was upon belligerent anti-Protestantism, underwent a remarkable transformation when the duke succeeded his brother to the French throne. Between 1583 and 1587, when Auger was Henry's spiritual adviser, he supported the king's moderate policies and was the leader of a faction of Jesuits which was politique and gallican in sympathies and opposed to another Jesuit faction which favored the militant policies of the Catholic League.[31] Finally, the pro-League authorities of Lyon arrested Auger in 1589 for his alleged part in a royalist conspiracy.[32] To make an obvious point, Emond Auger was a complex man, and his activities and attitudes defy simple categorization. Had he been consistently moderate, it would be easy to dismiss the allegations of his role in the Massacre at Bordeaux; had he always presented an uncompromising belligerence towards the Huguenots, the allegations would gain credence.

According to Henri Hauser, the sole basis for these allegations is the following passage from the *Mémoires de l'estat de France sous Charles Neufiesme*, edited by Simon Goulart:

> Edmond Augier [*sic*] . . . shouted every day, expressing his opinion from the pulpit, and thundered horribly, bitterly scolding the unconcern and tardiness of those at Bordeaux and the pusillanimity of the governor, so far as to say that his sword remained in the scabbard and that he went to sleep with his whore. As for the *procureur general* Mulet, this preacher attacked him also, saying that the mule [*mulet*] is a beast composed of an ass and a mare and that there was no mule on Noah's Ark during the deluge. On the day called the feast of Saint Michael, in speaking of the angels through which God executed his threats and vengeances, he cried out saying, "Who has executed the judgement of God at Paris? The

[28]Martin, *Henry III*, 29-30, 36-38.

[29]ARSI, GAL 84, f. 253, Manare to Nadal, Paris, 3 October 1572.

[30]*Lettres de Catherine de Médicis*, 4: 225, Catherine to Anjou, 30 May 1573.

[31]Cf. Martin, *Henry III*, esp. Chapter 15.

[32]Ibid., 222.

Angel of God! Who has executed it at Orleans? The Angel of God! Who has executed it in several other cities of the realm? The Angel of God! Who will execute it in the city of Bordeaux? It will be the Angel of God!" In short, all these sermons and discourses, full of invectives, had no other goal, and in public as in private he incessantly solicited the men to do at Bordeaux as had been done in Paris.[33]

The new evidence relevant to Auger's role in the Massacre at Bordeaux is, unfortunately, not unambiguous and is open to varying interpretations. Edmond Hay, writing on 11 October, did not mention any incendiary sermons or any other details of the Massacre:

Meanwhile our confessors and our preachers are quite profitably occupied, especially Father Emond. Many Huguenots, who previously said that he was a seditious and bloodthirsty man, have experienced his religious gentleness and mercy. He even saved the lives of many of them and, as we believe, persuaded many that the true and Catholic religion is the way to eternal life.[34]

Auger, writing on the 12th, reported on the Massacre but likewise gave few specific details and, moreover, as a Frenchman writing to a Spaniard in an Italian heavily influenced by Latin construction, produced a prose that poses problems of meaning.

Here the affairs of the Catholic faith go well, and the seditious have been castigated almost as in Paris, and on the third of this month the same was done in Toulouse. I fear, among so many just executions of the wicked, that there be irregularities [an uneven distribution of justice], but of the sort which Samuel and Elijah confronted. In a few months more than seven hundred of the people have been truly converted. May God prosper everything![35]

[33]"Massacre de ceux de la religion a Bordeaux le 3. jour d'octobre 1572," (Meidelbourg: Par Heinrich Wolf, 1579), 1: 380v-381.

[34]ARSI, GERM 134 II, f. 502: Interim confessarii nostri et concionatores utiliter satis occupantur maxime P. Emundus in quo multi Hugonoti experiuntur Christianam et religiosam mansuetudinem et misericordiam qui prius illum dicebant hominem seditiosum et sanguinarium. Multis enim vitam temporalem servavit et multis, ut credimus persuasit veram et Catholicam religionem quae via est ad vitam aeternam.

[35]Ibid., f. 504: Qui le cose della fede catholica vanno bene et si son castigati i seditiosi quasi come in Parigi, et il giorno 3 di questo medesimamente si fece in Tolosa; io temo fra tante giuste uccisioni de tristi di essere irregolare, ma di quella irregolaritá di Samuel, o d'Elia. Piú di 700 fra alcuni mesi del popolo si son ridotti da dovero. Idio prosperi il tutto.

Both letters contain material that supports as well as refutes Goulart's accusations. Hay's letter notes that the Huguenots believed Auger to be bloodthirsty and seditious. This might be a reference to Auger's provocative sermons in Bordeaux, but Auger certainly had such a reputation among Protestants long before the Massacre. Moreover, Hay declared that Auger saved the lives of many Huguenots who were evidently in danger at the time of the Massacre. It makes no sense for Auger to argue that the authorities in Bordeaux should follow the lead of Paris in executing "the enemies of God" and then save the lives of the very same "enemies of God." The problem with this interpretation is that authorities in Paris did precisely that, namely, save the lives of some Huguenots after ordering the Massacre. Auger's letter indicates that he definitely approved of the Massacre and linked it to the progress of the Catholic faith. He nonetheless tempered the approval (and here the problems of interpretation become acute) with comments on the "irregular" nature of the executions. On the other hand, he then qualified this statement by linking it to the Old Testament prophets Samuel and Elijah. The first probably refers to an incident in 1 Samuel 15:1-3 when Samuel proclaimed God's commandment to Saul: "Now go and smite Amalek, and utterly destroy all that they have; do not spare them, but kill both man and woman, infant and suckling, ox and sheep, camel and ass." Similarly, Elijah ordered the execution of the 450 prophets of Baal (1 Kings 18:40). Perhaps Auger's reference to the Old Testament prophets was an attempt to excuse his own role in fomenting the Massacre at Bordeaux. Such an interpretation is tempting but problematical to say the least. In short, a definitive verdict is not possible on the basis of the information contained in these letters. If this is indeed the final word on the role of the Jesuit Emond Auger in the Saint Bartholomew's Massacre at Bordeaux, it is because other evidence is unlikely to exist.

Bipartisan Justice and the Pacification of Late Sixteenth-Century Languedoc

Raymond A. Mentzer, Jr.
Montana State University

One of the more important, yet frequently forgotten features of the edict of Nantes in 1598 was the definitive establishment of bipartisan chambers of justice (*chambres mi-parties* or *chambres de l'Edit*) within the major parlements of France. Staffed by both Protestant and Catholic judges, these special courts were specifically empowered to adjudicate civil and criminal cases involving Protestants. The chambers had operated sporadically since 1576 and, as such, occupied an important role in the settlement of the religious question and the related warfare. Perhaps the strongest of these chambers was that which operated in the province of Languedoc. Although theoretically attached to the Parlement of Toulouse, it met in two early sessions at Lisle before finding a more permanent seat at Castres. Aside from the normal case load of any higher court, this bipartisan chamber addressed some rather complex questions related to the peace process. It supervised the orderly restoration of economic assets which Protestants had seized from the Catholic Church, mediated for the reduction of friction in the lingering religious rivalry, and carefully examined defendants who claimed royal amnesty for wartime acts that would have otherwise been considered criminal. While their relationship was far from amicable, the Protestant and Catholic magistrates of the *chambre de l'Edit* did cooperate for the mutual advantages of pacification.

THE EDICT OF NANTES, ISSUED IN 1598 provided the formal, negotiated structure for bringing to a close the years of war which accompanied the Reformation in France. Its most memorable feature was the accord of practical toleration to the Huguenots by granting them garrisoned surety towns. Less well known is another of the edict's basic provisions: the definitive establishment of bipartisan chambers of justice (*chambres mi-parties*) for the judgment of litigation involving Protestants. The edict envisaged these special chambers for the six major parlements of the realm and, as such, reflects a basic Protestant demand initially voiced in the edict of Beaulieu of 1576. The tribunals are commonly called *chambres de l'Edit* in honor of this earlier proclamation and not, as is often but mistakenly thought, as a result of the Nantes legislation. In fact, the notion that Protestant litigants, for both civil and criminal instances, ought to have access to courts staffed at least partially by Protestant judges can be traced to the very beginnings of the Wars of Religion. And the chambers themselves operated, albeit in sporadic fashion, throughout the two decades prior to the edict of Nantes and occupied an important but often overlooked role in working toward peaceful settlement of the religious question and the related warfare.[1]

Perhaps the strongest of these chambers was that which existed for the province of Languedoc. Justifiably fearful of prejudicial and harsh treatment by Catholic judicial magistrates, Huguenot leaders of the region had already sought to establish separate and wholly Protestant tribunals at every level in the 1560s. They enjoyed limited success in the exercise of consular as well as subalternate justice for those towns and areas under their political and military domination. The Parlement of Toulouse, a sovereign court whose jurisdiction extended over the entire province, was a far more perplexing obstacle. Unable to wrest control of it, the Calvinists were equally incapable of establishing a new, fully Protestant high court. The Parlement, more than any other tribunal, represented royal judicial authority and the conservative Catholic magistrates who sat on the bench held tenaciously to their power. Only with the general decline of Protestant fortunes following the Saint Bartholomew's Day Massacre of 1572 and the development of a Huguenot-Politique alliance did a compromise solution gradually emerge. The edict of Beaulieu in May 1576 contained the first official confirmation of bipartisan chambers attached to the various parlements and staffed by proportionate numbers of Protestant and Catholic judges.

Two early, ephemeral sessions of the *chambre de l'Edit* of Languedoc took place at Lisle, a small town about midway between the center of Catholic power at Toulouse and the Huguenot strongholds to the northeast. For six months in 1579-80 and just over two years in 1583-85, a Protestant president and six associate judges (*conseillers*) were joined by an analogous delegation of Catholic magistrates from the Parlement of Toulouse. A more sustained effort began at the Huguenot town of Castres in 1595 and was confirmed three years later by the edict of Nantes. The Castres chamber, ultimately staffed by two presidents and sixteen counselors drawn equally from each faith, was theoretically a part of the Parlement of Toulouse and would continue to sit, despite brief interruptions, until 1679.[2]

The concept of bipartisanism indelibly marked the Protestant settlement as well as the joint pacification process throughout Languedoc. When the alliance between Huguenots and Politiques first surfaced in the mid-1570s, Henri de Montmorency-Damville, provincial governor and chief of the Politique party, agreed to a bipartisan council of advisors (*conseil mi-partie*). With the

---

[1] Léonce Anquez, *Histoire des assemblées politiques des réformées de France (1573-1622)* (Geneva: Slatkine, 1970; reprint of Paris, 1859), 119-39, 197-204, and 456-502. Elie Benolist, *Histoire de l'édit de Nantes*, 5 vols. (Delft: A. Beman, 1693-95), 1: 235-37 and 457-58. Daniel Ligou, *Le protestantisme en France de 1598 à 1715* (Paris: SEDES, 1968), 13-14.

[2] Jules Cambon de Lavalette, *La chambre de l'Edit de Languedoc* (Paris: Sandoz et Fischbacher, 1872), 12-90. Raymond A. Mentzer, Jr., "The Formation of the *chambre de l'Edit* of Languedoc," *Proceedings of the Annual Meeting of the Western Society for French History* 8 (1980): 47-56.

suspension of hostilities at the end of the century, membership on the special commissions created for the execution and enforcement of the edict of Nantes also followed the principle of parity. Each of the two commissions empaneled for Languedoc had two officers, one Catholic and the other Protestant.[3] Like the magistrates who sat on the mixed bench of the *chambre de l'Edit*, these commissioners sought to assure the secure and continued practice of both faiths in accordance with the terms of the edict, the equitable enforcement of the law for all royal subjects, and the reduction if not elimination of threats to social peace arising from religious differences. Although the effort was bipartisan rather than nonpartisan and the opposing parties were far from a genuine reconciliation, they recognized the potential, mutual advantage of practical cooperation in adherence to royal policy.

The problem of re-establishing public order in the wake of protracted war was not new to France. The kingdom had faced this very question in the mid-fifteenth century at the conclusion of the Hundred Years' War. Many late-sixteenth-century issues bore a striking resemblance to the previous experience. Ownership of property seized or confiscated during the war had to be sorted out. Persons claiming benefit of various royal amnesties needed to be heard in a regular and orderly process. At the same time, criminals who had taken advantage of the lawlessness borne of prolonged strife deserved punishment. There was even an element of bipartisan accommodation when magistrates of the Burgundian faction were integrated into the Parlement of Paris.[4] On the other hand, the conclusion to the religious wars of the sixteenth century differed from the earlier situation in an important respect—no one had triumphed decisively. This fact imposed the unusual requirement that former enemies work together in pursuit of a sensible and functional settlement.

Aside then from the normal case load of any higher court, the bipartisan chamber at Lisle and later Castres had before it some rather complex questions related to the establishment of a durable accord and implementation of the various pacification edicts (of which Nantes was merely the last and most famous). Catholic bishops and abbots were anxious that ecclesiastical property seized by Protestants in the course of the religious wars be returned. Both sides recognized that considerable revenues were at stake. The Catholic prelates also sought re-establishment of Catholic worship in those areas where the Huguenots had suspended it. A second major issue focused on the many towns of Languedoc which possessed significant religious minorities. The rival confessional groups frequently clashed on a variety of matters and such conflicts, if left unresolved, held the potential for spawning a new round of

---

[3]François Garrisson, *Essai sur les commissions d'application de l'édit de Nantes* (Montpellier: Déhan, 1950), 50-55.

[4]André Bossuat, "Le rétablissement de la paix sociale sous le règne de Charles VII," *Le Moyen Age* 60 (1954): 137-62.

fighting. Few doubted the gravity of the affair for, after all, religious riots and massacres had been the scourge of the preceding forty years. Finally, a number of persons whose actions would normally have been considered criminal claimed benefit of the various royal amnesties. The essential thrust of the argument was that their deeds were legitimate acts of war and ought to be forgiven in return for obedience to the crown.

The ecclesiastical issues were probably the most intractable. Indeed, their solution would take the next three-quarters of a century, in the end coming less from the decisions of the courts than the royal pronouncements which gradually proscribed Protestantism in France. Still, the chamber did face immediate petition by the Catholic hierarchy and, for the moment, needed to find some middle ground between the competing faiths. Jean de Fossé, bishop of Castres, provides a particularly zealous example of the reassertion of episcopal authority. He seized the occasion of the installation of the court at Castres in April 1595 to visit his episcopal seat for the first time and to re-introduce Catholic clergy and services. The Catholic judges firmly maintained their right to assist at mass and the bishop took full advantage of the opportunity. Returning cathedral canons soon argued that the chapel assigned for regular worship was too small and insufficiently furnished. And the Catholic magistrates, while sometimes miffed by de Fossé's strident nature, were generally sympathetic to pleas for a larger church with a proper cross and adequate candelabra, chalices, and basins. For his part, the bishop ended a twenty-two-year hiatus when in 1596 he reinstated, with the approval of the *chambre de l'Edit*, the traditional public procession on the feast of Corpus Christi. Though the ceremony involved but a handful of persons and was conducted entirely outside the town walls, all shops were obliged to close for the occasion and the municipal consuls took special security precautions. Bishop de Fossé also set about the recovery of ecclesiastical property and, more particularly, episcopal revenues. He filed suit in the chamber for the restitution of certain benefices attached to his diocese and joined the canons of the cathedral chapter in demanding the return of a house and cellar (*maison et tinal*) which had fallen into the possession of a Protestant merchant. In similar fashion, members of various monastic foundations such as the Franciscans and Trinitarians returned to Castres and began rebuilding their war-ravaged monasteries as well as regaining legal control of disputed lands and the incomes attached to them.[5]

---

[5]Archives départementales de la Haute-Garonne (hereafter ADHG), B 173, fo. 306; B 174, fo. 110; Chambre de l'Edit, civil, 7 (15 et 26 juin 1595), 9 (10 juillet 1598), 13 (4 janvier et 2 mars 1600), 14 (13 septembre 1600). Archives départementales, Tarn, G 264, fo. 116. Bibliothèque Nationale, Collection Dupuy, 63, fo. 94-94v. Jean Faurin, *Journal de Faurin sur les guerres de Castres*, ed. Charles Pradel (Marseilles: Lafitte, 1981; reprint of Montpellier, 1878), 217, 223-24, and 233-35. Jacques Gaches, *Mémoires sur les guerres de religion à Castres et dans le Languedoc (1555-1610)*, ed. Charles Pradel (Geneva: Slatkine, 1970; reprint of Paris, 1879-94), 452 and 462.

The persistence of the litigants in these property disputes suggests economic necessity as well as ideological or religious motivation—a point amply illustrated by an incident involving several mills in the region around Mauvesin. The case also makes plain the difficulties which the chamber faced in sorting out such matters. The Dominicans of Mauvesin claimed that the mills, two situated in or adjacent to the town and two others slightly to the east along the Gimone river, had belonged to the monastic house since the fourteenth century. They passed into possession of Denis Mauléon, seigneur of Savaillan, in the course of the Huguenot assumption of power at Mauvesin. The King of Navarre, who as vicomte of Fezensaguet had feudal rights over the mills, invested Mauléon with the property. During one of the respites from the fighting in the late 1570s, the Dominicans sought restoration of their convent at Mauvesin and reintegration of the lost mills. The *chambre mi-partie*, then sitting at Lisle in its earliest session, heard the arguments in late October 1579 and decided in favor of the monks. Yet the resumption of fighting shortly thereafter made enforcement of the judgment difficult. Twenty years later, Jacques de Mauléon who had succeeded his father as seigneur of Savaillan continued the family's legal battle with the Dominicans. The dispute went first to a subalternate judge at Gimont and when he reaffirmed the ruling of 1579, Mauléon appealed to the *chambre de l'Edit*. The appeal fared no better and the Dominicans retained possession.[6] The rule of law as interpreted by a bipartisan magistracy prevailed. Neither party contested the decision as inequitable or prejudicial on the basis of religion; nor did anyone feel the need to resort to armed force.

A somewhat more urgent challenge for the chamber's judges was the necessity for prompt resolution of the seemingly endless string of factional squabbles which were the aftershocks of nearly a half century of war. Most incidents were minor, resulting from petty frictions. Yet the magistrates acted quickly, especially if the dispute pitted Catholic against Protestant. They dispatched two judges to calm tempers at Lautrec when in December 1596 a group opposed to the municipal consuls forcibly wrested control of the town gates. The chamber pointedly warned the citizens of Mende against aiding the Sieur de Montmorency-Fosseuse, governor of Gévaudan, who refused to demobilize his troops or raze the town's citadel in compliance with royal orders; and, as we shall see, it punished several persons who failed to take heed. The court issued a warrant for the apprehension of three men from the village of Le Faget who took up arms and organized illicit assemblies in "contravention of the edicts of pacification." Although the trio had long since fled, it charged them with *lese majesty* and confiscated their property. In a case with

<hr/>

[6]ADHG, Chambre de l'Edit, audience, 1 (22 octobre 1579); civil, 11 (28 mai 1599), 12 (11 septembre 1599).

distinct confessional tones, the Huguenot habitants of Béziers asked the chamber that they might be permitted to assemble for worship in the adjacent suburbs or nearby hamlet of Boujan. As it stood, they had to travel some four leagues (about twenty kilometers) to Florensac for services. The court assured the petitioners that they enjoyed full benefit of the pacification edicts, but declined to intervene in this instance, suggesting instead that they seek remedy from the king. Perhaps the judges were wary of altering a situation which, though inconvenient, appeared to keep frictions at a minimum. Equally likely, the magistrates were divided among themselves and, in a circuitous fashion, followed the normal practice of referring such cases to the crown. A more frequent source of sectarian irritation was burial practice and the use of cemeteries. The family of a Catholic woman from Castres protested when, upon her death, she was buried in Protestant ground according to the Reformed ceremony. The *chambre de l'Edit* ordered her disinterment for Catholic reburial and enjoined the municipal officers of Castres henceforth to inform the appropriate curé or vicar upon the death of a Catholic. In another instance, the Huguenot minority at the Catholic village of Saint-Pargoire enlisted the chamber's aid in forcing the consuls to purchase land for a Protestant cemetery and, in the meanwhile, to allow Protestant burial in the communal graveyard.[7]

Criminal defendants claiming benefit of the general amnesties contained in the many edicts issued throughout the religious wars represent a final major difficulty in the pacification process for the magistrates of the *chambre mi-partie*. The cases involved grave offenses—murder, arson, theft, assault, as well as other ill-defined "acts of hostility"—and came to the chamber on appeal from subordinate jurisdictions, typically courts of the various seneschals. The critical issue was pardon for acts of war and the necessity therefore of distinguishing such deeds from normal criminal offenses.

The judges of the bipartisan tribunal which sat at Lisle in 1579-80 heard at least ten defendants request dismissal of charges in accordance with the peace negotiated at Nérac in February 1579. Guillaume Leclerc, accused of having burned a house and two barns near Cahors, countered with a claim of immunity because, he argued, the action had occurred in the course of waging war. When the Seneschal of Armagnac condemned Jean de Bimont, seigneur of Tournecoupe, for unlawful "force" and "violence" against the person and property of the Countesse of Montret, the case went to the *chambre de l'Edit* where Bimont too invoked the edict's amnesty clause. A corporal found it more difficult to convince the court that the rape of two women and repeated armed attack of a minor judicial official were anything other than criminal.

[7]Ibid., Chambre de l'Edit, civil, 6 (2) (19 décembre 1596), 7 (6 avril 1596), 8 (22 mars, 13 mai et 15 octobre 1597), 11 (15 avril 1599), 14 (2 décembre 1600). Dom Claude de Vic and Dom J. Vaissète, *Histoire générale de Languedoc*, 16 vols., ed. A. Molinier (Toulouse: Privat, 1872-1904), 11: 870-74.

The magistrates refused to hear the appeal of another soldier who had stolen a horse from a carter. They returned his case to the Seneschal of Quercy for trial. A half dozen men imprisoned at Mirabel, a village near Montauban, requested discharge from accusations of murder, battery, and theft. Again, they asked the charges be dropped under the terms embodied in the articles of the Conference of Nérac.[8]

Although the basic question raised by these cases—exoneration for what would otherwise be a crime—continued to plague the chamber for the next two decades, the magistrates appear to have become progressively more willing to grant the practice as well as the principle of amnesty. They declared that Anthoine Aude, appealing a decision of the Seneschal of Quercy in 1585, enjoyed benefit of the edicts of pacification and, accordingly, released him from further prosecution. Pierre Hebrart and Pierre Jaquin, condemned by the Seneschal of Carcassonne for the theft of cattle "during the troubles," successfully pressed a similar argument before the chamber's judges at Castres in 1595. Pierre Mas, a merchant from Serignan near Béziers, obtained discharge despite his murder of Louis Galles. Quashing a lower court ruling, the chamber granted a cobbler of the Rodez region benefit of amnesty. Jean de Morerio petitioned in 1597 for dismissal of his condemnation by the presidial court of Toulouse for a murder which he had committed nearly a decade earlier. After two years of trial maneuvering, complicated by an additional accusation of embezzlement, the court discontinued process and released de Morerio. It exonerated Jean de Bouffard, sieur de Lagrange, for his seizure of the chateau of Puechassault, virtually ignoring the furious protests of the chateau's owner. The magistrates of the chamber readily accepted the royal *lettres d'abolition* presented by Marc-Antoine d'Avessens, seigneur of Saint-Rome, in remitting punishment for unspecified "acts of hostility" committed in July 1598.[9]

Pleas for amnesty in other causes were less successful. A merchant from Chirac, high in and among the Protestant strongholds of the Cévennes mountains, failed to win dismissal of criminal charges stemming from his participation in the Sieur de Montmorency-Fosseuse's defiant refusal to surrender the garrison at Mende in 1597. The chamber denied his request for release and returned him to the Seneschal of Nîmes-Beaucaire for continuance of trial. The court was almost as severe with the consuls and syndic of Mende who had served during the disturbance of 1597. In spite of their petition for amnesty

[8]ADHG, Chambre de l'Edit, audience, 1 (7 et 13 août, 29 octobre, 5 novembre, 3, 10 et 17 décembre 1579). *Edits des guerres de religion*, ed. A. Stegmann (Paris: Vrin, 1979), 158-70.

[9]ADHG, Chambre de l'Edit, civil, 5 (8 mars 1585), 6 (12 décembre 1595), 11 (27 avril 1599); criminel, 1 (4 janvier, 20 février, 4 et 15 mars, 10 avril, 13, 14 et 31 mai,10 et 24 septembre, 22 octobre, 31 octobre, 4 décembre 1597), 2 (11 février, 14 et 17 avril, 17 juillet, 4 août, 4 septembre 1598), 3 (23 et 26 février, 12 mai 1599).

under the terms of the edict of Nantes, the chamber refused to absolve them of all responsibility in the deaths of two prominent inhabitants. It voided the murder charges, but levied heavy fines payable to the victims' heirs.[10]

What can be said of the notion of bipartisanism and its application to the judicial system of early modern Languedoc? The general principle was certainly double-edged. While bipartisanism at first offered the Protestants greater security, it held little promise as the foundation for a lasting settlement. Its employ invariably meant concessions by the Huguenot minority. Acceptance of the Politique plan for mixed courts, as a part of the union struck in the mid-1570s, entailed abandonment of the original demand for separate Protestant tribunals. The bipartisan commissions set up after 1598 for the enforcement of the edict of Nantes had a dual assignment: legalization of Protestant worship and, more ominously, re-establishment of Catholicism. In the next century, the crown invoked the instrument of bipartisanism to restrict further the Huguenot position. At Castres, for example, membership in the town's governing consulate and on the faculty of the municipal college became *mi-partie* through a succession of royal proclamations in the early 1630s.[11] Both institutions would be exclusively Catholic within two generations.

Bipartisan justice was, on the other hand, a beneficial mechanism in the recognizably modern problem of conflict resolution and restoration of internal peace for a state divided by civil war and religious strife. The mixed court proved valuable in solving certain immediate and specific issues: the slow yet orderly restoration of economic assets to the Catholic Church, conservation of a fragile religious and political equilibrium amid the lingering confessional frictions, and the careful scrutiny of those cases where defendants claimed royal amnesty. Protestant and Catholic magistrates, though hardly amicable, did recognize mutual advantage in advancing the peace process and thus cooperated for the reduction of religious tensions and implementation of the delicate structure of coexistence.

[10]Ibid., Chambre de l'Edit, criminel, 2 (5 juin, 14, 21 et 23 juillet, 18 août, 9 novembre, 2 décembre 1598), 3 (5 et 18 mars 1599), 5 (7 février 1600).

[11]Camille Rabaud, *Histoire du Protestantisme dans l'Albigeois et le Lauragais*, 2 vols. (Paris: Sandoz et Fischbacher, 1873-98), 1: 143-44 and 275-76.

Melanchthon on Resisting the Emperor:
The *Von der Notwehr Unterricht* of 1547

Luther D. Peterson
State University of New York at Oswego

The "Magdeburg *Confession*" of 1550 brought together about a quarter-century of Lutheran thinking on the question of political resistance–whether superiors may be actively opposed, and if so under what circumstances and by whom. Probably the most important vernacular book to precede that treatise was *Instruction Concerning Self-Defense* (*Von der Notwehr Unterricht*), published in 1547 in the midst of the Schmalkaldic War. Though it appeared under the name of Justus Menius, it was essentially the work of Philipp Melanchthon. It is a book that has been little-studied. This article shows that Melanchthon indeed found justifiable reasons for resistance by lower magistrates and subjects–the latter less clearly so than the former. He proclaimed a right of self-defense and the duty of protection of others, which he found valid at all times. If a superior can be judged a tyrant, these grounds justify a resistance movement and an attempt at his removal. Melanchthon used private law for this, and structured his argument according to the Lutheran idea of orders of creation.

FROM HIS EARLIEST PUBLICATIONS, PROFESSOR ROBERT M. KINGDON has drawn the attention of Reformation scholars to the problem of political resistance: whether a right or perhaps even an obligation exists to resist political authority, and, if so, by whom may this be done and under what circumstances.* In examining the sources of Huguenot resistance theory, Kingdon demonstrated that Theodore Beza had espoused resistance in the early 1550s, much earlier than had been previously thought, and that he was deeply influenced in this by the German Lutherans, particularly by the bold *Confession, Instruction and Admonition of the Pastors and Preachers of the Christian Church at Magdeburg* of 1550.[1]

*The research for this article was funded by a *Vollstipendium* of the Herzog August Bibliothek, Wolfenbüttel, B.R.D., and a Grant-in-aid of the SUNY Research Foundation. The author wishes to thank both institutions for their generous support.

[1]See "The First Expression of Theodore Beza's Political Ideas," *ARG* 46 (1955): 88–100, and "Les idées politiques de Beza d'après son traitté de l'authorité du magistrat en la punition des hérétiques," *BHR* 22 (1960), 566–69. The *Confession* appeared in German and Latin: *Bekentnis Vnterricht vnd Vermanung / der Pfarrhern vnd Prediger / der Christlichen Kirchen zu Magdeburgk; CONFESSIO ET APOLOGIA PASTOrum & reliquorum ministrorum Ecclesiae Magdeburgensis.* Both eds.: Magdeburg: Michel Lotther, 1550. Nine pastors signed it; its principal author was Nicolaus Gallus.

133

The Magdeburg *Confession* was indeed an influential tract in its day and has rightfully received a good deal of scholarly attention in our century.[2] It appeared at a time when Magdeburg, still defiant of the emperor and Catholicism after the Protestant defeat in the Schmalkaldic War, faced an imperial army led by elector Moritz of Albertine Saxony. Not widely recognized, however, is the fact that the *Confession* brought to a climax more than a quarter century of Lutheran thought on political resistance. As its authors stated, it did not attempt to repeat all previous arguments in favor of resistance, but rather intended to present additional ones.[3] In the process they found occasion to deride those current enemies whom they labeled the "Adiaphorists"—Philipp Melanchthon and the other theologians of Wittenberg and Leipzig, who they believed were betraying the Evangelical faith by cooperating with Moritz's religious policy. In contrast to their present lack of courage, these were the very ones who during the war had publicly justified resistance: at that time these "proved such self-defense (*notwehr*) sufficiently, both from God's Word and natural recognition, which God has planted in the human heart."[4] The *Confession* spoke correctly here, for during the Schmalkaldic War (1546-47) Melanchthon and his colleague Johannes Bugenhagen printed tracts, disputations, and letters of Luther justifying resistance, with introductions to tie the Reformer's ideas to the present moment, and fellow theologian Georg Major and jurist Basilius Monner authored respectively a parody of the emperor's declaration of war and a study of the constitutional grounds for revolt.[5] Printed in the vernacular, they were intended to be read by a wide audience and to shore up Protestant resolve. Given the probable consequences of defeat, a modern scholar has labeled their efforts a case of "Evangelical courage."[6] Except for Monner's book, the arguments of these tracts were mainly from Scripture and natural law and supported a right and duty of defense, as the

[2] For contemporary influence see Kingdon, "First Expression," 93-96 and n 20; idem, "The Political Resistance of the Calvinists in France and the Low Countries," *Church History* 27 (1958): 227-28; Quentin Skinner, *The Foundations of Modern Political Thought* (Cambridge: Cambridge University Press, 1978), 2: 209-10; Esther Hildebrandt, "The Magdeburg *Bekenntnis* as a Possible Link between German and English Resistance Theories in the Sixteenth Century," *Archiv für Reformationsgeschichte* 71 (1980): 240-52. Notable recent studies are Skinner, 207-10, 217-19; Cynthia G. Shoenberger, "The Confession of Magdeburg and the Lutheran Doctrine of Resistance," (Ph.D. diss., Columbia University, 1972); Oliver K. Olson, "Theology of Revolution: Magdeburg, 1550-1551," *Sixteenth Century Journal* 3 (1972): 56-79.

[3] Three additional arguments, to be precise; see *Bekenntnis* K1b; *CONFESSIO*, F3a.

[4] *Bekenntnis*, H3b; *CONFESSIO*, E4a. The "Adiaphorists" are labeled "enemies" on H2a (*Bekenntnis*) and E2b (*CONFESSIO*).

[5] See Oskar Waldeck, "Die Publizistik des Schmalkaldischen Krieges," *ARG* 7 (1909/10), 37-49, and my "The Philippist Theologians and the Interims of 1548: Soteriological, Ecclesiastical, and Liturgical Compromises and Controversies within German Lutheranism" (Ph.D. Diss., The Univeristy of Wisconsin, 1974), 452-63.

[6] Curt Christmann, *Melanchthons Haltung im schmalkaldischen Kriege*, Historische Studien, no. 31 (Berlin, 1902), 54.

Confession stated. These arguments received their longest and most thorough expression in still another German tract from the Wittenberg presses, *Von der Notwehr Unterricht, Nützlich zu Lesen* (*Instruction Concerning Self-Defense, Necessary to Read*), printed in 1547 under the name of Justus Menius.[7] I suspect that more copies of this were printed than any other book on resistance prior to the *Confession*, and since it nevertheless has been little studied,[8] I wish to examine it in the following as a contribution to the theme for which we are so indebted to the work of Professor Kingdon.

*   *   *

Von der Notwehr exists in two quite different versions, the first based on Menius's manuscript with revisions by Melanchthon, particularly in the second half, and the second for which Melanchthon in correspondence took full credit. The second version was best known at the time, reprinted more than once, and translated into Latin,[9] and therefore is the text under examination here. Melanchthon's version at seventy-eight pages was four pages shorter than the first, but still is long, rambling, and repetitious. It retains the divisions of the first, with a preface followed by a part he entitled, "Instruction Concerning Self-Defense, by Justus Menius," and then sections labeled "First Part," "Second Part," a brief "How Self-Defense is a God-Pleasing Work," and "Third Part." Some of the book will interest us little. The last part is a statement of Lutheran religious teachings, set out here so that "the God-fearing soldier may know that he fights or suffers for the sake of true, necessary things," with the result that he should be ready to risk his life for this doctrine according to his calling (*Beruff*).[10] An otherwise unremarkable preface rejoindered the right of self-defense to the "many disagreeable people" who told the Evangelicals that their princes could not resist the emperor: would

[7]See n10 below. Menius was a student of both Luther and Melanchthon who, spending most of his career in Eisenach and Gotha, is sometimes called "the Reformer of Thüringia"; for him see Gustav L. Schmidt, *Justus Menius: der Reformator Thüringens*, 2 vols. (Gotha: Perthes, 1867).

[8]The treatise is briefly discussed in the following: Schmidt, *Justus Menius* II: 20–26; Christmann, "Melanchthons Haltung," 5, 52–53, 156–57, as well as references to Melanchthon's revisions in chap. 3; Waldeck, "Publlizistik," 44–47; Schoenberger, "Confession," 52–55; and my "Philippist Theologians," 455–56.

[9]*Von der Notwehr vnterricht: Nützlich zu lesen. Durch Justum Menium. Witteberg. M.D.XLVII.* Colophon: *Gedruckt zu Witteberg / bey Veit Creutzer. M.D.XLVII.* Signatures A(1a–4b)–D, a–f. Signature references in the text of this article are to this edition, which is a second, slightly revised printing of the second version. This was reprinted again in 1549 (n.p., n.pub.) and in both eds. of Friedrich Hortleder, *Keyser vnd Königlichen Maiestete / Auch dess heiligen Rö. Reichs / geistlicher vnd weltlicher Stände.* . . . vol. II: *Handlungen vnd Ausschreiben . . . Von Rechtmässigkeit / Anfang / For- vnd endlichen Außgang deß Teutschen Kriegs / Keyser Carls deß Fünfften / wider die Schmalkaldische Bundsoberste.* . . . (1st ed., Frankfurt/M., 1618, 2d ed., Gotha, 1645), Book 2, no. 29. Latin ed.: *DE DEFENSIONE CONCESSA HVMANO GENERI IVRE naturae, Scriptum Justi Menij, Ex Germanica lingua in Latinum conuersum. VITEBERGAE ANNO M.D.XLVII.* A distinguishing mark of the first German edition is its signatures: A(1a–4b)–L. I am preparing a brief article explicating the differences in the two versions and Melanchthon's reasons for extensively editing Menius's manuscript.   [10]B3b; the "Third Part" is pp. c2b–f3b.

these not protect their wives, daughters, and youth against the "unjust atroci-ties" of Italians, Spaniards, and Hussars? (A4a). This argument reappears (b4a), as do others sounded in the second chapter ("Instruction . . . "): that the pope caused the Schmalkaldic War to destroy the Evangelical church, and that the Protestant cities, princes, and electors had been obedient to the emperor in all temporal matters (B2a-b). Furthermore, the religious issues which the emperor and pope intended to resolve by the force of arms should be settled in a free general council (B2b), the convening of which contemporary readers would have known Martin Luther to have repeatedly demanded. The second chapter ends by announcing that the treatise will show how far one is obliged to obey superiors and that self-defense and protection are proper against unjust power (B3b).

Already one may observe hints of two different theoretical bases for diso-bedience and resistance. This first of these is suggested by the *Self-Defense* in the title. Here one need not take God and God's will into account, but rather self-preservation and protection are deemed simply rights of nature. Quentin Skinner has focused attention on a private-law theory of resistance espoused by some medieval jurists and theologians on the basis of Roman and canon law. The Roman Digest, they observed, justified the violent action of self-defense, which it considered a basic law of nature, in the case of adultery or in repelling unjust force. Canon law dealt with the case of an "unjust" judge: one who proceeded when the case in question was under appeal, who acted outside his lawful jurisdiction and the result was "notorious injury" (*atrox injuria*), or who within his jurisdiction acted unjustly and caused irreparable harm. In all these circumstances the judge lost his authority and could be resisted as a private person. In the fourteenth century William of Ockham and Jean Gerson appealed to these natural rights to assert that subjects could depose their rulers. In late 1530 the private-law arguments were taken up by the Lutheran theolo-gians to justify the opposition of the Protestant princes and cities to the emperor. Early in the following year they appeared in Luther's somewhat evasive *Warning to his Dear German People* and over the next decade in a few of Melanchthon's Latin writings. But prior to the Schmalkaldic War these argu-ments appeared mainly in private opinions (*Gutachten*) which the theologians addressed to the Saxon court.[11]

The second basis, that soldiers had callings that involved defending their faith, unsurprisingly suggests that the Lutherans conceived of resistance within the religious context. To be sure, Luther and Melanchthon from their

[11]Skinner, *Foundations*, 124–26, 197–204. For the *Gutachten*, see Heinz Scheible, ed., *Das Widerstandsrecht als Problem der Deutchen Protestanten, 1523–1546*, Texte zur Kirchen- und Theologiegeschichte, no. 10 (Gütersloh: Mohn, 1969), 89–94; see also Hans Lüthje, "Melanchthons Anschauung über das Recht des Widerstands gegen die Staatsgewalt," *ZKG* 47, n.s. 10 (1928): 525–35.

earliest reflections upon society stressed obedience to higher authority as a religious duty. Luther's conception of this world rested on an Augustinian idea of two kingdoms, with two regiments to effect God's purposes within the worldly kingdom: a church to gather and nurture God's own, and temporal government to maintain order and protect God's own. The fourth commandment's injunction to honor parents was for Luther the model for authority and obedience. He regarded this commandment as the link between the two tables of the Law, and thus a witness to God's will for society.[12] Hence his conviction that whereas equality existed in the spiritual kingdom, here inequality and hierarchy governed, with obedience demanded of child to parent and subject to ruler. He continually appealed to Romans 13:1-7 in support not only of the proper behavior of subjects, but also of the divine origins of the hierarchies: "Let every person be subject to the governing authorities" because they have been instituted by God (v. 1). By the late 1520s Luther had fused these images into the idea of the orders of creation. God had established in the beginning three hierarchies or orders—the family, the state, and the church—by which to structure society and further his purposes within the world. All people were set within the household order as parents or children or servants and the state as ruler or soldiers or officials or subjects, and Christians were also in the church as ministers or members of the congregation. "Orders" (*Ordnungen*), "hierarchies" (*Hierarchien*), "offices" (*Ämter*), "estates" (*Standen*), and "regiments" (*Regimenten*) testified to the static nature of the conception, and "calling" (*Beruf*) to the sense of duty to God with which one acted within these orders.[13] This conception of society placed the Lutherans among those whom Thomas Brady has recently labelled the "Augustinian rear-guard fighters" of history, still asserting a religious function to the state. These opposed an idea which would soon dominate: the state as "an omnipotent yet impersonal power," and as "a form of public power separate from both the ruler and the ruled, and constituting the supreme political authority within a certain defined territory."[14]

Although the conception was fundamentally conservative, placing each order's activity within divine purpose, it also had a radical corollary—each order also had limits beyond which it could not legitimately act. Also, it recognized in addition to clergy and magistrates another office involving authority

[12]Ernst Kinder,"Luthers Ableitung der geistlichen und weltliche 'Oberkeit' aus dem 4. Gebot," in *Für Kirche und Recht: Festschrift für Johannes Heckel z. 70. Geburtstag*, ed. Siegfried Grundmann (Cologne & Graz: Böhlau, 1959), 272, 275-77.

[13]The best discussion of orders of creation is Wilhelm Maurer, *Luthers Lehre von den drei Hierarchien und ihr mittelalterlicher Hintergrund*, Bayerische Akademie der Wissenschaften, Philosophisch-Historische Klasse, Sitzungsberichte, 1970, no. 4 (Munich, 1970); see also Thomas Brady, "Luther and the State: the Reformer's Teaching in Its Social Setting," in *Luther and the Modern State in Germany*, ed. James D. Tracy, Sixteenth Century Essays & Studies, no. 7 (Kirksville, Mo.: Sixteenth Century Journal Publ., 1986), 33-36.

[14]Brady, "Luther," 31-32; the quotes are from Skinner, *Foundations*, 352, 358.

within society, that of housefather or more generally parents. Luther discussed resistance in the context of the orders in a disputation of 1539,[15] but the argument first appeared on the popular scene in the wartime tracts of the Wittenbergers. The burden of *Von der Notwehr* was to justify resistance to higher political authority without authorizing uncontrolled rebellion, and the orders of creation proved useful for the purpose. One does not find here a detailed theoretical discussion of the orders, but rather throughout the concept was presupposed, as such terms as order or ordinance, office, and calling indicates, and it formed the basis of the book's argument for defense and protection in the "Second Part." One final note: with its focus on the temporal order, the book gave rather little attention to the household order, nor very much to the church order.

Turning then to the two substantial chapters, the "First Part" on disobedience and the "Second Part" on resistance, the reader is confronted immediately with a typical Lutheran image of society and with a special pleading of innocence. God gave humankind the spiritual and temporal regiments. The office of preaching was the keystone to the spiritual, and the rest had to obey it (B4b–C1b). The temporal regiment, founded on law, existed to maintain discipline and peace (C2a) and to protect and sustain the church (a3a). It placed the ten commandments and other divine law before the people, and needed to make more specific laws for specific circumstances. Those regents who did this were to use sound reason, and the results had to concur with divine and natural law. The temporal regiment must then enforce external compliance to these laws (C2b–3a). Melanchthon next produced Romans 13 and insisted obedience here ought to stem not from mere fear of punishment, but rather from the dictates of conscience. Nobody in a thousand years stated this demand for obedience as clearly and forthrightly as we Lutherans, Melanchthon claimed,[16] and therefore he rejected the accusation (presumably from Catholic opponents) that the Evangelicals were rioters or taught revolution.

Melanchthon's temporal regiment was conceived in accordance with the Lutheran image of a divinely-ordered society, and was therefore expressed in the language of orders of creation. He then held the ideal up to the light of experience, finding that few rulers used their offices as they were ordained, but rather to further idolatry and engage in murder (C2a, 4a, a3b). Many, that is to say, contravened their obligations to one or both tables of the Law, and if their failures were thus seen in religious terms, then understandably the Bible would be Melanchthon's recourse in cases where they had ordered their subjects to follow them. When a ruler ordered one to do something forbidden

---

[15]This was the "*Zirkulardisputation*," in Scheible, *Widerstandsrecht*, 94–98, and *WA* 39/II:39–51. See Rudolf Hermann, "Luthers Zirkulardisputation über Matth. 19:21," *Lutherjahrbuch* 23 (1941): 35–93.

[16]Luther had written the same, dating it from the apostolic age; Brady, "Luther," 32, n 4.

in God's law, the latter for the sake of his soul could not obey, and *Von der Notwehr* here employed a by-now standard Lutheran text for justifying disobedience, "We must obey God rather than men" (Acts 5:29).[17] Should opponents maintain that there could not be limits to one's obedience to the ruler, or if a guideline was needed to ascertain that limit, Melanchthon was ready with another passage, the familiar "Give to Caesar the things that are Caesar's and to God the things that are God's" (Matt. 22:21)—Caesar was due *only* that which belonged rightly to his office.[18]

The arguments for disobedience in *Von der Notwehr* followed those Luther had used as early as his *Of Temporal Authority: to What Extent it Should be Obeyed* of 1523, and therefore were unexceptional. However, since the Reformers regarded interference by governments in the religious sphere as particularly serious, they often gave the impression that only in such cases was disobedience acceptable. Melanchthon's mention of murder reminds us that enforcing Mosaic law encompassed also what we think of as "purely" temporal, and thus that these religious grounds for disobedience were indeed broad. Also, he felt it necessary to oppose advice he attributed to "popes and Turks" that for the sake of peace and unity counseled toleration of the errors of parents and governments. Peace and unity were admirable ideals, and also God-given objectives of temporal authority, but could not be acceptable at the price of destruction of God's law and endangerment of the individual's soul (D1b). Simply put, where a superior in any order commanded something that contravened God's law or will, the inferior could not obey. Melanchthon's argument here, as was true of Luther in his early arguments for disobedience, remained solely within the religious framework of the orders of creation.

In the "Second Part" Melanchthon proposed to demonstrate that active defense, and not only disobedience, was proper under certain circumstances. But since active resistance so clearly contradicted Romans 13 in spirit as well as word, Melanchthon utilized both orders of creation and the private law argument to argue that one might oppose the emperor. More accurately, he employed private law arguments to bolster an argument based upon the concept of orders of creation. Then he added a brief nod to feudal law, and finally refuted four arguments of his opponents. In an unsystematic way he showed when a government or magistrate was no longer to be tolerated, and explained what acts were then permissible or in fact demanded. He did not address directly a third question, who may carry out this resistance, but his argument suggested answers to this as well.

---

[17]Luther used this text as early as *Of Temporal Authority* of 1523. See Skinner, *Foundations* 17, and Gunnar Hillerdal, "Der Mensch unter Gottes Regiment: der Unterthan und das Recht," in Günther Vogt, ed., *Luther und die Obrigkeit* (Darmstadt: Wissenschaftliche Buchgesellschaft, 1972), 36.

[18]D2a; this text also appears in *Of Temporal Authority*.

"He who resists the authorities resists what God has appointed" (Rom. 13:2a, RSV). Luther gave expression to the orders of creation in translating this. He rendered the last words as *Gottes ordnung*, thus "resists God's order (or ordinance)," highlighting God's purpose in establishing government instead of those people in the governmental offices. Melanchthon pointed to Luther's translation to claim that only when the authorities ruled in accordance with godly order were they to be obeyed: "Therefore this statement [i.e., Rom. 13] should not be extended beyond the office (*Ampt*) which is God's ordinance (*ordnung*) to the confirmation of all tyranny and evil." Private law concurred that obedience was proper only *in casu iustae iurisdictionis* (b1a). But Melanchthon's goal here was resistance, not merely disobedience. He found that the papacy had no legitimate jurisdiction in the temporal order, so that in claiming authority over king and princes the pope was openly against God's order and was a thief and tyrant. Therefore the Schmalkaldic League was correct in protecting itself (a4a). As if to reply to the obvious objection that the enemy, ostensibly at least, was the emperor, not the pope, Melanchthon next produced two examples of just resistance within the temporal realm. Trebonius stabbed his superior (Julius Caesar, as readers would have known), and in this was not opposing God's ordinance but rather atrocious evil and the devil's will.[19] Second, the wife of a ruler of Thessalonia who killed him because of his cruel torture of martyrs was also not resisting God's ordinance (a4b).

For Evangelicals the pope's political activities perverted and threatened destruction of the temporal order, and therefore demanded resistance. Temporal tyranny, as in the case of Caesar or the Thessalonian, could result in the same, and Melanchthon appealed to natural law, "a light planted in human reason," to justify active resistance. Reason enabled men to recognize when rulers inflicted atrocious injury (*atrox iniuria*) on their subjects. In such a circumstance, and if no magistrate should step in with help, natural law permitted (*erleubet*) one to defend himself and "there are many cases" where this commanded (*geboten*) husbands to protect wives, fathers their children, and magistrates their subjects.[20] Did the Gospel that told Christians to turn the other cheek contradict this natural right? No, Melanchthon claimed, the Gospel rather confirmed natural law, and also permitted to Christians those positive laws of a state which agreed with reason (b1a-b). Were the Gospel to tell Christians to suffer and not defend themselves, it would be a "political document" and further oppression and slavery (d1b). To be sure, to assert a *right* of self-defense Melanchthon would have had to call upon a natural right

[19]Melanchthon here agreed with the republican interpretation of Caesar's death argued by the Florentine civic humanists ca. 1400; see Hans Baron, *The Crisis of the Early Italian Renaissance*, 2d ed. (Princeton: Princeton University Press, 1966), esp. chaps. 3, 5.

[20]b1a; see also c1a, d3a. The condition that left first redress to a magistrate was repeated on p. b3b.

and to have insisted upon its independent jurisdiction, since Lutherans had generally counseled Christians to suffer. A *duty* of protection, however, stemmed more directly from Luther's conception of the redeemed Christian who made himself a servant of the needs of fellow humans (the ethic of "Christian love"). Here the religious idea of office—whether in the house or temporal order—involved its holder in obligations towards those in his or her charge, and among these was that of protection. In fact Melanchthon often referred to both a right of self-defense and a duty of protection, and in the other instances duty was a consequence of one's Christian obligations to fellow humans. Turning to the present situation, Melanchthon judged that the emperor had attacked the Schmalkaldic League with foreign troops and deceit with the intent of overcoming the Evangelicals, and that the elector and princes were protecting wives, children, clergy, schools, and subjects. "Protection is an ordained work"; the defense raised by the Protestant leaders was therefore according to order.[21]

Melanchthon felt obligated to distinguish between justifiable defense on the one hand and riot and rebellion on the other. The decision here hinged on judgments both of the inferior's intent in opposing a superior and of the latter's overall performance of his office. Justifiable resistance against ordained authority must be for purposes of protection. Unjustified rebellion for him was violence carried out without a calling (*Beruff*) and intended to raise oneself up. Absalom's opposition to his father David, for example, was prompted by "unmeasureable arrogance" and ambition instead of either self-defense or protection of others (b2a, see 2 Sam. 15-18). Also, one must tolerate occasional lapses or failures of otherwise good regents. David, Jehoshaphat, Hezechiah, Cyrus, and Augustus, despite faults, desired the good and more often than not did rightly in their office. Violence perpetrated to remove these from office for such faults was rioting (b2a-b). On the other hand, "A tyrant is that sort of regent whose will is not good; who devotes himself to atrocities or evil," even when some act of his may be beneficial. Caligula, Nero, Diocletian, and the like were his examples, and he continued by praising the two men who led the revolts against the thirty tyrants of Athens and Spartan control of Thebes, two fathers (William Tell was one) who acted to protect their children, and Obediah's hiding of priests from the evil designs of Queen Jezebel. He asked whether housefathers of Rhodes would not have acted properly in removing a tyrant for violating the wives of some subjects (b3a-c1a). By justifying resistance in his present moment, he implied Charles V's place among a most unsavory crowd!

Interestingly, in the midst of this argument Melanchthon took up the case of Uriah, Bathsheba's husband. Though subjects should tolerate the failures of rulers like David, had Uriah the opportunity to protect his wife he would have

---

[21]b1a, *ordentlichen defension*; b2a, *"schutz oder defensio ein geordnet werck ist."*

been right in so acting: "the *casu defensionis* of the subject (*Unterthan*) remains" (b2b). This remarkable exception to the argument here was couched strictly in terms of a husband's duty of protection. He has then an office, one which moreover must be regarded as without equal in his order and which justifies his opposition if need be to the highest authority in another order.

Melanchthon also employed the feudal relationship of lord and vassal to argue the rights of inferiors. His example was Emperor Trajan, who while handing a sword to a new marshal supposedly said, "I give you this sword to protect the empire and my body, if I do rightly, and against me if I do wrongly" (c2b). Melanchthon was answering potential objections. Some might not accept the argument asserted in the orders of creation and private law, that the princes' authority was independent of the emperor, but rather insist that they must be considered his agents. Trajan's lesson was that still the princes must be ready to act independently, according to what they deemed best for the empire as a whole.[22]

Before ending the "Second Part," Melanchthon addressed three arguments for simple obedience drawn from Scriptures and one that called upon the example of Luther. While his answers repeated much already discussed, some of his comments are worth noting. The first was Jesus' words to Peter at Gethsemane, "All who take up the sword will perish by the sword" (Matt. 26:52b). This was God's judgment against murder, not defense, and one could judge the difference by determining intent and by considering office. One knew his own conscience, and though he could not read someone else's heart, he—and the courts—could judge that person's intent using reason. Also, those in the preaching office should not bear the sword. Thus Peter did wrongly in drawing the sword and the pope was wrong in raising up this war. On the other hand, God gave princes the sword of protection, so the Protestant leaders had not "taken" it up (c1b-3a). The second argument was 1 Peter 2:18: "Servants, be submissive to your masters with all respect, not only to the kind and gentle but to the overbearing." This gave occasion for Melanchthon to repeat the distinction between acts that were "notorious injury" and those whose burdens were not so great. The prime example of the former was a lord's violation of the wife or children of a servant (*Knecht*). This the servant should oppose "according to his calling and ability." Injury was quite literally a decisive criterion of what was not to be tolerated. A pious wife was to be patient with a rowdy husband, "but she is not obliged to be patient if his acts towards her are injurious, with hitting by which she would lose her health." The pattern of rights and duties was maintained. Whereas she had a right of

---

[22]c1a–b. Melanchthon apparently regarded this pre-feudal incident as an example of the feudal *diffidatio*. See also Richard Benert, "Lutheran Resistance Theory and the Imperial Constitution," *Il Pensiero Politico* 7 (1973): 28; Benert notes that Melanchthon used the example in the 1543 ed. of *Loci communes*, as did Luther and Monner also.

self-defense, Melanchthon said the servant would sin if he did not defend his family (c3b-4a). The third argument was the example of David not killing King Saul when he had the opportunity. As far as Melanchthon was concerned, David had indeed suffered *notoria iniuria* at Saul's hand, giving him the right of self-defense, but he did not want to give an example of regicide in this first instance of monarchy. More importantly, David at this time had no office, and protection of others was not involved. Hence his patience was a "special act" and "a voluntary indulgence" done for the sake of general peace (c4a-b).

Finally, recalling his well-known demand for obedience, some claimed the Schmalkaldic League's actions contradicted Luther. This Melanchthon dismissed without discussion: "In the *Warning* [*to his Dear German People*] and in other writings, Dr. Martin Luther declared that defense was just" (d1b). Those today who still write as if Luther taught obedience pure and simple, might take note of these words of his closest colleague.

* * *

Von der Notwehr is extraordinary in its support of resistance to civil superiors, and for that matter to household superiors also. Melanchthon here accepted a personal right of self-defense, which seems valid in all threatening circumstances, but over which *a la* David, one ought to exercise judgment. Furthermore, household or temporal office carries the duty of protecting those in its care. If the superior's acts are such that "tyranny" and "notorious injury" fit, he is to be opposed and removed from office, if possible. And those acts may be violations of either table of the Mosaic law, so it would not be correct to say that the Lutherans justified resistance solely for what we would label religious reasons. If the superior's acts are more generally good, the judgment about which Melanchthon trusts to the reason of the inferior officeholder, then apparently the inferior's opposition should be limited if possible to the bare act of protecting those oppressed, perhaps like Obediah. In Melanchthon's view, Pope Paul III and Emperor Charles V were both, if on varying grounds, guilty of tyranny and *atrox iniuria*, and all should join behind the Schmalkaldic League banner to oppose them. This was an incendiary tract befitting its wartime purposes.

Extraordinary also is the answer or answers readers were offered, had they asked the question "Who may lead resistance?" The book was addressed to the current conflict between an elector, princes, and cities against their superior. The primary and probably sole intended answer was that these inferior magistrates were justified in their actions, and the German people should lock arms behind them. Nevertheless, Melanchthon's examples praised even common subjects, men and women alike, who resisted authorities and in some instances had led movements of resistance. According to Quentin Skinner, Melanchthon "insist[s] that 'it is never permissible' for private individuals 'to engage in acts of sedition' on their own behalf against any legally constituted authority."[23] His evidence is a few Latin treatises written in the decade prior to the war. With respect to *Von der Notwehr*, his claim is not correct, for here there is no prohibition of violence on the part of subjects and plenty of examples to the contrary. The book thus appears seditious. But this is precisely where its orders of creation argument proves valuable, for according to that parents are not simply private individuals but, just as lower magistrates, are indeed legally constituted authorities. Thus although he offered no indication of office in the cases of the two opponents of tyranny in Athens and Thebes, usually Melanchthon did identify the household office of subjects whose resistance he supported. That is to say, William Tell, the wife of the Thessalonian tyrant, and the husbands of Rhodes are examples of just resistance because they held offices in the household order that obligated them to protecting others.

There was a dilemma posed by *Von der Notwehr*. The private law argument did in fact suggest that individual subjects may legally resist authority. Melanchthon did not back away from that consequence, hoping instead that the orders of creation would restrain its seditious thrust. But what if his readers did not take "office" and "order" and "calling" seriously? In the same moment Basilius Monner's book placed the constitutional argument, which specifically limited resistance to lower magistrates, into discussion.[24] The Magdeburg *Confession* three years later, while pointing in approval to the previous discussion and also utilizing private law theory, emphasized the constitutional duties of lower magistrates, and this was what the Calvinists took away from the Lutheran experience of resistance. So *Von der Notwehr* deserves our attention not merely because of its length and thoroughness, but also because it turned out to be the high water mark for an argument that perhaps was "too hot to handle."

ABBREVIATIONS

ARG	*Archiv für Reformationsgeschichte*
BHR	*Bibliothèque d'Humanisme et Renaissance*
SCJ	*Sixteenth Century Journal*
WA	*D. Martin Luthers Werke: Kritische Gesamtausgabe.* Weimar: Böhlau, 1883–.
ZKG	*Zeitschrift für Kirchengeschichte*

[23]*Foundations*, 203.

[24]For a discussion of the constitutional argument, see ibid., chap. 4, and pp. 195–96, 204–11.

Celibacy and Clericalism in Counter-Reformation Thought: The Case of Robert Bellarmine

Robert W. Richgels
Viterbo College

This essay studies the thought on priestly celibacy of the most prominent controversialist of the Counter-Reformation, Robert Bellarmine. It shows the close interdependence between celibacy and clericalism that his thought exhibits. Bellarmine defines the clergy as the elite of the church, both in rank and role, set above the laity in every way. They alone have authority and charge of holy things, to a laity that is passive. Bellarmine argues that celibacy is necessary in order to uphold this sacred role of the priest, and in order to clearly distinguish clergy from laity and maintain the all-important line between them.

CELIBACY WAS ONE ISSUE, AMONG THE MANY, which divided Catholics and Protestants in the Reformation. Are vows of celibacy legitimate Christian practice, and should they continue to be required of the clergy? These were the basic questions. To both of these of course the Protestants said no. Protestant thinkers denounced vows of celibacy as a violation of God's law and part of the delusion that divine favor could be won through human works. In addition, they were regarded as a profound insult to the high esteem due to Christian marriage, which was blessed by God and properly open to all.[1] The Catholics of course took the other side, in defense of celibacy. They continued to define virginity as an intrinsically higher and holier state than marriage and continued to require vows of celibacy for their priests.[2]

This essay studies the thought of one prominent Catholic theologian of the sixteenth century, Robert Bellarmine, on this matter of celibacy for priests. Another characteristic of Counter-Reformation Catholicism that is often noted is its intense clericalism, that is, its increased emphasis on papal and episcopal authority and its strong sense of the superiority in function and worth of clergy over laity.[3] This essay will examine the close interdependence

---

[1]A good summary of Protestant views in these matters is Derrick Sherwin Bailey, *Sexual Relation in Christian Thought* (New York: Harper, 1959), 167–72. See also Steven Ozment, *When Fathers Ruled: Family Life in Reformation Europe* (Cambridge: Harvard University Press, 1983), 3–25.

[2]Bailey, *Sexual Relation*, 179; *New Catholic Encyclopedia*, s.v. "Celibacy, History of."

[3]See H. Outram Evennett, *The Spirit of the Counter-Reformation* (Cambridge: Cambridge University Press, 1968), 92–100; William Bouwsma, *Venice and the Defense of Republican Liberty* (Berkeley: University of California Press, 1968), chaps. 6 and 8.

between celibacy and clericalism that Bellarmine's thought exhibits in his major theological work, the *Controversies*.

Bellarmine (1542-1621) was an Italian Jesuit who became the most prominent Catholic controversialist of the Counter-Reformation. From 1576 to 1588 Bellarmine was Professor of Controversy at the Roman College, where he delivered a series of lectures designed as a thorough refutation of Protestant thought on all matters and a comprehensive exposition of the correct Catholic view. Between 1586 and 1596 these lectures were published as the *Controversies*.[4] As a result of their appearance and immediate acceptance all over Catholic Europe, Bellarmine was recognized at once as the chief theological spokesman for the Roman cause. Building upon the decrees of the Council of Trent, his work was very influential in setting the basic Catholic position on most of the vital doctrinal issues of the day.[5]

Bellarmine was a leading advocate within the Roman church of its policy of clericalism, both through his *Controversies* and other activities of his career. In 1597 he became theological advisor to the pope in Rome, and, except for a brief interruption of three years from 1602 to 1605 when he served as Archbishop of Capua, he spent the rest of his life in that role. He was named Cardinal in 1599. He served as chief troubleshooter for Rome in many of the great religious affairs of the day, including the admonishment of Galileo in 1616, always defending the preeminent role of the papacy to direct and decide on a wide range of matters.[6] One other affair in which Bellarmine had considerable involvement is the clash of the papacy with the Republic of Venice in the early years of the seventeenth century over immunity of the clergy from control by the civil government. William Bouwsma has studied this matter extensively and has shown the great extremes to which the Roman leadership of the church went in its statement and defense of clerical honor and privilege. He presents the papal government as committed to a strictly hierarchical view of things in which lay people are an always inferior order below the clergy, and in which the concerns of lay life are of secondary importance, with even civic and political matters being subordinate to superior clerical control.[7]

---

[4]Its full Latin title is *Disputationes de controversiis Christianae fidei adversus hujus temporis haereticos.*

[5]*Dictionaire de théologie catholique*, s.v. "Bellarmin"; *Dictionaire d'histoire et de géographie ecclésiastiques*, "Bellarmin"; James Brodrick, *Robert Bellarmine* (London: Burns & Oates, 1961), 85–87. For Bellarmine's reliance on Trent, see Robert W. Richgels, "Robert Bellarmine's Use of Calvin in the *Controversies*," (Ph.D. dissertation, University of Wisconsin–Madison, 1973), 177–78.

[6]Broderick, *Robert Bellarmine*, describes these Roman years at length in his biography of Bellarmine. For a more concise treatment, see *Dictionaire de théologie catholique*, s.v. "Bellarmin," cols. 569–74.

[7]Bouwsma, *Venice and the Defense of Republican Liberty*, 312–29 and 420–44.

Rome took the position that the clergy composed a separate and superior order.... For Possevino, therefore, it was simply 'monstrous,' in a very exact sense, 'for ecclesiastics to obey laymen,' as the Venetians proposed, 'just as it is monstrous that the head should be subject to the feet, the greater to the less, those who are consecrated to the divine cult to profane men.'

Roman theologians were clear that the church was a visible institution ... of which the clergy, as Bovio expressed it, constituted 'the more important part,' so that it was proper to limit the term *church* merely to its clerical members. In the church the laity rightly had no authority whatsoever.[8]

Bouwsma shows Bellarmine taking a leading role in this in arguing all aspects of the papal position.

Priests, [Bellarmine] declared, must not be judged by other men because, in relation to the laity, the clergy are gods. A man who despises a prelate despises God himself, and it is far worse for a layman to disobey a prelate than for a prelate to injure a layman. Pursuing the same line of thought, he pointed out the superiority of holy orders, as a sacrament, to baptism.[9]

The *Controversies* were published several decades before the Venetian affair and before Bellarmine took up his position within the papal government. His task in the work was discussion of not just one issue but of the entire range of theological and doctrinal matters under debate at the time. When he does turn to a discussion of the church, however, these same strongly clerical attitudes are very evident. His entire understanding of the church is full of the concepts of hierarchy and rank. He defines the church, for example, as "the community of men united by their profession of the same Christian faith and their communion in the same sacraments, *under the rule of their legitimate pastors, above all the one vicar of Christ on earth, the Roman Pontiff.*"[10] In another place he refers to the church as a "gathered multitude in which there are prelates and subjects (*Praelati et subditi*)."[11]

Hierarchy and rank are also evident in an elaborate analogy that Bellarmine develops when discussing those who are members of the church.

[8]Ibid., 442 and 452.

[9]Ibid., 442–43. For the full account of Bellarmine's role, see chap. 8.

[10]*De conciliis*, 3: 2. Italics mine. The edition of the *Controversies* used in this study is that in Robert Bellarmine, *Opera Omnia*, ed. Justin Fèvre, 8 vols. (Paris, 1870–73; reprinted Frankfurt: Minerva, 1965). All translation is my own.

[11]*De conciliis*, 3: 13.

He compares the church on earth to an army drawn up for battle, composed of three ranks: clergy, monks, and laity. The clergy, he says, are the highest of these ranks who are the leaders or the leaders' aides. In this army it is Christ of course who is the ultimate "commander" (*imperator*), but, since he is in heaven, on earth it is the pope who gives orders in his place. Below the pope are the bishops, who command smaller bands, with priests as their officers. Deacons, sub-deacons, and others in minor orders are the standard bearers and message carriers, while monks are guards, scouts, and forward commanders. The laity comprise the common foot soldiers. This is God's true church, Bellarmine says, "arranged and divided clearly by God's wisdom and divine plan into three ranks of soldiers." Just how fundamental this system of hierarchy is to his understanding of the church becomes clear as he goes on. For the first charge he hurls against the Protestant "heretics" on this matter is that they so confuse the clergy and laity together as to do away with the concept of clergy entirely. For them, "there remains only the laity."[12] For Bellarmine they are for certain two different orders, and the clergy are set above the laity in every way. The clergy are "the first and most noble order" in the church, "the lot and inheritance (*sors et haereditas*) of the Lord, who are consecrated to divine worship," while the laity "are like the lower order, the common people (*plebeii ac populares*), from whom no ecclesiastical function is expected."[13]

What then of celibacy? What is its role in all this? Bellarmine makes it very clear that it has an essential role to play in this hierarchical system. Celibacy is a vital indicator of high status and role, one very important way clergy are distinguished from laity.

The charge is made by Bellarmine against the Protestants that they have abolished the clerical order and put in its place only certain designated men whom they call ministers.[14] How do we know they have no clergy? By the fact, among others, that they have no celibacy. "These [ministers] they want not to have power over the people, nor to be bound by the laws of celibacy, nor to be free of public courts, but in the manner of the laity they direct them to join in marriage, procreate children, engage in secular business, and be subject to the public courts."[15] Abolishing celibacy thus dissolves the line between clergy and people. If priests would marry, he explains, "clergy would hardly be distinguished from laity, and as would be the people, so would be the priest." This would interfere with the proper administration of the sacraments, he charges, as experience in the time of Pope Gregory VII indicates. In Germany priests began to take wives, and such contempt for the sacraments

---

[12]*De membris ecclesiae*, Preface.
[13]Ibid., 1: 1.
[14]Ibid., Preface.
[15]Ibid.

followed that the laity began to administer them. "Celibacy is necessary to the honor of the priesthood," he concludes.[16]

In defining clerical marriage as a serious threat to the proper administration of the sacraments, Bellarmine is making a serious indictment of it indeed. For he later presents the sacraments as the single most important factor in the process of human salvation. They confer grace directly to the soul of the recipient by virtue of the act itself, he says, and "are the true and immediate causes of justification."[17] Anything that would interfere with their proper administration therefore, like clerical marriage, would be a serious blow to the entire salvation-rendering function of the church.

But celibacy is necessary not just to the proper administration of sacraments. It is necessary for the proper fulfillment of all aspects of the priest's role within the structure of the church. The duties of a priest, Bellarmine says, involve, in addition to administering the sacraments, his gifts of sacrifice, prayer, teaching, exhortation, care for the poor, and the like. For these the priest needs to be hospitable, kind, sober, just, holy, learned, and pure, and marriage and sexual intercourse, he insists, make very difficult every one of these. The demands of wife and children on one's time and treasure impede the priest's ability to teach, exhort, and care for others. Prayer is made difficult by the threat to mental concentration that sexual intercourse poses. "For prayer requires an elevated, purified, and tranquil mind. The act of intercourse, however, . . . seriously dulls the mind's sharpness and drags it down to lower things, as it also disorders the soul and makes it in some way carnal." It is the priestly role of offering sacrifice though that above all is undermined, because of the inevitable sordidness involved in the sexual act. Bellarmine explains that to offer sacrifice "the highest purity and sanctity are required," but "it cannot be denied that the act of intercourse itself is transfused with a certain impurity and pollution." Even within matrimony, "it cannot be performed without some pollution and turpitude–that the wantonness of the bodily members sufficiently proves, as well as the human shame in the act, which always seeks a secret place." For all these reasons, sexual intercourse by priests he calls a "sacrilege."[18]

So for Bellarmine celibacy is certainly no small matter. It touches on nearly every important aspect of the life of the church as he understands it. It is essential for maintaining the priests' function as leaders and agents of holy things and dispensers of grace and salvation to the laity through the sacraments. It is a vital mark of the elite within the hierarchical structure of the church, a necessary means of maintaining the fundamental difference between clergy and laity. Bellarmine clearly sees celibacy and the basic clerical nature

---

[16]Ibid., 1: 19.

[17]*De sacramentis in genere*, 2: 1–2.

[18]*De membris ecclesiae*, 1: 19.

of the church as intimately interdependent. In his view, to relinquish one would be to also relinquish the other.

Given all this, it is difficult to see Bellarmine accepting a church that would not require celibacy of its priests. Yet strong as his case is against priestly marriage, he does admit, even actively argue, that the requirement of clerical celibacy is not something unchangeable in the church, for it is not a thing commanded by divine law. He agrees with Aquinas, Cajetan, and Soto and disagrees with two other sixteenth-century Catholic thinkers, John Major and Josse Chichtove, in seeing it as only a decree of the church and thus in theory dispensable. He does assert though that it is an ancient practice, originating with the apostles, and one that certainly should not be done away with.[19]

There seems to be a bit of difficulty in all of this, however. If one accepts what Bellarmine says against priestly marriage–that it seriously jeopardizes the church's salvation-rendering function by undermining administration of the sacraments, for example, or that it renders the priest so polluted and carnal through sexual intercourse that it is no less than a sacrilege–it is difficult to see how God could have neglected to forbid it outright in his church in the first place.

That God did forbid it was a view held by some Catholic thinkers in the sixteenth century, and it was a view argued at the Council of Trent when clerical celibacy was being discussed. The view was rejected though, mainly because of the obvious difficulties of reconciling it with known approved practice in centuries past of priests who were married.[20] When Trent did decree continuance of mandatory celibacy it did so referring to it only as an "ecclesiastical law" (*lege ecclesiastica*).[21]

Bellarmine of course was well aware of the work of Trent, and he does cite its decree to support his case for the ecclesiastical origin of the practice.[22] He was also well enough aware of the historical record of the church of having allowed priests to live in marriage[23]–something it of course could not rightly do if such practice were forbidden outright by God. Thus in fact Bellarmine had little choice but to argue as he does, even if somewhat awkwardly.

Bellarmine is writing the *Controversies* as a sort of official spokesman for the Catholic cause in Europe, and his views have wide impact, not only in his time but for centuries to follow. He was named saint by the Catholic Church

---

[19]Ibid., 1: 18–19.

[20]*New Catholic Encyclopedia*, s. v. "Celibacy, History of."

[21]Session 24, Canon 9, in *Canons and Decrees of the Council of Trent*, ed. H. H. Schroeder (Saint Louis: Herder, 1941), 453.

[22]*De membris ecclesiae*, 1: 18.

[23]Ibid.

in 1930, and in 1931 declared Doctor of the Church. The case he presents for the close and necessary relationship between celibacy and clericalism perhaps reveals something quite fundamental in Catholic thought in the post-Tridentine era. It may also help explain why priestly celibacy has so tenaciously survived up to this point, despite the many pressures upon it and the significant changes that have taken place in so many other aspects of the church in recent years. Perhaps Bellarmine has captured something essential in the logic of Catholic thought: that priestly celibacy is no incidental matter at all, but something bound up with the very nature itself of the church; that celibacy must remain for the church to remain hierarchical, clerical, and sacramental. To allow priestly marriage may be to tamper with the fundamental reality of the church, and, though many may be the changes in other areas, that would be one change yet too radical for any church leaders to consider.

Families Unformed and Reformed: Protestant Divorce and Its Domestic Consequences*

Thomas Max Safley
Wabash College

The "polarity" between interest and emotion in pre-modern family life serves as the essential focus of "Families Unformed and Reformed." Since publication of *The Making of the Modern Family* by Edward Shorter in 1975, historians have labored mightily to distinguish material and psychological forces in the household. Many have insisted with Shorter that the rise of the transcendental—sentiment and emotion—characterizes the modern family and distinguishes it from its predecessors. A younger generation, influenced by historical anthropology and Marxist theory, has responded that the application of twentieth-century psychology to families in the sixteenth and seventeenth centuries is anachronistic and blinds the historian to pre-modern emotional forms. Furthermore, they assert the survival of a material basis for family life well into the modern period.

Safley tests the dialectic of interest and emotion through application of a single, well-documented case of divorce, which originated in the German Protestant city of Isny im Allgaeu between 1677 and 1681. Using several first-person statements by the litigants themselves, he demonstrates that the terminology of modern scholarship fails to conform to historical experience. The marital dispute centered on issues of domestic authority and sexual compatibility, the older husband yearning for a subservient, industrious helpmate and his young wife struggling to preserve her self-determination. In this case, interest was not simply a matter of material calculation but was loaded with psychological content. Interest cannot be separated from emotion. Safley concludes by insisting on the analysis of the interrelationship of interest and emotion, both present and inseparable in the pre-modern family.

"SENTIMENT," WROTE EDWARD SHORTER IN 1975, "makes personal happiness the most important objective in the selection of a mate, ahead of such traditional criteria as family interest and dowry size. . . . When we encounter young men passing up fat dowries to wed their heart's desire, we shall know we're standing before romance."[1] The "sentimentalization" of the family has since become a focus for historical scholarship. Many eminent historians of sexuality and marriage, such as Lawrence Stone, Jean-Louis Flandrin, Steven

---

*This paper was first presented at the annual meeting of the American Historical Association in 1985.

[1]Edward Shorter, *The Making of the Modern Family* (New York: Basic Books, 1975), 17.

Ozment, and Michel Foucault, have seen it as one of the most important sources of modern family life.[2]

Without questioning the central place of "sentimentalization" as a factor in the making of the modern family, it is possible to doubt the essential conflict between material interests and human emotions in the pre-modern one. As Hans Medick and David Sabean have suggested, the modern family, despite its putative emotional basis, is by no means free of the material rights and responsibilities which help determine personal relationships. Likewise, the language of family experience, the means of expressing emotions, varies over time and space.[3] To assume, therefore, that an emphasis on "fat dowries" implies an absence of human "sentiment" is at once to misunderstand pre-modern family life and to commit the cardinal sin of anachronism. Interest and emotion were, indeed, closely connected. Their essential congruence, acknowledged and shared by all family members, determined the solidarity and survival of the family.

One means of assessing the interrelationship of interest and emotion in marital and familial life in early modern Europe is a case study of divorce. Divorce litigation often resulted in voluminous documentation offering potential insights into the values, expectations, and behavior of the married couple. Especially valuable are the occasional first-person statements which, in the context of accusation and exoneration, reflect the forces shaping inner-familial relations.

One such case is that initiated by Hans Jerg Zachen, a *Zimmermeister* or master builder of the Lutheran free imperial city of Isny im Allgaeu, against his wife, Dorothea Langin, on 10 August 1677.[4] Their dispute may be summarized as follows. Soon after the death of his first wife, Zachen decided to remarry and sought the hand of Barbara Langin, the elder sister of Dorothea. Although Barbara was unenthusiastic about the match, Dorothea stepped forward and announced her willingness. Then it was Zachen's turn to have misgivings. After some thought, however, he agreed, and the parties signed a formal contract. Shortly thereafter, Dorothea developed reservations about her future husband and refused to complete the marriage. Her parents remonstrated with her and convinced her to proceed. The union of Zachen and Langin was duly consecrated and consummated. Unfortunately for all concerned, it did not last long. Within weeks of her marriage, Langin felt her

---

[2]Michel Foucault, *Histoire de la sexualité* (Paris: Éditions Gallimard, 1976-84); Lawrence Stone, *The Family, Sex and Marriage in England, 1500-1800* (New York: Harper & Row, 1977); Jean-Louis Flandrin, *Families in Former Times: Kinship, Household and Sexuality* (Cambridge: Cambridge University Press, 1979); Steven Ozment, *When Fathers Ruled: Family Life in Reformation Europe* (Cambridge, Mass.: Harvard University Press, 1983).

[3]*Interest and Emotion: Essays on the Study of Family and Kinship*, ed. Hans Medick and David Warren Sabean (Cambridge: Cambridge University Press, 1984), 11.

[4]Stadtarchiv Isny, Fasz. 604, *Ehescheidung und Dissidien, Memoriale*, 3 January 1680.

worst fears entirely justified. She abandoned her husband and fled to the neighboring city of Lindau, where she entered service to support herself. Zachen responded by suing for divorce on grounds of malicious abandonment. The marital court of Isny issued citations to Langin, which ordered her to appear before the court to answer charges. Rather than appearing in person, she sent a legal representative who lodged a counter-suit. Langin charged that her husband abused her, causing her to fear for life and limb. Furthermore, she alleged that Zachen was impotent, that the child of his first marriage was by his own admission not his own. On 6 March 1681, the court finally granted Zachen a divorce, with permission to remarry as he wished, and awarded him compensation for damages caused by Langin's behavior.

The question of compensation was difficult because Langin was still alive and her residence well known. Under such circumstances, the court hoped for eventual reconciliation. In a quandry and under pressure from Zachen, the court sought the opinion of Sigmund Schleicherd, a jurist from the city of Ulm. Schleicherd wrote that a case of malicious abandonment might be treated like adultery: the abandoning party, the wife in this case, would lose her marital portion to her injured husband. He might further claim the value of his wife: in Schleicherd's words, "what is attributed in the case of the spouse's death."[5] As a result, the court ordered the wife's father, Hans Lang, to pay a long list of damages, which included, among other things, fifty *gulden* for the dowry, fifteen *gulden* stolen by Langin when she fled, and sixty-six *gulden* for Zachen's legal expenses. Total compensation was over 163 *gulden*, a considerable sum. In addition, Hans Lang was ordered to replace his daughter's personal property, four dresses and underclothing as well as bedding, which she illegally removed from her husband's house.[6] Indeed, the estate of Dorothea Langin was treated as if she were legally deceased; it passed to her husband as sole heir.

Taken in its broad outline, the case of *Zachen* v. *Langin* is no different from thousands of other divorce cases originating in the Protestant free imperial cities of southern Germany and the reformed city-states of Switzerland between 1500 and 1700. A husband or wife petitioned for divorce on the grounds of some clear violation of marital responsibilities, such as adultery, abuse, or abandonment. The magistrates of those communities which legalized divorce and remarriage reviewed each case with a care and skepticism born, one imagines, both of experience in human affairs and distrust of legal innovations. A verdict was reached, usually within several weeks or months, and the couple passed out of the purview both of the court and of the historian.

[5]Ibid., *Memoriale*, 15 October 1680.
[6]Ibid., *Verzeichnis*, 5 March 1681.

Nonetheless, *Zachen* v. *Langin* is unique and instructive. This case extended over four years and created a dossier of some four hundred folio pages of manuscript. Among the various legal documents are several statements and letters by the litigants themselves. As such, this divorce provides both an invaluable study of marital failure and unusual perspectives on the interests and emotions of domestic life.

In a letter addressed to the marital court of Isny some time early in 1678, Zachen reviewed his marriage. He recalled learning of Langin's interest in marrying him from her brother-in-law, Albrecht Buhler. At the time, he did not think she would make a very good housekeeper, but he recognized her insistence as God's will. As a sign of his agreement, Zachen gave his future bride a ring and a gold ducat. He then sent two honorable men to speak with her father and conclude an agreement. There was some disagreement over the testamentary status of Zachen's child; he wanted to guarantee his offspring's inheritance as part of the marital agreement but finally agreed to parity between his child and his second wife. Zachen and Langin shook hands, and her father poured wine over their joined hands, wishing them health and happiness. As a sign of his confidence in the future, Zachen entrusted Langin with the key to his household goods, *"meinem Hauswesen."*[7]

It is tempting to view the marriage of Zachen and Langin in crass, commercial terms. Zachen's emphasis on a wife's ability to keep house seems utilitarian. The exchange of coin and ring as tokens of earnest and the shaking of hands recall a business transaction more than a betrothal. Finally, giving his fiancée the keys to the cellar seems consistent with the other indications of interest ruling emotion.

Yet, a closer assessment suggests a different interpretation. Zachen used the word *vertraut*, that is, entrusted.[8] Likewise, he was willing to forego the guaranteed rights of his child to provide suitably for his bride. He evidently trusted Langin to care for her stepchild in the event of his death. It would be pointless to deny the practical, material considerations in this marriage. These were, however, neither bereft of nor contrary to the emotional needs of husband and wife. Zachen saw Langin as a companion and helpmate, a trusted figure. Love and passion might follow, but a solidly amicable and practical foundation seemed secure.

The collapse of that foundation came suddenly and inexplicably. Zachen learned of Langin's last-minute hesitation from her sister. That woman claimed her sister had neither love nor desire for him and would soon return the marriage gifts he had given her. Zachen turned to Langin's parents, who convinced her to marry according to the agreement. Nonetheless, several weeks later, Langin disappeared and never returned. Zachen claimed he had

---

[7]Ibid., *Brief*, 1678.
[8]Ibid.

never understood his wife's behavior and still had no idea why she had left. If she intended to behave in this manner, he wished to divorce her and remarry. He closed his letter with a plea for swift justice saying cryptically that the absence of a wife was ruining his household.

A second, undated, letter—presumably written in 1678 as well—from Zachen to the court added new material to this tale of trust betrayed. He had come into possession of a letter from Langin to her brother-in-law, Albrecht Buhler. Zachen entered it in evidence because it contained material pertinent to his case.

This personal letter is the first direct statement from Langin. Apart from references to her family, directed to her brother-in-law, Langin offered a running stream of abuse aimed at her husband. Calling her husband a rotten apple, a swindler, and a thief, Langin left little doubt as to her feelings about him.[9] She claimed that since leaving Zachen she felt reborn. She asked rhetorically what he would want with a wife when he could as easily get a dog. If need be he could lay with a serving girl as it would not injure his accursed soul.[10] Encouraging her brother-in-law not to worry about her, she declared that she had found work and was spending her nights dancing and drinking. In fact, while writing she claimed to have a glass of schnapps before her as a nightcap. She intended never to return to Zachen.

The references to a dog and a maid seem to be the solid points in this torrent of vilification. Together they suggest that Langin rejected a certain style of life, rejected the companionship and housework which were the lots of pets and servants. She may also have objected to the physical abuse and sexual attention which these creatures were expected to accept from their masters. Striking, too, is Langin's independence, her willingness to support herself and defy convention.

Zachen entered this letter in evidence noting primly that it demonstrated both Langin's immorality and her malice. Her drinking and dancing were scandalous in his eyes, and her abuse demonstrated that this was a clear case of malicious abandonment. He counted himself more hurt than offended, remembering wistfully the peace of his first marriage. He offered his vision of the ideal marriage when he claimed that he never had to strike his first wife.[11] His second marriage obviously had not lived up to his expectations.

Langin's procurator responded both to this evidence and to the charge by offering a statement on behalf of Langin. Admitting the authenticity of the letter, she interpreted it differently. She never led an immoral or godless life. The references to drinking and dancing were deliberate sarcasm—the word

---

[9]Ibid.
[10]Ibid.
[11]Ibid.

used was *burla*, or joke—chosen because she knew Zachen strongly disapproved of both.[12] The procurator then entered Langin's charge. She claimed that her husband abused her, on one occasion threatening her with an ax and causing her to fear for life and limb. Furthermore, Zachen was impotent. Langin claimed her marriage had never been consummated and that her husband had confided to her that his child was the result of an adulterous relationship by his first wife. Although these offenses could serve as grounds for divorce, Langin requested a judicial separation because, in her words, she "could live perfectly well without a man."[13] The procurator closed his presentation with the claim that Zachen was at fault for the breakdown of marital harmony.

At this point it is impossible to ignore the sexual tension in this case. Given Langin's apparent independence and her firm assertion that she needed no man, why did she find it necessary to lodge the fantastic accusation of impotence? The existence of Zachen's child was *prima facie* evidence to the contrary. Furthermore, proven deadly abuse was sufficient grounds for divorce according to the marital statutes of Isny. After all, the courts usually did a brisk business in cases of domestic violence and sexual offense. This may be simply another instance of spite, a demonstration of Langin's despair and frustration.

What is less usual is the alleged joke or *burla*. In addition to any abuse, this may be evidence of a more profound sort for the lack of sympathy between Zachen and Langin. Although it is not possible to determine their ages, Zachen was probably older than his wife. This was, after all, his second marriage, and she had been living in her father's household at the time. Likewise, the different temperaments are clearly revealed in their statements. Langin appears an aggressive and independent woman. Zachen seems quieter, describing himself as a patient man, who valued a steady, dependable spouse. It seems reasonable to surmise, therefore, that differences of age and temperament accounted for Langin's actions as much as the alleged abuse. She wished to enjoy life rather than succumb early to the drudgery of housekeeping. Zachen probably saw these impulses as frivolous as well as immoral. An older man, he might have had less tolerance for the entertainments of youth. Zachen and Langin conceived their interests in quite distinct manners, and she was not prepared to accept either his ideal of a wife or his authority as *Hausvater*.

As this divorce makes clear, interest was both material and psychological, merging with emotion. Zachen demanded companionship and obedience as well as housekeeping from his wife. Langin, while not necessarily averse to physical labor—she was more than able to support herself—was not prepared to surrender her pleasure and self-sufficiency. Here, the weakness of intellectual dichotomies, whether materialism and sentimentality or interest and emotion,

---

[12]Ibid., *Memoriale*, 1678.

[13]Ibid. "weil sie aber gar wohl Ohnemanne sein kann. . . ."

is manifest. Distinct in theory, they merge and become barely distinguishable in practice. Far from representing poles in a continuum, interest and emotion appear interactive and omnipresent in the experience of married couples.

Zachen's answer to Langin's case was devastating. He repeated coolly his assessment of her letter as proof of malicious abandonment. Far from a joke, the matter was evil and slanderous. What wife, he asked the court, would say such things of her husband? He denied categorically the charge of deadly abuse, noting cogently that the City Council, which had been investigating rumors concerning discord in their marriage before Langin's departure, would have separated them had there been any truth in the accusation. Zachen also denied being impotent. Indeed, Langin had occasion to know for, as he put it, she once exclaimed, among many "coarse" expressions, that "he was a man like a stallion and she could not outlast the thing."[14] It is worth noting that the issues of abuse and impotence were not seriously raised again.

In a final letter to the court, again undated but probably written in July 1678, Langin made her final, direct statement to the marital court. She referred to her husband's behavior as tyranny.[15] She repeated the allegation of physical abuse, adding that in one instance she was bedridden for four days as a result. Langin ended her statement by admitting rather forlornly that she could produce no witnesses to Zachen's many abuses.

Langin had no intention of surrendering her youth or her pastimes. As such, she expected her husband's rule to be mild—neither abusive nor tyrannical. Expressed in material terms, she would contribute her labor to the domestic economy but expected some degree of control over the distribution of its wealth as well. She expected to be able to afford an occasional evening at a dance or in a tavern. Once again, it is possible to construe the evidence in such a way that material interests and personal emotions, far from being mutually exclusive, are actually inseparable and dependent on one another.

The marital court of Isny heard testimony in the case of *Zachen* v. *Langin* during 1678. For the next two years the case hung suspended in a legal limbo. Learned opinion held that no verdict could be issued. On the one hand, Langin had made serious charges against her husband that could not be adjudicated in her absence. On the other hand, Zachen's case could not be resolved.[16] Although she steadfastly refused to attend court sessions, Langin made no secret of her refuge. She was merely contumacious and not dead. Therefore, the court hesitated to pronounce judgment, hoping at worst that she might yet appear in court and at best that the couple might be reconciled.

During the years 1678 to 1680 Zachen kept a steady pressure on the magistrates. He complained that his case was not progressing and begged for

[14]Ibid., *Brief.* "ich were ein Mann wie ein Pferd und sie konte das ding nicht ausdauern."
[15]Ibid., *Brief.*
[16]Ibid., *Memoriale.*

a full divorce. On 23 November 1680 the court finally issued a temporary separation pending the satisfactory participation of Langin.[17] On 26 November, Zachen addressed a petition to the court.[18] For years he had said that his household and conscience were endangered by the lack of a wife. Now he made his strongest appeal. He was unable to keep house and conduct business at the same time. For years he had hired strangers at great expense to tend his household and care for his child. He warned that he faced imminent financial ruin as a result. In addition to the material dangers posed by this unresolved state of affairs, Zachen hinted darkly that there were spiritual dangers as well. For the first time he stated openly his intention to sue for damages caused by his wife's absence.

Zachen arrived at the market value of a wife as companion and housekeeper. Given the legal opinion of Sigmund Schleicherd and the award of damages cited above, the magistrates appear to have been prepared to consider such a notion. The idea of a value-added theory of marriage, such as Zachen seems to have held, should remove any doubt of the close association between material interests and personal emotions in early modern marriage. In the case of Zachen at least, material considerations seem to have been more profound, and to have determined the content of emotions.

In early modern marriage, neither interest nor emotion were absent, contrary to some recent scholarship. Indeed, it may not be possible to separate them. The problem resides, at least in part, in the vagueness of the term, interest. For Zachen and Langin, interest could not be stripped of its emotional content and limited strictly to economic concerns. The issues of sexuality and entertainment suggest clearly the corporeal and material reality of emotion.

Otto Brunner remarked as part of his theory of the entire house—*das ganze Haus*—that interest and emotion, rationality and sentimentality, community and individual, *Gesellschaft* and *Gemeinschaft*, exist in a state of tension within the early modern household.[19] Domestic success, both in moral and economic terms, depended largely on a correspondence between these concerns and a resolution of that tension. Any failure to balance interest and emotion created a crisis not only for the family but also for the community.

Hans Zachen's petition suggests that divorce could occur where emotions threatened interests. Interest bound the married couple to kin and community, establishing economic and sentimental ties and necessitating regulation and intervention. Interest and emotion constitute neither a dialectic nor a dichotomy. Rather, they are congruent elements in the historical experience of family life.

---

[17]Ibid., *Ehegerichtsprotokolle*, 23 November 1680.

[18]Ibid., *Brief*, 26 November 1680.

[19]Otto Brunner, *Neue Wege der Verfassungs- und Sozialgeschichte* (Göttingen: Vandenhoeck & Ruprecht, 1968), 111.

Frail, Weak, and Helpless:
Women's Legal Position in Theory and Reality

Merry E. Wiesner
University of Wisconsin–Milwaukee

Women's theoretical legal position deteriorated in Germany during the sixteenth century. Academic jurists supported the reception of Roman law, which viewed women as mentally and physically weak. Thus as territories revised their law codes, they often re-introduced gender-based guardianship, limited mothers' rights to their children, and restricted the ability of married women to administer their own property. They did not make gender distinctions in criminal procedure, however, and both sexes were required to confess in capital crimes, which led to judicial torture. In their drives for public order and systematic procedure, governments more vigorously prosecuted individuals who broke the law, becoming less willing to make exceptions in the case of women. In Protestant areas, new courts of marriage and morals replaced Catholic church courts, introducing stricter laws concerning adultery and clandestine marriage.

The actual impact of these changes may be seen in court and city records from Nuremberg. The number of married and single women who bought and sold property independently decreased, as did the number of married women who made separate wills. Punishments for moral crimes increased in severity, and widows and single women were increasingly required to have male guardians represent them in court. The reality of women's inferior legal status lagged somewhat behind the theory, but by the seventeenth century women throughout Germany found it increasingly difficult to act as independent legal persons.

THE SIXTEENTH CENTURY IN GERMANY saw several major changes in law codes and legal structures. Humanist lawyers encouraged the introduction of Roman law, favoring it over Germanic law because it was systematic and comprehensive: it gradually replaced or augmented older Germanic law codes in civil matters. The *Carolina Constitutio Criminalis*, a standardized code of criminal procedure drawn up for Charles V, was gradually adopted in most of the territories of the Empire. The Reformation ended the power of canon law, forcing Protestant areas to devise new ordinances in regard to marriage and morals, and to establish new courts to replace Catholic church courts, or expand the jurisdiction of existing courts. There was also change in Catholic areas, for the decrees of the Council of Trent—particularly the decree Tametsi—cleared up many ambiguities in canon law regarding marriage.

All of these changes in civil, criminal, and church law had an impact on the legal position of women in Germany. Civil codes established their rights

161

to buy, sell, and trade property, act in legal capacities without guardians, control their children, inherit and will cash and goods, and carry out other financial transactions. Criminal procedures determined how female suspects would be treated, and what sort of punishments would be meted out. Church law largely determined their rights to marry and divorce, and set penalties for sexual crimes and deviance.

In the first half of this essay I wish to discuss how women's theoretical legal status changed during the sixteenth century. The second half will turn from theory to reality, examining women's actions in courts and other legal bodies to assess the actual impact of these changes.

The realm of legal theory in regard to women may itself be divided into two levels. The first is the level of pure theory, the discussion among jurists of "woman" in the abstract. This was provoked by a gloss on the Roman law of homicide by the French humanist jurist Jacques Cujas in which he asserted—perhaps flippantly—that a woman (*mulier*) is not a human being (*homo*).[1] Though he was using this to satirize the scholastic inflexible approach to language, other jurists, as well as theologians, took him seriously and set out to prove that women are human.[2] No one argued, however, that this shared humanity should imply legal equality.

Academic jurists found justification in both Roman and German law for excluding women from a wide variety of legal functions. Roman law stressed women's alleged physical and mental weakness, her *levitas, fragilitas, infirmitas et imbecillitas*, and held women, along with peasants and the simple-minded, as not fully responsible for their own actions. Germanic law based women's secondary status on their inability to perform vassal service and duty to obey their husbands: the age of this tradition was alone grounds for its acceptance among jurists, who regarded *mores* and *consuetudo* (traditions and institutions) as adequate grounds for most laws. Academic jurisprudence thus made clear distinctions between men and women, and further subdivided women according to their relationship to a man; a woman's legal status was determined by her marital status as maiden/wife/widow, and occasionally also by her physiological status as virgin/pregnant/nursing mother/mother.

The second level of legal theory is made up of codes which transformed these ideas into actual laws and regulations. During the late fifteenth and sixteenth centuries most areas of Germany revised their civil codes to include procedures and principles drawn from Roman law. This had less of an impact on women than one might expect, however, for, of all branches of law, family

---

[1]Ian MacLean, *The Renaissance Notion of Woman* (Cambridge: Cambridge University Press, 1980), 70.

[2]Ibid., 71-81; Manfred P. Fleischer, "Are Women Human? The Debate of 1595 Between Valens Acidalius and Simon Geddicus," *The Sixteenth Century Journal* 12 no. 2 (1981): 107-21.

law was the most resistant to change. Jurists began to use Roman terms for such things as a woman's dowry (*dos*), but did not give women the absolute rights to their dowry that they possessed under traditional Roman law. Such dowry rights meant that a woman had a claim to part of her husband's income, and rights vis-à-vis his creditors, both of which were perceived as un-German.[3] Only in a few parts of Germany did a widow have absolute right to a certain part of her husband's estate as she did to her "widow's third" under English common law.[4]

Roman law did have an impact in the area of guardianship. The oldest Germanic codes had required that every woman have a male legal guardian because she was not capable of bearing arms; this gender-based guardianship gradually died out in the later Middle Ages as court proceedings replaced trial by combat and trial by ordeal. Women everywhere in Germany were regarded as legally capable of holding land and appearing in court on their own behalf. In the sixteenth century, gender-based guardianship reappeared, now based on Roman ideas of women's mental weakness and *fragilitas*. Though Roman law itself did not have gender-based guardianship, its rules for the guardianship of children were carried over to the guardianship of women.[5] Roman ideas about guardianship also affected mothers' rights to their children. Early German codes had known only fatherly authority, but the idea of joint parental authority over children had grown gradually in the Middle Ages. This died again with the reception of Roman law, with its concept of *patria potestas*.[6]

These trends were common throughout Germany, but there were variations because each territory of the empire devised its own code, combining Roman and traditional law as it deemed appropriate. Thus to explore women's legal position in detail it is necessary to look at a specific political entity. I have chosen the free imperial city of Nuremberg, which served as a model for other cities and princely territories.

Nuremberg revised its civil law code in 1484 and 1564, and in marriage and family matters there is little difference between the two Reformations, as such revisions are termed. Both recognize two types of marriage, which, with minor variations, were found throughout Germany. The first and much more common type involved communal ownership of all property (*Gütergemeinschaft*); in the words of the code "man and wife marry their goods together as well."[7] Theoretically the wife's approval was necessary for any transaction

---

[3]Marianne Weber, *Ehefrau und Mutter in der Rechtsentwicklung* (Tübingen: J. C. B. Mohr, 1907), 237-41; Rudolf Huebner, *A History of Germanic Private Law*, tr. Francis S. Philbrick (Boston: Little Brown, 1918), 633.

[4]Hans Thieme, "Die Rechtsstellung der Frau in Deutschland," *Recueils de la Sociètè Jean Bodin* 12 no. 2 (1962): 372.

[5]Huebner, *History of Germanic Private Law*, 67.

[6]Ibid., 365.

[7]*Der Verneurte Reformation der Stadt Nürnberg 1564* (Nuremberg, 1564), Sec. 28: 1.

which concerned family property, for she was co-owner of all movables and immovables. In actuality, during the sixteenth century husbands were gradually given more rights to act alone or for their wives in all financial matters. Though women remained co-owners, they were no longer considered co-administrators.[8] The Nuremberg city council recognized that women had often lost their say in family financial matters, and in the 1564 code required widows to pay off only half of their husband's debts.[9] It also did not leave a woman totally at the mercy of her husband's whims while he was alive. If a wife could prove that her husband was *in Abfall* (going to waste), losing money through gambling, drink, unwise investments or simply bad luck, she had the right to take over "the value of her dowry and his matching payment from his property and goods into her own management."[10] The council was not only protecting widows and other women with these provisions, of course, but also keeping them from requiring public support—a fortunate conjuncture of its paternalism and fiscal conservatism.

In the second type of marriage, only part of the property of each spouse was considered marital property (*Heyratsgüter*).[11] This limited community of goods was termed *Güterverbindung*, and was more common for landed families who wished to maintain family ownership of certain pieces of property. It was originally less favorable for women than a marriage with total communal ownership, for everything the couple earned during the course of the marriage belonged solely to the husband, who also had the *usufruct* of all his wife's property during the course of the marriage. In actuality, it became more favorable for women, for they retained the right to co-administer their own property. By the late sixteenth century, *Güterverbindung* was termed *das Gesetz für die Weiber* (the law for women) in Nuremberg.[12]

In both types of marriage, a woman theoretically lost the ability to carry out financial transactions without the approval of her husband. The guiding force behind these restrictions was the concept of *weibliche Freiheit*, "female freedom" in exact translation. Basically this meant that women had the "freedom" to declare their signatures invalid on contracts and agreements, saying they had been pressured or misled or had not understood what they were doing. Authorities justified *weibliche Freiheit* by noting it protected women, though it was actually greater protection for their husbands, of course. The Nuremberg city council recognized that some married women were in occupations which required that they buy and sell goods or loan and borrow

---

[8]Weber, *Ehefrau und Mutter*, 230.

[9]*Reformation 1564*, Sec. 33: 9.

[10]Ibid., Sec. 28: 5.

[11]Ibid., Sec. 27: 2.

[12]Bertha Kipfmuller, *Die Frau im Rechte der freien Reichsstadt Nürnberg* (Dillingen: Schwäbische Verlagsdruckerei, 1929), 35.

money. It specifically exempted "female tailors, shopkeepers, hotel-keepers, and market-women" from any restrictions, exceptions which were also made in other cities.[13] Unmarried women and widows over the age of 18 who owned their own property could make contracts, borrow, and lend without a man as co-signer; not until the seventeenth century was gender-based guardianship made law in Nuremberg.[14]

Women could appear in court as witnesses in civil cases, if no male witnesses were available, but could not be used as witnesses for a will. Pregnant women were given special rights as witnesses; along with other "dangerously ill" people, they were allowed to give their testimony before a case had been officially opened, in case they were no longer available once it had been opened.[15] A woman could freely make her own will, and had the right to a certain share of her parents' estate (*Legitima*). Despite the Lutheran insistence on parental approval for marriage, a daughter could not be disinherited for marrying against her parents' will if it could be shown that the parents had not found her a husband before she was 22; sons could be disinherited for this at any time.[16] Because children were viewed as tangible property belonging to their father's family, a married woman had less legal control of her own children than did her husband's father. If she remarried, she lost all control of her children by her first husband, which was not the case with a man who remarried.[17]

Though women were clearly unequal in terms of civil legal rights, they were most definitely equal in terms of civil responsibilities. Female heads of household—about 12 percent of the total number of households in both 1497 and 1561—were responsible for paying taxes and providing soldiers for the city's defense.[18] If a female citizen moved out of Nuremberg, she was required to pay the same tax that men were for giving up citizenship rights.

[13]Andreas Baader, ed., *Nürnberger Polizeiordnungen aus der 13. bis 15. Jahrhundert.* Vol. 63 of Bibliothek des literarische Verein Stuttgart (Stuttgart: Literarische Verein, 1862), 30.

[14]*Reformation 1564*, Sec. 19: 5.

[15]Otto Reiser, "Beweis und Beweisverfahren im Zivilprozess der freien Reichsstadt Nürnberg" (Jur. Diss., Erlangen, 1955), 45, 74.

[16]Albrecht Purucker, "Das Testamentrecht der Nürnberger Reformation" (Jur. Diss., Erlangen, 1948), 7.

[17]This was actually more liberal than in other cities which accepted Roman law more completely, in which a widow had no rights over her own children, whether she remarried or not. In Nuremberg, only if a mother did not properly care for her children's affairs was her guardianship lifted. (Dieter Beck, "Die Rechtstellung der Minderjährige nach Nürnberger Stadtrecht" [Jur. Diss., Erlangen, 1950], 52.)

[18]Otto Puchner, "Das Register des Gemeinen Pfennigs (1497) der Reichsstadt Nürnberg als bevölkerungsgeschichtliche Quelle," *Jahrbuch für fränkische Landesforschung*, 34/35 (1974/75), 936; Rudolf Endres, "Zur Einwohnerzahl und Bevölkerungsstruktur Nürnbergs im 15/16. Jahrhunderts," *Mitteilungen des Verein für Geschichte der Stadt Nürnberg* 57 (1970): 263.

Non-citizen women, including domestic servants, who wanted to live in the city had to apply annually for permission.[19]

Women were also equal to men in terms of their liability in criminal cases: *weibliche Freiheit* applied only to civil law. Nuremberg did not have a uniform code of criminal law, but after 1532 used the *Carolina* to systematize procedure. The *Carolina* was heavily influenced by Roman law, which required a confession or absolute proof in capital cases, and saw punishment as a matter of state concern and not simply up to the discretion of the injured party. Though the requirement of a confession or eyewitnesses appears to be a humane and just one, in actuality it sanctioned judicial torture, particularly in cases where proof was difficult to obtain, such as witchcraft or infanticide.[20] Pregnant women and nursing mothers were to be handled more mildly than other suspects, but women who pretended to be pregnant in order to get preferential treatment were to be dealt with more harshly once this was discovered. Women who were to be executed were generally buried alive until 1515, when the council decided to switch to drowning "in consideration of what a horrible death being buried alive is for women and that such punishments are no longer being carried out in many imperial areas."[21] They were drowned from 1515 to 1558, when the city executioner recommended that they be beheaded because the Pegnitz river which flowed through the city had been frozen several times when he was supposed to carry out an execution. The council accepted his reasoning and also came to the conclusion that a beheading had more shock value than a drowning, when no one could see the actual death.[22] Men were generally beheaded, or hung if they had committed a "dishonorable" crime like theft. For lesser crimes, corporal punishment, mutilation, and banishment were prescribed for both women and men, though a wife was generally included in her husband's banishment—including that for adultery!—while the opposite was not the case.[23]

In theory, the most dramatic legal change in sixteenth-century Nuremberg was the ending of the jurisdiction of the Catholic church in marriage and morals cases. By January 1525, marriage cases were no longer going to the bishop's court at Bamberg, and the city council asked for an official opinion (*Gutachten*) from the city's jurists and theologians about what should be

[19]Gunther Düll, "Das Bürgerrecht der freien Reichsstadt Nürnberg vom Ende des 13. Jahrhunderts bis Anfang des 16. Jahrhunderts" (Jur. Diss., Erlangen, 1954), 122.

[20]Carl Ludwig von Bar, *A History of Continental Criminal Law*, tr. Thomas S. Bell (Boston: Little, Brown, 1916), 220.

[21]Hermann Knapp, *Das Lochgefängnis, Tortur und Richtung im Alt-Nürnberg* (Nuremberg: Heerdegen-Barbeck, 1907), 73.

[22]Ibid., 71; *Meister Franntz Schmidts Scharfrichters in Nürnberg all sein Richten*, ed. Albrecht Keller (Leipzig: Wilhelm Heims, 1913).

[23]Düll, "Das Bürgerrecht," 71.

done.[24] Though Andreas Osiander, the Lutheran pastor in the city's main church, wanted to establish a consistory, the council decided instead to turn over jurisdiction in marriage cases to the regular city civil court. The court's name was changed from *Stadtgericht* to *Stadt- und Ehegericht*, and it was also to handle morals cases like blasphemy and non-attendance at church.[25] As in all Protestant areas, marriage was no longer considered a sacrament, but a legally binding marriage now required the presence of a pastor and witnesses. Clandestine marriages were strictly forbidden, and parental approval was stressed as highly desirable, though, as we have seen, not absolutely necessary in the case of daughters. Luther recommended that fathers be given the right to annul marriages which their children had entered into without their approval, even if they had been consummated, but Nuremberg followed the more moderate ideas of Melanchthon and the Wittenberg jurists on the matter.[26]

Turning now from theory to reality, the changes in the sixteenth century are less dramatic than one might expect, and may best be seen as long-term trends which continue on into the seventeenth and eighteenth centuries. The number of women who bought and sold property independently gradually decreased. In the fifty-year period from 1484 to 1534, 23 percent of those buying or selling houses or land were women; from 1534-84, 18 percent; and from 1584-1624, 16 percent.[27] Most of the sales which involve widows or single women (*Jungfrau*) from the first half of the sixteenth century made no mention of guardians at all, and some specifically state that the woman herself appeared before the court. In the last half of the century, widows more often appeared with male advisors, either their sons, brothers, or guardians (*Vormunder, Advocaten, Curatores*) or else the men brought the case alone on behalf of the women. Because wives were co-owners of marital property, their names always appear on contracts, but the number of married women who bought and sold property on their own declined. In addition, by the end of the sixteenth century, a specific explanation was always given when a married woman appeared alone in court—her husband was ill, away fighting, gone on a business venture—whereas in the early part of the century this was not deemed necessary. These trends are the result of ideas about female *fragilitas* and *imbecilitas*, and also of the growing professionalization of the legal system. As more formal legal language was required in supplications and arguments, those without university training, which included all women, could no longer argue their own cases.

[24]Nuremberg Staatsarchiv, Rep. 51, Ratschlagbücher, vol. 4, fol. 190 (January 17, 1525).

[25]Judith Harvey, "The Influence of the Reformation on Nuremberg Marriage Laws: 1520-1535" (Ph.D. Diss., Ohio State University, 1972).

[26]George Howard Joyce, *Christian Marriage: An Historical and Doctrinal Study* (London: Streed and Ward, 1948), 118.

[27]Nuremberg Stadtarchiv, Rep. B7/I, II, III, Grundverbriefungsbücher (Libri Litterarum), vols. 2-132.

A similar trend is apparent in wills. Women often used their wills to express religious convictions by endowing funds for preachers and teachers, and also to assist other women with donations for poor expectant mothers or funds for trousseaus for poor girls.[28] During the sixteenth century, wills made jointly by husbands and wives became more common, with donations to specifically female charities decreasing.[29]

Most of the changes in criminal procedure applied equally to women and men, but women were often the only ones to suffer punishment in cases of fornication, for they alone bore the proof of their actions. Punishments for moral crimes increased in severity throughout the sixteenth century, and even setting out a foundling was criminalized.[30] It is not surprising that the most common capital crime among women was infanticide, and that almost all of these women were unmarried.[31] Women were more likely than men to be put up to public ridicule, forced to wear a stone collar (*Lasterstein*) or sit in the stocks for fighting in public, blasphemy, or scolding, all particularly "unfeminine" activities. The wives of wealthier citizens could also be forbidden to wear a *Schurz*, a type of veil which indicated their social standing, if the council felt their conduct had been in some way unseemly. Rarely were women fined, because that would have penalized their husbands as well.

The municipal marriage court made no immediate break with tradition in cases of divorce and remarriage. It did allow divorce in cases of adultery, but initially continued to prohibit the remarriage of either party. Gradually it began to allow the innocent party to remarry, but still preferred that he or she leave the area or at least donate something "ad pias causas."[32] There was no relaxation in the canonical impediments to marriage, despite Osiander's arguments to the contrary. In general, though marriage had become a matter for temporal authorities, the city council was unwilling to break sharply with Catholic practice because it was attempting to keep peace with the emperor at all costs.

In terms of both theory and reality, women's legal position clearly deteriorated in the sixteenth century. The parts of Roman law which placed women

[28]J. C. Siebenkees, *Nachrichten von Armenstiftungen in Nürnberg* (Nuremberg: Schneider, 1792), passim; Idem., *Nachrichten von der Nürnbergischen Armenschulen und Schulstiftungen* (Nuremberg: Schneider, 1793), 71. For a discussion of women's and joint wills elsewhere in Germany, see R. Po-Chia Hsia, "Civic Wills as Sources for the Study of Piety in Münster, 1530-1618," *The Sixteenth Century Journal*, 14 no. 3 (1983): 321-48.

[29]Purucker, "Das Testamentrecht," 52.

[30]Karl Roetzer, *Die Delikte des Abtreibung, Kindstötung sowie Kindsaussetzungen und ihre Bestrafung in der Reichsstadt Nürnberg* (Jur. Diss., Erlangen, 1957), 86.

[31]Ibid., 103; *Meister Franntz*, passim.

[32]Kipfmuller, "Die Frau im Rechte," 18. For Protestant reluctance to allow divorce elsewhere in Germany, see Thomas Max Safley, *Let No Man Put Asunder: The Control of Marriage in the German Southwest* (Kirksville, Mo.: Sixteenth Century Journal Publishers, 1984), 131.

in a dependent or secondary position were incorporated into traditional codes, while those which gave them specific independent rights were not. Governments came to view law as a tool for shaping society, expanding their civil, criminal, and church codes to make them more systematic and comprehensive, and more vigorously prosecuting those who violated these codes. This had a particular impact on women, who had often slipped through the cracks of the older, looser codes, or whose infractions were simply ignored. Governments gradually became less willing to make exceptions in the case of women, for they felt any laxness might disrupt public order. Thus Nuremberg began to insist that all women moving away formally renounce their citizenship; all women who conducted business apply formally for the right to do so; all widows have a male city official write their will and take their inventory; all couples marry in the approved manner.[33] The reality of women's inferior legal status lagged somewhat behind the theory, but by the seventeenth century women throughout Germany found it increasingly difficult to act as independent legal persons in the way their grandmothers had. They were human beings, but not persons.

[33]Nuremberg Staatsarchiv, rep. 52b, Amts- und Standbücher, No. 303, fols. 206-7; Rep. 78, Nürnberger Testamenten, No. 1253 (1562-82); Nuremberg Stadtarchiv, Inventarbücher, nos. 1-4, 16-17 (1529-84); Rep D15/I, Heiliggeistspital Inventarbücher, nos. 4021-6771 (1563-1600); Emil Sehling, ed., *Die evangelische Kirchenordnungen des XVI. Jahrhunderts*, Vol. 11: *Bayern*, part 1; *Franken* (Tübingen, 1962), 140-305.

TABULA CONGRATULATORIA

Frederic J. Baumgartner
Robert G. Clouse
Nancy Conradt
John Patrick Donnelly
Joseph S. Freedman
Jerome Friedman
W. Fred Graham
Rudolph W. Heinze
Maryanne Cline Horowitz
Robert A. Kolb
Robert D. Linder
A. Lynn Martin
Raymond A. Mentzer, Jr.
Donald Nugent
Luther D. Peterson
Robert W. Richgels
Thomas Max Safley
Merry E. Wiesner

Scholarly Publications
of
Robert M. Kingdon

He has touched on highly important questions and events. His work is one that breaks new ground a genuine contribution to an understanding of religious history.

Carl S. Meyer

Book Length Publications

1. **Geneva and the Coming of the Wars of Religion in France, 1555-1563** Geneva: Droz, 1956.

   "It is somewhat astonishing that until now there has been found no satisfactory clue to the puzzle of how the Huguenot minority had become so large by 1562. The growth of the Huguenot party has largely been taken for granted, but Kingdon has opened a vein which makes this book a contribution to knowledge. . . . The author writes well; but my Protestant soul is shocked when Mary Tudor is called Bloody Mary."
   Quirinus Breen, American Historical Review 62 (1957): 449

2. Editor, with J.-F. Bergier, **Registres de la Compagnie des Pasteurs de Genève au temps de Calvin**, 2 volumes. Geneva: Droz, 1962, 1964.

   "The editing by Kingdon, Bergier and Dufour fulfills all of the exacting standards to be expected in a work bearing the imprint of Mlle. Droz. . . . The information accumulated by Mr. Kingdon in the writing of his earlier volume, *Geneva and the Coming of the Wars of Religion*, enabled him to supply an amazing number of footnote biographies of Huguenot pastors who were fanning out from Geneva for the conversion of French Switzerland, France and the Jersey Islands."
   Roland H. Bainton, Archiv für Reformationsgeschichte,
Texte und Untersuchungen 55 (1964): 279-80.

   "These deliberations of the Genevan Pastors are an important source not only for Genevan history but also for the study of Calvinist influence abroad, especially in France during the outbreak of the Wars of Religion. The editors provide copious notes identifying persons, places and events mentioned in the text. This is a major research source; in addition, exciting and illuminating reading for any student of the Reformation."
   Charles G. Nauert, Jr., American Historical Review 69 (1963): 219

171

"The standards and methods of the editors, brilliantly demonstrated in their 1962 edition of the Compagnie's minutes from the Servetus trial to Calvin's death, are virtually unchanged. The present volume is a painstakingly exact reproduction from the Genevan archives, replete with accurate and helpful annotations."

E. W. Monter, *Archiv für Reformationsgeschichte, Text und Untersuchungen* 56 (1965): 2:273.

3. Editor, William Cecil, **The Execution of Justice in England**, and William Allen, **A True, Sincere, and Modest Defense of English Catholics**, in Folger Documents of Tudor and Stuart Civilization. Ithaca: Cornell University Press, 1965.

"Professor Kingdon's attractively printed editions in modern spelling of Sir William Cecil's *The Execution of Justice in England* and William Cardinal Allen's reply to Cecil will be welcomed both by students of 16th century political thought and by those particularly interested in the problem of Catholic recusancy. While there have been modern editions of both books, neither of these earlier editions is readily obtainable or adequately annotated. Professor Kingdon's annotations are thorough without being pedantic."

Roger B. Manning, *Archive für Reformationsgeschichte* 58 (1967): 270-71.

4. **Geneva and the Consolidation of the French Protestant Movement, 1564-1572**. Geneva: Droz, and Madison: University of Wisconsin Press, 1967.

"Mr. Kingdon has added considerably to our knowledge of the precise ways in which Geneva, particularly as represented the Theodore Beza, influenced the formation of the Reformed Church in France during the crucial years between the death of Calvin and the Massacre of St. Bartholomew. . . . Kingdon relies heavily upon material drawn from the unpublished records of the Genevan Company of Pastors. He has unearthed interesting evidence of Beza's participation in an abortive attempt to enroll Swiss mercenaries for service in the Huguenot army, although not until after the Massacre of St. Bartholomew was Beza prepared to state clearly the doctrine of resistance to established authority is permissible if undertaken in the name of true religion."

Wallace K. Ferguson, *American Historical Review* 73 (1968): 1562.

"Kingdon's great familiarity with manuscript evidence and rare pamphlets has enabled him to bring order to the *affaire Morély* and put into proper perspective a subject whose importance for the history of the Reformed Protestantism has been masked by the confusion and obscurity which had engulfed it. . . . The author's meticulous scholarship is constant as he moves from one topic to another."

E. William Monter, *Journal of Modern History* 4 (1969): 89-90.

"Kingdon, an established Reformation historian, has produced an excellent study of the French Protestant movement from Calvin's death in 1564 to the disruption of the St. Bartholomew's Day Massacre in 1572. Thoroughly documented by significant new research in the libraries and archives of Geneva and Zurich, it should be added to any collection concerned with the Reformation."

Choice Magazine 5 (1968-9: 1150

"From this resume of Kingdon's book, it is evident that he has touched on highly important questions and events. His work is one that breaks new ground, a genuine contribution to an understanding of the religious history of France. The volume deserves wide acclaim and careful study."

Carl S. Meyer, *Concordia Theological Monthly* 40 (1969): 186-91

"Kingdon has already produced a distinguished book, *Geneva and the Coming of the Wars of Religion in France, 1555-1563* (Geneva, 1957). In this book he directs himself to two controversies which racked French Protestantism both in Geneva and France during the period of the wars of religion. . . . This is an admirable book based on fresh archival studies."

Roland H. Bainton, *Journal of Religious History* 5 (1968): 75-76

5. Editor, Théodore de Bèze, **Du droit des magistrats**. Geneva: Droz, 1971.

"Footnotes identify and verify references to classical and medieval writings, Roman law and Scripture. Appendixes include other statements by Beza on resistance, extracts from town council registers, a letter from Josias Simler commenting on Beza's theory, and an index, from a later Latin edition of Beza's replies to traditional objections to the doctrine of resistance. An excellent bibliography and glossary also help make this an extremely useful edition of a classic of political thought."

Thomas N. Tentler, *American Historical Review* 78 (1973) 92

"Careful scholarship is the continuing hallmark of the volumes of the *Correspondance*, whose meticulous editors provide such satisfying notes identifying and elucidating each person and event, and this at increasingly greater cost to themselves as they must work with more and more unedited materials after 1564. Kingdon's introduction and notes also provide the scholar with needed information both for more profitable reading of the text and for further research. With such publications, over-due interest in the latter half of the sixteenth century is indeed well nour-ished and encouraged."

Jill Raitt, *Church History* 40 (1971): 486-87

6. Editor, **Transition and Revolution: Problems and Issues of European Renaissance and Reformation History**. Minneapolis: Burgess Publishing Co., 1974.

"Professor Kingdon has performed a valuable service by combining the contributions of several well-known scholars of the Renaissance and Reformation. . . . What makes the volume particularly useful is the juxta-position of original interpretative essays and excerpts from primary sources pertaining to the subject at hand. . . . They raise the volume beyond the typical 'problems and issues' text and make it an original contribution."

Hans J. Hillerbrand, *Renaissance Quarterly* 29 (1976): 408

7. **The Political Thought of Peter Martyr Vermigli: Selected Texts and Commentary**. Geneva: Droz, 1980.

"Professor Kingdon, who drew attention some years ago to the relative neglect of Vermigli's political thought, has now supplied a convenient selection of the most relevant texts, with a short introductory essay. Slightly modernized versions of the sixteenth-century English transla-tions are followed by facsimilies of the original Latin text. . . . The substance of the texts presented is, however, sufficient for the reader to evaluate Vermigli's political doctrines—and no doubt to agree readily with the editor that they merit attention. . . ."

J. H. Burns, *Journal of Ecclesiastical History* 33 (1982): 501-2

"In his beautifully produced mixture of Introduction, and English (and Latin) contemporary texts, Robert M. Kingdon adds nothing but decently apportioned caviar to that essential question, raised especially since the Colloquy of Marburg: how could Protestantism survive in a politically piecemeal, politically hostile, internecine fashion, since it never united its ever-spawing tender consciences into a unified organization labelled 'the true faith'? In getting under the skin of that subject by pulling together the painfully political statements of a commonplace honest preacher and teacher, Kingdon has produced the most thoughtful and important book on Reformation Europe that I have read in years."

Gerhard Benecke, *English Historical Review* 98 (1983): 413

8. **Church and Society in Reformation Europe**. London: Variorum, 1985.

"Variorum reprints of London has aided research significantly by gathering together stoutly bound reprints of articles by . . . Robert M. Kingdon, [and] presents a useful compendium of Kingdoniana published over thirty-five years in seven countries, in five periodicals and twelve Festschriften. . . . Without conscious theological loyalty to Calvin, Kingdon, in an integral, secular way, continues the rationality of the French Protestant tradition along with Calvin's passion for faithfulness, truth, and order. This volume is a learned treat for those to whom French Protestantism remains a living tradition, and it can be instructive as well to others."

Lowell H. Zuck, *Church History* 55 (1986): 106-7

Article Length Publications

1. "The First Expression of Theodore Beza's Political Ideas," *Archiv für Reformationsgeschichte* 46 (1955): 88-100.

2. "Findings of Manuscripts Relating to French Calvinist Pastors," *History of Ideas News Letter* 1 (1956): 15-18.

3. "The Library of an Early Calvinist Pastor," *History of Ideas News Letter* 3 (1957): 5-9.

4. "The Business Activities of Printers Henri and François Estienne," in *Aspects de la propagande religieuse* (Geneva: Droz, 1957), 258-75.

5. "Laissez-faire or Government Control: a problem for John Wesley," *Church History* 26 (1957): 342-54.

6. "The Political Resistance of the Calvinists in France and the Low Countries," *Church History* 27 (1958): 220-33.

7. "The Economic Behavior of Ministers in Geneva in the Middle of the Sixteenth Century," *Archiv für Reformationsgeschichte* 50 (1959); 33-39.

8. "The Plantin Breviaries: a case study in the sixteenth-century business operations of a publishing house," *Bibliothèque d'Humanisme et Renaissance* 22 (1960): 133-50.

9. "Les idées politiques de Bèze d'après son *Traité de l'authorité du magistrat en la punition des herétiques*," *Bibliothèque d'Humanisme et Renaissance* 22 (1960): 566-69.

10. "Concerning Theodore Beza," *Bibliothèque d'Humanisme et Renaissance* 23 (1961): 415-22.

11. "The Continuing Utility of Burckhardt's Thought on Renaissance Politics," in *Jacob Burckhardt and the Renaissance: 100 years after* Miscellaneous Publications of the University of Kansas Museum of Art, no. 42, (1960).

12. "Genève et les réformés français: le cas d'Hugues Sureau, dit du Rosier," *Bulletin, Société d'histoire de d'archéologie de Genève* 12 (1961): 77-87.

13. "Christopher Plantin and his Backers, 1575-1590: a study in the problems of financing business during war," in *Mélanges d'histoire économique et sociale en hommage au professeur Antony Babel* (Geneva, 1963), 303-16.

14. "Calvinism and Democracy: some political implications and debates on French Reformed Church government, 1562-1572, *American Historical Review* 69 (1964): 393-401.

15. "Patronage, Piety, and Printing in Sixteenth-Century Europe," in *A Festschrift for Frederick B. Artz* (Durham, N.C.: Duke University Press, 1964), 19-36.

16. "Some French Reactions to the Council of Trent," *Church History* 33 (1964): 149-56.

17. "The Renaissance and the Reformation, 1300-1648," in *National Council for the Social Studies: 34th Yearbook* (1964).

18. "William Allen's Use of Protestant Political Argument," in *From the Renaissance to the Counter-Reformation: essays in honor of Garrett Mattingly*, ed. C. H. Carter (New York: Random House, 1965), 164-78.

19. "Démocratie et l'église: aspects de la querelle disciplinaire chez les calvinistes au XVIe siècle," *Bolletino della Società di Studi Valdesi* 120 (1966): 47-53.

20. "Problems of Religious Choice for Sixteenth-Century Frenchmen," *Journal of Religious History* 4 (1967): 105-12.

21. "New Editions of Manuscript Records of the Calvinist Reformation,' *Renaissance Quarterly* 20 (1967): 88-96.

22. "Pourquoi les réfugiés huguenots aux colonies américaines, sont-ils devenus épiscopaliens?" *Bulletin de la Société de l'histoire du protestantisme français* 115 (1969): 487-509; "Why Did the Huguenot Refugees to the American Colonies become Episcopalian?" *The Historical Magazine of the Protestant Episcopal Church* 49 (1980): 317-35.

23. "The Deacons of the Reformed Church in Calvin's Geneva," in *Mélanges d'histoire du XVIe siècle offerts à Henri Meylan* (Geneva: Droz, 1970): 81-90.

24. "Social Welfare in Calvin's Geneva," *American Historical Review* 76 (1971): 50-69.

25. "The Control of Morals in Calvin's Geneva," in *The Social History of the Reformation* ed. L. P. Buck and J. W. Zophy in honor of Harold J. Grimm (Columbus: Ohio State University Press, 1972), 3-16.

26. "Calvinism and Democracy," in *The Heritage of John Calvin*, ed. by J. H. Bratt (Grand Rapids: Eerdmans, 1973), 177-92.

27. "Quelques réactions à la Saint-Barthélemy à l'extérieur de la France," *Actes du colloque l'Amiral de Coligny et son temps* (Paris: Société de l'histoire du protestantisme français, 1974), 191-204.

28. "Reactions to the St. Bartholomew Massacres in Geneva and Rome," in *The Massacre of St. Bartholomew*, ed. A. Soman (the Hague: Nijhoff, 1975), 25-49.

29. Was the Protestant Reformation a Revolution? the case of Geneva," in *Church, Society, and Politics*, ed. D. Baker (Oxford: Blackwell, 1975), 203-22.

30. "Publishing at the Officina Plantiniana: a review article," *Library Quarterly* 46 (1976): 294-98.

31. "The Control of Morals by the Earliest Calvinists," in *Renaissance, Reformation, Resurgence*, ed. P. de Klerk (Grand Rapids: Calvin Theological Seminary, 1976), 95-106.

32. "L'emploi des impressions clandestines par le gouvernement d'Elisabeth dans sa politique française," in *Théorie et pratique politiques à la renaissance*, ed. A. Stegmann (Paris: Vrin, 1977), 247-58; "The Use of Clandestine Printings by the Government of Elizabeth I and its French Policy, 1570-1590," in *European History and its Historians*, ed. F. McGregor and N. Wright (Adelaide University Union Press, 1977), 47-57.

33. "Peter Martyr Vermigli and the Marks of the True Church," in *Continuity and Discontinuity in Church History: essays presented to George Huntston Williams*, ed. F. F. Church and T. George (Leiden: Brill, 1979), 198-214.

34. "Protestant Parishes in the Old World and the New: the cases of Geneva and Boston," *Church History* 48 (1979): 290-304.

35. "The Political Thought of Peter Martyr Vermigli," in *Peter Martyr Vermigli and Italian Reform*, ed. J. C. McLelland (Waterloo, Canada: Wilfrid Laurier University Press, 1980), 121-39.

36. "The Function of Law in the Political Thought of Peter Martyr Vermigli," in *Reformatio Perennis: essays on Calvin and the Reformation in honor of Ford Lewis Battles*, ed. B. A. Gerrish (Pittsburgh: Pickwick, 1981), 159-72.

37. "The Church: Ideology or Institution?" *Church History* 50 (1981): 81-97.

38. "Teaching: Garrett Mattingly," *American Scholar* 51 (1982): 396-402.

39. "Pamphlet Literature of the French Reformation," in *Reformation Europe: a guide to literature of the French Reformation*, ed. S. Ozment (St. Louis: Center for Reformation Research, 1982), 233-48.
40. "Calvinism and Social Welfare," *Calvin Theological Journal* 17: 212-30.
41. " 'Disciplines' réformées du XVIe siècle français: une découverte faite aux Etats-Unis," *Bulletin de la Société de l'histoire du protestantisme français* 130 (1984): 69-86.
42. "Calvin and the Family: the work of the Consistory in Geneva," *Pacific Theological Review* 17 (1984): 5-18.
43. "Calvin's Ideas about the Diaconate: social or theological in origin?" in *Piety, Politics, and Ethics: Reformation Studies in honor of George Wolfgang Forell*, ed. C. Lindberg (Kirksville, Mo.: Sixteenth Century Journal Publishers, 1984), 167-80.
44. "Calvin and the Government of Geneva," in *Calvinus Ecclesiae Genevensis Custos*, ed. W. H. Neuser (Frankfurt: Lang, 1984), 49-67.
45. "The Reformation and the Family," in *On the Way: occasional papers of the Wisconsin Conference of the United Church of Christ* 2 (1984): 12-25.
46. "Calvin and 'Presbytery': the Geneva Company of Pastors," *Pacific Theological Review* 18 (1985): 43-55.

Shorter Publications
More than 100 book reviews in the following periodicals:

> *American Historical Review*
> *American Sociological Review*
> *Archiv für Reformationsgeschichte*
> *Bibliothèque d'Humanisme et Renaissance*
> *Business History Review*
> *Canadian Journal of History*
> *Catholic Historical Review*
> *Church History*
> *History of European Ideas*
> *Journal of the American Academy of Religion*
> *Journal of Ecclesiastical History*
> *Journal of Interdisciplinary History*
> *Journal of Modern History*
> *Journal of Religion*
> *Library Quarterly*

Renaissance Quarterly
Review of Religion
Schweizerische Zeitschrift für Geschichte
Speculum
William and Mary Quarterly

Articles in

Dictionary of the History of Ideas: studies of selected pivotal ideas (1)
Encyclopedia Americana (8)
Encyclopedia Britannica Macropedia (1)
New Catholic Encyclopedia (4)
Theologische Realenzyklopädie (1)
Twentieth Century Encyclopedia of Religious Knowledge (16)

Foreword to *Shapers of Religious Traditions in Germany, Switzerland, and Poland, 1560-1600*, ed. Jill Raitt (New Haven: Yale University Press, 1981).

For Student Use:

1. With R. D. Linder, *Calvin and Calvinism: Sources of Democracy?* in *Problems in European Civilization* (Boston: Heath, 1970).
2. *Transition and Revolution: Problems and Issues of European Renaissance and Reformation History* (Minneapolis: Burgess, 1974), ed. and author of one chapter.

Library of Congress Cataloging-in-Publication Data

Regnum, religio et ratio.

(Sixteenth century essays & studies; v. 8)
Bibliography: p. 171
Includes index.
1. Europe—Civilization—16th century. 2. Europe—Civiliza-
tion—17th century. 3. Reformation. 4. Church history—16th
century. 5. Kingdon, Robert McCune, 1927-. I. Kingdon, Robert
McCune, 1927-. II. Friedman, Jerome. III. Series.
CB367.R44 1987   940.2'32   87-16328
ISBN 0-940474-08-5

Index